ECONOMIC CONVERGENCE AND MONETARY UNION IN EUROPE

SAGE Publications

Association for the Monetary Union of Europe
National Institute of Economic and Social Research

The Association for the Monetary Union of Europe was set up in 1987 as a voice of Europe's business community, expressing the need for monetary stability and a single European currency. It does so by taking public positions on matters related to European Monetary Union in the European media. It is conducting research in order to clarify some of the issues in the public debate. The Association also organises seminars and publishes material in order to raise the knowledge on EMU and the practical use of the Ecu.

The National Institute of Economic and Social Research is an independent non-profit-making body whose object is to increase knowledge of the social and economic conditions of contemporary society. It conducts and publishes research by its own staff and in cooperation with the universities and other academic bodies.

ECONOMIC CONVERGENCE AND MONETARY UNION IN EUROPE

Edited by

Ray Barrell

SAGE Publications

Association for the Monetary Union of Europe
National Institute of Economic and Social Research

SAGE Publications Ltd
6 Bonhill Street
London EC2A 4PU

SAGE Publications Inc
2455 Teller Road
Newbury Park, California 91320

SAGE Publications India Pvt Ltd
32, M-Block Market
Greater Kailash – I
New Delhi 110 048

ISBN 0-8039-8720-X
ISBN 0-8039-8721-8 pbk

Printed in Great Britain by Billing and Sons Ltd, Worcester

Contents

Contributors and Participants

Robert Anderton, National Institute of Economic and Social Research
Ray Barrell, National Institute of Economic and Social Research
Iain Begg, Department of Applied Economics, Cambridge
Professor Christian Bordes, University of Bordeaux
Professor John Bradley, ESRI, Dublin
Stefan Collignon, Association for the Monetary Union of Europe, Paris
Dr Willy Friedmann, Deutsche Bundesbank
Professor Eric Girardin, University of Bordeaux
Jan Willem in't Veld, National Institute of Economic and Social Research
Bénédicte Larre, OECD, Paris
Malcolm Levitt, Barclays Bank
James McHugh, Oriel College, Oxford
Professor David Mayes, National Institute of Economic and Social Research
Dr Enno Langfeldt, Kiel Institute of World Economics
Professor Paolo Onofri, Prometeia, Bologna
Michael Posner, European Science Foundation, Strasbourg
Stefania Tomasini, Prometeia, Bologna
Raymond Torres, OECD, Paris
Karl Whelan, ESRI, Dublin
Professor John Williamson, Institute for International Economics, Washington

Other participants
Sam Brittan, Financial Times
Andrew Britton, National Institute of Economic and Social Research
Guglielmo Caporale, National Institute of Economic and Social Research
Pietro Catte, Bank of Italy
Bob Corker, IMF
Bernard de Maigret, Association for the Monetary Union of Europe, Paris
Christopher Dow, National Institute of Economic and Social Research

Professor John Driffill, Queen Mary and Westfield College, London
Neal Hatch, Bank of England
Brian Henry, Bank of England
Andrew Holder, HM Treasury
David Lomax, National Westminster Bank
Helen MacFarlane, Bank of England
Giuseppina Madonia, University of Kent
Chris Mellis, HM Treasury
Dr Stefano Micossi, Confindustria, Rome
Dr Carlo Monticelli, Bank for International Settlements
Nigel Pain, National Institute of Economic and Social Research
Nikitas Pittis, National Institute of Economic and Social Research
Eirik Svindland, DIW, Berlin
Mark Vanhuekelen, European Commission
Peter Westaway, National Institute of Economic and Social Research
Garry Young, National Institute of Economic and Social Research

Preface

Michael Posner

It was a pleasure to chair this quiet, thoughtful, constructive conference held at the National Institute on 12–13 December 1991. The Association for Monetary Union in Europe provided funds, and in association with the Institute organised a discussion on nominal convergence amongst the economies of Europe. The theme was excellently timed: we had in front of us the Maastricht texts which prescribed the convergence criteria which could in a few year's time trigger the final phases of EMU, and we had very much in mind the *real* cost of achieving that *nominal* convergence over the next few years in countries such as the United Kingdom and Italy.

To someone like myself who had been away from the frontline of this topic for a few years there were a few surprises:

– Everyone agreed that monetary and fiscal pressure could, fairly quickly and permanently, squeeze out inflationary pressures; the temporary losses, and how to minimise them, were recognised as an important issue; the permanent losses (if the non-inflationary equilibrium unemployment levels were high and rising) were recognised as important, but belonging to another branch of policy discussion.

– Everyone seemed to assume that fixed (perhaps irrevocably locked) exchange rates were a very useful, perhaps even uniquely necessary, nominal anchor of the system. It was as if the half a dozen fiercely fought passionate arguments and policy switches (from fixed to floating, from free to managed, from jumps to crawls) of the last quarter century had never happened!

– Everyone placed great emphasis on 'confidence', its feedback to individuals' behaviour, the way an extra dose of confidence could make unnecessary an extra dose of monetary restriction. This too evoked the past, and left at least one participant with an uneasy feeling that an element of faith healing lurked somewhere in the jungle of econometric equations.

There was indeed a handsome forest of econometrics around, but it was kept well in the background. An important and recurrent theme (in the National Institute paper, in the Onofri and Tomasini paper, and in the Bordes and Girardin paper) was the search for evidence that EMS/ERM had provided for its participants over the last few years a route to nominal convergence that was quicker or cheaper than the conventional one-country squeeze. Several of the careful and scholarly tests gave encouragingly positive results. But one of the German participants, noting that all the convergence tests were between country *n* and Germany, suggested that convergence in the recent past had perhaps been achieved more by a relative weakening in German performance than by a relative strengthening in the performance of others. On the whole, however, my own feeling was that the optimists had the better of the argument on this central point.

A careful paper by Friedmann convinced us that the recent lessons of German monetary union, although important, had few general implications. Bradley provided a clear path through the complexities of Irish/United Kingdom monetary relationships. John Williamson, who intervened constructively in the discussion throughout, opened what may well be an important long-term debate on the external relations of EMU – long-term in its durability, possibly quite immediate in its implications for the building of EMU.

There were a few heterodox voices, which I did my best to support. Mayes and Begg wrote of 'cohesion', and although they admitted that nominal convergence was a stronger necessity for EMU than was real convergence, they left an impression in my mind at least that the possibility of EMU for the Europe of all twelve present EC members raised social questions undiscussed at Maastricht and unresolved at this NIESR/AUME conference. There were some who spoke of exchange-rate changes over the next few years as a possible precondition of avoiding larger fractures in the future, but these voices were even more isolated than their predecessors of thirty years ago.

I found it pleasant to attend a truly European meeting of economists. Whatever the continuing parochialism of many University departments, and of many political debates, the brightest and best amongst the young (and younger middle-aged!) talk the same (intellectual) language, use the same econometric methods, address the same issues. And, for an economist like myself, who spends most of his time with natural scientists whose logic is so much simpler, a pleasure to refresh the flow of thought processes along arteries grown a little furry with age.

Michael Posner
December, 1991

1

Macroeconomic Convergence in Europe: Achievements and Prospects

Robert Anderton, Ray Barrell and Jan Willem in't Veld

Economic convergence within the EMS member states is a precondition for further moves to economic and monetary integration. The Delors Report has set out a path towards EMU in three stages, where transition to the next stage depends on some degree of convergence being achieved in the previous stage. In October 1990, the European Council in Rome agreed that 'in order to move on to the second phase (of economic and monetary union), further satisfactory and lasting progress toward real and monetary convergence will have to be achieved' (Press communique, European Council, Rome, 28 October 1990). The treaty text from the Maastricht Summit states that before the start of the second phase in January, 1994, the Council shall assess the progress made with regard to economic and monetary convergence, and in particular with regard to price stability and balanced public finances.

Before transition to the third stage, and not later than December 1996, progress made in economic convergence must be reassessed. Each country will be assessed individually before it is decided whether or not they can go forward to union. The Protocol referred to in Article 109F of the treaty sets out four criteria for transition to the third stage relating to inflation performance, budget positions, exchange-rate stability and interest-rate convergence. First, each prospective member state must have 'a price performance that is sustainable and an average rate of inflation observed over a period of one year before the examination that does not exceed that of the, at most, three best performing member states in terms of price stability by more than 1.5 percentage points. Inflation shall be measured by means of the consumer price index (CPI) on a comparable basis'. The protocol states that the government budgetary criterion shall not be met if there is a Council decision that an 'excessive' deficit exists for the member state concerned. Another protocol referred to in Article 104B stipulates that the planned or actual general government deficit should not exceed 3 per cent of GDP and the gross nominal government debt to GDP ratio should not exceed 60 per cent. This criterion refers to the general government, that is, central, regional and local government and social security funds. The third criterion relates to a country's record in the ERM. Any prospective candidate for the third stage must have respected the normal, that is, narrow, fluctuation margins in the ERM 'without severe tensions for at least the last two years before its examination', ruling out devaluations that come about from an initiative of the country concerned. The fourth criterion states that nominal long-term interest rates must not have exceeded that of the, at most, three best performing member states in terms of price stability by more than 2 percentage points in the last year before examination.

The analysis of convergence

In this introductory chapter we will discuss the convergence achieved so far in Europe and assess the prospects of further convergence in the coming years.[1] In general terms convergence can be defined as the narrowing of international differences in the development of certain economic variables. As a requirement for a system of stable exchange rates, a distinction must be made between *nominal* convergence, which is the convergence of the development of costs and prices and their underlying determinants, *real* convergence of working conditions and living standards and the convergence of economic institutions or *structures*. Real convergence is one of the fundamental objectives of a fully-integrated Europe, but it is a long-term process and it is not a necessary condition for a successful transition to an economic and monetary union. The paper by Begg and Mayes in the *National Institute Economic Review* of November 1991, analyses the issues around real convergence. This chapter is mainly concerned with nominal convergence but the convergence of economic structures is also briefly discussed.

In a monetary union inflation rates must be similar, and hence it is prudent to insist that countries demonstrate that they are willing and able to converge in this respect before the union is finalised. This demonstration involves getting inflation rates into line, and doing so without strain. The strain would show up in indices of competitiveness, in unemployment and in external balance. Lack of strain implies some conditions on underlying economic variables, such as fiscal and external balances. Convergence of price performance can only be maintained when such underlying factors do not put pressure on prices to diverge again. This does not of course mean that fiscal and current account balance are required, rather that they must be consistent with internal and external equilibrium.

If a region is far away from its non-accelerating inflation rate of unemployment (NAIRU), or its fundamental equilibrium exchange rate (FEER), then this cannot be a sustainable situation and some sort of adjustment towards equilibrium will take place. A prolonged overvaluation of the real exchange rate associated with a current account imbalance is not sustainable. Such a situation will lead to lower exports, higher imports and the gradual decumulation of wealth. These will all lead to lower demand and this will put downward pressure on prices. Of course, current account deficits will be easier to finance in a fully-integrated Europe with free capital flows, but this will be at the cost of higher interest payments. Such a situation does not rule out an economic and monetary union, but it has implications for the costs of adjustment. An economy cannot continually diverge from its NAIRU and FEER because the automatic stabilising mechanisms in the economy will eventually produce adjustment. The further a country is away from equilibrium, and the longer this lasts, the more painful will be the adjustment.[2]

The transition from high to low inflation also involves reducing nominal interest rates and (in some cases) reducing fiscal deficits. It is arguable that this transition should be made before joining EMU. Fiscal balance is not required for all countries, nor is a full convergence of public debt positions. But it is generally accepted that a situation of prolonged fiscal deficits and a rising debt to GDP ratio is not sustainable. The increasing burden of servicing the public debt reduces fiscal flexibility. If countries are not in a monetary union this burden may put upward pressure on real interest rates, and may ultimately lead countries to resort to monetary financing or inflation as methods to reduce the real debt stock. Once inside a union individual countries face fewer financing problems, and hence they may feel some relaxation of the pressure to observe fiscal discipline. A minimum political requirement for transition to EMU may well therefore be that all countries are on a sustainable debt path. This rules out countries that have not managed to bring the medium-term trend of public debt under control. For this trend to be stabilising, the primary surplus, the overall public sector balance excluding interest payments, must exceed the product of the desired, or initial, debt to GDP ratio and the difference between the long-term nominal interest rate and nominal growth rate.[3] We will show below that not all Community countries have achieved this target.

In the following we will review the progress that has been made so far in the European Community in achieving the necessary convergence of the most important economic variables. We consider not only the countries that are members of the EC at present, but also include Austria in our comparison, as Austria has *de facto* followed the D-Mark over the past ten years and has arguably achieved closer convergence to Germany than many ERM countries. We will first discuss the exchange-rate developments and the realignments in the ERM. Next we review consumer price indices, as well as different cost measures and measures of competitiveness and real exchange rates. We will also look at the performance of monetary variables such as short and long-term interest rates. We will then consider measures of external and internal imbalances.

Exchange-rate developments

Since its inception in 1979, the ERM has seen twelve realignments. The first years were characterised by frequent tensions within the system and some large realignments. These were partly caused by large differences in countries' external positions but mainly by continuing inflation differentials, which were a reflection of divergent economic performances. These divergences provoked expectations of exchange-rate realignments and speculative capital flows that put irresistible pressure on the system to realign. Table 1.1 shows all the changes in parities that have taken place since 1979. Only after 1983, when several countries' domestic economic policies changed, did a stable exchange rate in the EMS become the objective for monetary policy. Only then were serious efforts made to achieve the nominal convergence needed for exchange-rate stability. It is often said that the ERM became hard at that time. During the first ten years, the Italian lira participated in the ERM in wider fluctuation margins of 6 per cent around bilateral central rates and only since 1990 has it adopted normal margins of 2.25 per cent. Spain and the United Kingdom joined the ERM in 1989 and 1990 respectively and have opted also for the wider fluctuation margins of 6 per cent. Over the last decade, the Italian lira has devalued most, by more than 40 per cent, followed by

Table 1.1　*Changes in EMS central rates (per cent change in central rate)*

Dates of realignments	Belgian franc	Danish kroner	German mark	French franc	Irish punt	Italian lira	Dutch guilder
24/09/1979	0.0	−2.9	+2.0	0.0	0.0	0.0	0.0
31/11/1979	0.0	−4.8	0.0	0.0	0.0	0.0	0.0
02/03/1981	0.0	0.0	0.0	0.0	0.0	−6.0	0.0
05/10/1981	0.0	0.0	+5.5	−3.0	0.0	−3.0	+5.5
22/02/1982	−8.5	−3.0	0.0	0.0	0.0	0.0	0.0
14/06/1982	0.00	0.00	+4.25	−5.75	0.00	−2.75	+4.25
21/03/1983	+1.5	+2.5	+5.5	−2.5	−3.5	−2.5	+3.5
21/07/1985	+2.0	+2.0	+2.0	+2.0	+2.0	−6.0	+2.0
07/04/1986	+1.0	+1.0	+3.0	−3.0	0.0	0.0	+3.0
04/08/1986	0.0	0.0	0.0	0.0	−8.0	0.0	0.0
12/01/1987	+2.0	0.0	+3.0	0.0	0.0	0.0	+3.0
08/01/1990	0.0	0.0	0.0	0.0	0.0	−3.7	0.0

the French franc and the Irish pound. The Dutch guilder has continually shadowed the D-Mark closely and has only devalued by 2 per cent in 1979 and 1983 against the D-Mark. The Austrian schilling has depreciated only 10 per cent against the D-Mark over the period 1979 to 1991, and has been virtually pegged to the D-Mark since 1981.

Prices and costs

The general trend of the last decade suggests an emerging nominal convergence among ERM members. In particular, consumer price inflation differentials have narrowed dramatically over the 1980s. Table 1.2 and charts 1.1 and 1.2 show that the Netherlands and Belgium, and more recently France, Ireland and Denmark, have achieved the greatest inflation convergence towards German rates in absolute terms. Inflation in the Netherlands has actually been lower than that in Germany since 1987 and Austria has also achieved close convergence to German rates. France, Denmark and Ireland have managed to bring their inflation rates down to close to the German rate after having all experienced very high inflation during the first half of the 1980s. Ireland in particular has seen a dramatic decline in its inflation rate from a peak of 19 per cent in 1981 to below 4 per cent in the second half of the decade.

Chart 1.3 shows the inflation rates of the ERM countries that had not achieved convergence to German rates by the end of 1990. Italy has reduced its inflation differential *vis-à-vis* Germany from 15 percentage points in 1980 to 3 points at present. Spain has achieved a similar inflation differential. The United Kingdom has, after a diverging inflationary trend in recent years, achieved closer convergence since the beginning of this year. It should be noted that although this general disinflationary experience is also common among many non-ERM countries, their experience has not been as strongly associated with shrinking inflation differentials. However, there is no doubt that the recent inflationary upsurge in the newly unified Germany has exaggerated the impression of inflation convergence. Much of the convergence achieved can be attributed to the increase in the rate of inflation in Germany from around zero to 4 per cent. Furthermore, forecasts by the National Institute, such as those published in the November 1991, *Review*, suggest that a high inflation rate will persist for the next few years in the newly unified Germany.

Price inflation convergence in several ERM member countries has been associated with the steady implementation of austerity packages with the process beginning around 1982. Since the election of a new coalition government in the Netherlands in 1982, both the real minimum wage and the ratio of unemployment benefits to average earnings have been

Table 1.2   *Consumers' expenditure deflators (per cent rate of change over previous year)*

	Germany	Netherlands	Belgium	Austria	France	Denmark	Ireland	Italy	UK	Spain	Portugal	Greece
1978	2.75	4.56	4.21	4.10	9.18	9.21	7.96	13.28	9.09	18.90	20.6	12.8
1979	4.28	4.36	3.89	4.59	10.79	10.51	14.75	14.34	13.52	16.58	24.3	16.6
1980	5.78	7.07	6.29	6.40	13.25	10.62	18.67	20.63	16.31	16.55	21.4	22.0
1981	6.43	6.30	8.59	7.55	13.00	12.00	19.63	18.10	11.22	14.30	20.4	22.4
1982	5.25	5.27	7.91	6.03	11.59	10.27	14.99	16.93	8.70	14.61	21.0	20.7
1983	3.36	2.77	6.97	3.41	9.67	6.80	9.10	15.13	4.76	12.29	25.8	18.1
1984	2.73	2.17	6.07	5.60	7.66	6.37	7.44	11.82	5.09	10.88	28.1	17.9
1985	2.04	2.21	5.93	3.31	5.78	4.35	4.93	9.00	5.37	8.22	19.6	18.2
1986	-0.50	0.33	0.70	1.92	2.67	2.87	4.30	5.78	4.40	8.78	14.7	22.2
1987	0.60	-0.17	1.69	0.90	3.15	4.58	3.26	5.02	4.31	5.36	8.6	15.5
1988	1.40	0.67	1.37	1.60	2.64	4.89	2.51	5.29	5.05	5.14	10.1	14.2
1989	3.05	2.06	3.37	2.72	3.45	5.02	3.89	6.26	5.59	6.72	13.0	14.7
1990	2.49	2.43	3.45	3.16	2.94	2.59	3.23	6.23	4.72	6.70	13.4	20.0
1991(a)	3.70	2.69	3.33	3.81	3.10	2.81	3.04	6.70	5.40	6.07	11.5	17.5

Source: NIESR database and Datastream.
(a) Includes forecast.

Chart 1.1 *Consumer price inflation differential for the Netherlands, Belgium and Austria vis-à-vis Germany*

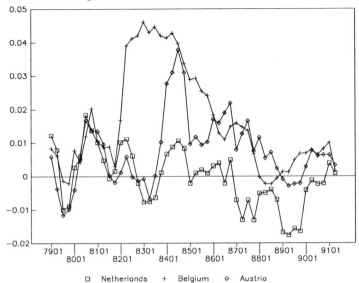

□ Netherlands + Belgium ◇ Austria

Source: NIESR database.

Chart 1.2 *Consumer price inflation differential for France, Denmark and Ireland vis-à-vis Germany*

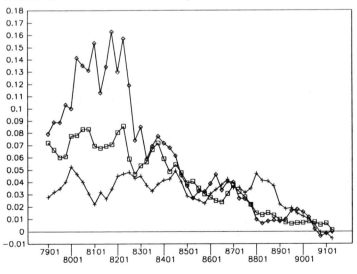

□ France + Denmark ◇ Ireland

Source: NIESR database.

Chart 1.3   *Consumer price inflation differential for Italy, Spain and the United Kingdom vis-à-vis Germany*

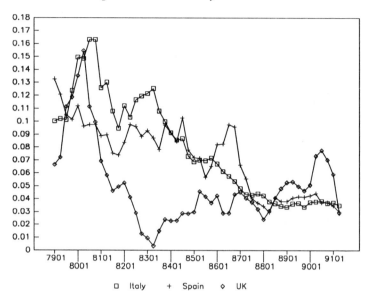

□ Italy   + Spain   ◇ UK

Source: NIESR database.

reduced, followed in 1984 by cuts in nominal public sector wages.[4] In 1982 Belgium introduced a deflationary policy package of increased taxes, reduced public expenditure, suspension or elimination of wage indexation and the freezing of some prices.[5] Also in 1982, Denmark implemented measures consisting of 'tight fiscal policy, wage guidelines, suspension of wage indexation ... and a fixed exchange-rate policy' (Anderson and Risager, 1988). In 1982 Ireland also adopted a policy of higher tax rates and tighter money, froze special pay increases in the public sector and 'hardened-up' on the exchange rate. Also in 1982, France introduced a temporary freeze on prices and wages and announced a reduction in budget deficit plans.[6] Italy began the process of dismantling wage indexation (the Scala Mobile) in 1983.[7]

As table 1.3 shows, the above measures helped to reduce the rate of increase in unit labour costs, relative to Germany, for many ERM countries. However, Italy has been less successful in this respect. Non-convergence of Italian unit labour costs has been associated with falling export profit margins. This seems to support the hypothesis that, because of greater exposure to foreign competition, prices in the traded-goods sector are under more pressure to converge than the non-traded sector. Further evidence of this is contained in the 1990/91 OECD Country Survey on Italy (p. 88) which demonstrates that the prices of Italian

Table 1.3 *Unit labour costs (per cent rate of change over previous year)*

	Germany	Netherlands	Belgium	Austria	France	Denmark	Ireland	Italy	UK	Spain	Portugal	Greece
1978	3.15	5.73	3.81	9.43	9.52	9.31	13.20	11.99	10.38	21.08	20.63	16.20
1979	3.98	5.18	5.51	1.84	9.88	7.96	20.98	14.65	14.01	16.71	15.35	20.68
1980	7.66	5.50	4.28	5.13	13.67	10.63	20.99	17.94	21.04	11.90	22.43	18.73
1981	4.74	2.61	6.29	8.31	12.50	9.15	15.40	20.63	9.74	12.25	20.80	23.49
1982	4.19	4.44	3.62	3.53	11.67	9.66	14.88	15.89	4.56	11.88	19.79	28.26
1983	0.22	-0.30	3.03	2.12	9.19	6.35	11.08	13.86	3.39	10.90	19.96	19.92
1984	0.65	-2.95	4.75	3.92	5.77	3.41	6.01	8.38	4.22	4.79	18.25	18.91
1985	1.94	0.63	4.75	3.44	4.47	3.65	5.10	8.82	4.39	6.05	19.21	20.95
1986	2.96	1.77	2.47	4.93	2.30	3.98	7.44	5.33	4.09	9.66	14.34	10.44
1987	2.67	2.25	0.60	2.15	2.04	9.29	0.40	5.37	3.52	6.16	10.98	11.23
1988	0.30	0.30	-1.20	-0.10	1.30	1.90	3.20	5.60	6.80	5.60	15.40	18.40
1989	0.60	-1.60	1.32	2.40	2.67	1.77	-0.29	6.16	8.99	7.77	12.30	15.96
1990	2.87	2.63	3.60	3.13	3.46	1.16	1.75	9.63	11.25	8.70	14.97	22.14
1991(a)	4.72	3.16	3.86	4.08	3.90	1.81	3.53	7.00	6.64	6.79	15.17	13.50

Source: NIESR database and Datastream.
(a) Includes forecast.

services are rising rapidly compared with other sectors and Italy seems to be an 'outlier' in this respect compared to other ERM members.[8] Chart 1.4 gives a comparison of French and Italian manufacturing export profit margins. The slower growth of French unit labour costs seems to have allowed France to converge in terms of manufacturing export prices without severely squeezing profit margins.

Although inflation differentials have narrowed, they have not disappeared. As a result price levels for many ERM members are continually diverging. Given that no substantial currency realignments have occurred since 1987 this means that real exchange rates have appreciated for several ERM countries. In particular, in CPI terms, the Italian real exchange rate has increased by over 15 per cent since 1987 and, in its brief period of EMS membership, Spain has experienced a 10 per cent real appreciation. Ireland, Denmark and France have also experienced less severe real appreciations. There seems little change in fundamentals to justify these real appreciations. On the contrary, Barrell and in't Veld (1991) argued that France and Italy have experienced a depreciation of their FEERs over the 1980s. The recent real appreciations will therefore make future nominal adjustments more difficult. Charts 1.5–1.7 plot relative normalised unit labour costs which are commonly used as a measure of the real exchange rate. Once again it is possible to divide these countries into three groups with Denmark, Germany and the Netherlands experiencing real appreciation since 1985. These reflect the nature of their economies rather than the emergence of structural problems. The second group consists of Austria, Belgium, France and Ireland where real exchange rates have been constant in recent years. The third group contains the United Kingdom, Italy and Spain. All have previously used the nominal exchange rate to overcome the effects of inflation differentials. Since they have eschewed the use of this instrument they have appreciated in real terms, reflecting emerging competitiveness problems.

Although not members of the ERM, Greece and Portugal belong to the EC and may participate in a future monetary union if sufficient economic convergence is achieved. However, tables 1.2 and 1.3 reveal that substantial adjustment is required within these countries if acceptable growth rates for prices and unit labour costs are to be attained.

Interest rates

Short-term interest-rate differentials have narrowed considerably among ERM members. The Netherlands have followed the most credible policy since the inception of the ERM with the Dutch guilder virtually moving in line with the D-Mark. As a consequence, the Dutch/German interest-rate

Chart 1.4 *French and Italian manufacturing export profit margins,*
1980=100

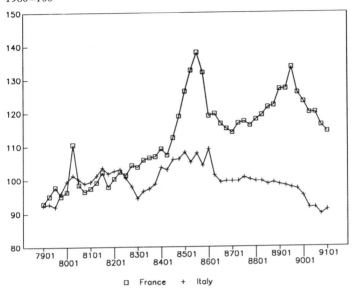

Source: NIESR database.

Chart 1.5 *Relative unit labour costs for Germany, Netherlands*
and Denmark, 1985=100

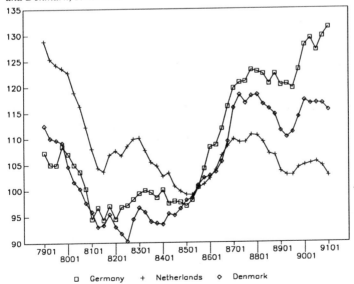

Source: NIESR database.

Chart 1.6　*Relative unit labour costs for France, Belgium, Austria and Ireland, 1985=100*

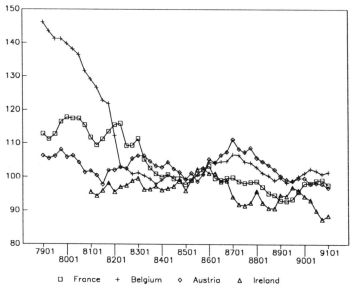

Source: NIESR database

Chart 1.7　*Relative unit labour costs for Italy, Spain and the UK, 1985=100*

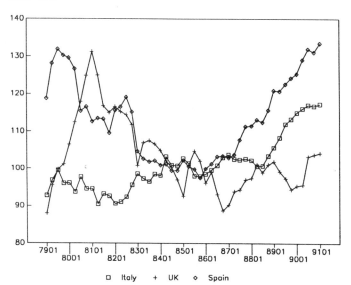

Source: NIESR database

differential is now almost zero and has been for some time. The same can be said of interest rates in Austria. Chart 1.8 plots interest rates in these countries along with that in Germany. Throughout the rest of the ERM member countries, interest rates that were almost double that of Germany in the pre-ERM period are now within 1 or 2 percentage points of the German rate. These remaining ERM countries can be divided into two distinct groups, those where interest-rate convergence has recently taken place, and those where it has not. This latter group consists of Italy, Spain and the United Kingdom. Even though the differential has been cut to around 2 percentage points this has been at least in part the result of rising rates in Germany rather than falling rates in the United Kingdom, Spain or Italy. German short rates are 6 points higher than in the middle of 1988 whilst rates in the United Kingdom are only 2 points higher. Chart 1.9 plots interest-rate differentials for these three countries against Germany.

The third group of ERM countries forms a central lane in contrast to the fast and slow groups described above. As chart 1.10 shows, interest rates in France and Belgium, and to a lesser extent in Ireland, have been moving together for some time, and between 1989 and 1991 the differential against Germany narrowed from around 1.5 per cent to approximately zero. Some of this narrowing has been associated with policy announcements. A good example is shown by the effects of the

Chart 1.8   *Short-term interest rates for Germany, the Netherlands and Austria*

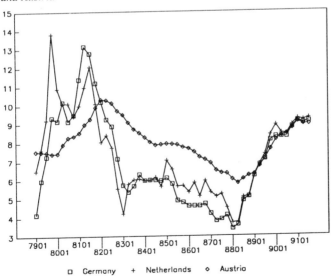

□ Germany   + Netherlands   ◇ Austria

Source: NIESR database

Chart 1.9   *Short-term interest differentials for Italy, the UK and Spain vis-à-vis Germany*

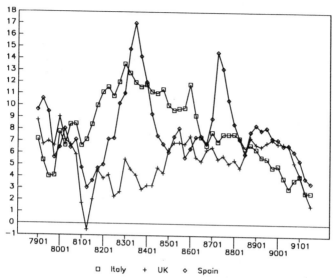

Source: NIESR database

Chart 1.10   *Short-term interest differentials for France, Belgium and Ireland vis-à-vis Germany*

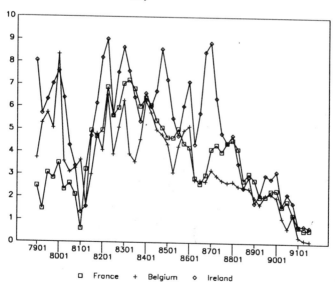

Source: NIESR database

Belgian announcement in March 1990, that the Belgian franc would be pegged to the D-Mark. The interest-rate differential against the D-Mark disappeared almost immediately. In late 1991 Dutch, Belgian, Danish and Austrian short rates were all within one third of a per cent of German rates, whilst French and Irish rates have recently moved to within a half percentage point of German rates. It is even possible that French rates may fall below those in Germany in 1992. Short rates in the United Kingdom and Italy remain about 1½–2 points above those in Germany, whilst Spanish rates (buoyed up by capital inflow controls) have maintained a differential of over 3 percentage points. This period of interest-rate convergence has been combined with the virtual elimination of substantial capital controls, and France and Italy have virtually eradicated onshore/offshore interest-rate differentials.

The Maastricht Treaty makes great play of the role of convergence of long-term interest rates. Longer-term interest differentials have not generally shown such clear evidence of convergence as short-term rates, and this is especially the case for Italy, Denmark, Spain and the United Kingdom. Table 1.4 gives long-term interest rates for the EC countries, and chart 1.11 plots long rates on a quarterly basis for the major four over the same period. Long rates embed expected future short rates, and hence if short rates are expected to converge (as is necessary in a monetary union) then long rates must already show signs of doing the same. The

Chart 1.11   *Long-term interest rates*

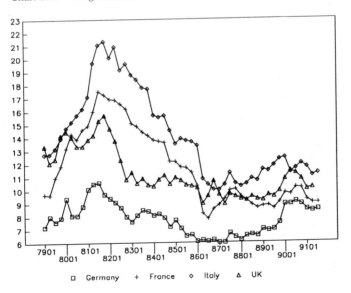

Table 1.4 *Long-term interest rates (per cent)*

	Germany	Netherlands	Belgium	Austria	France	Denmark	Ireland	Italy	UK	Spain	Portugal	Greece
1978	6.13	7.74	8.45	8.21	10.61	17.46	12.83	13.05	12.07	11.93	19.33	11.08
1979	7.58	8.78	9.70	7.96	10.85	17.41	15.07	13.02	12.95	13.31	20.50	13.08
1980	8.45	10.19	12.20	9.32	13.78	19.14	15.35	15.25	13.91	15.96	20.50	16.75
1981	10.13	11.52	13.78	10.61	16.29	19.29	17.27	19.36	14.88	15.81	20.90	18.00
1982	8.94	9.93	13.45	9.92	16.00	20.46	17.06	20.22	13.09	15.99	23.83	16.00
1983	8.07	8.23	11.80	8.17	14.37	14.40	13.90	18.30	11.27	16.91	28.83	18.00
1984	7.98	8.10	11.96	8.02	13.40	14.04	14.61	15.60	11.27	16.52	31.50	18.00
1985	7.04	7.33	10.61	7.77	11.87	11.57	12.64	13.71	11.06	13.37	30.13	18.00
1986	6.17	6.36	7.93	7.33	9.12	10.55	11.06	11.47	10.06	11.36	22.50	18.00
1987	6.24	6.35	7.83	6.94	10.22	11.92	11.27	10.58	9.59	12.77	19.06	18.04
1988	6.48	6.10	7.85	6.67	9.22	10.60	9.49	10.54	9.67	11.74	17.20	18.73
1989	7.03	7.21	8.64	7.13	9.15	10.22	8.95	11.61	10.19	13.80	19.75	20.38
1990	8.82	8.99	10.06	8.74	10.42	10.98	10.09	11.88	11.81	14.60	21.70	25.30
1991(a)	8.50	8.90	9.60	8.60	9.60	10.00	9.50	11.50	10.05	13.10	22.10	25.80

Source: NIESR database and Datastream.
(a) Includes forecast.

evidence from recent changes in long rates suggests that short rates are expected to converge in Germany, France, Belgium, the Netherlands, Austria and even Ireland. However, the United Kingdom, Italian and Spanish long rates show fewer signs of an expected convergence in short rates. This may not only be due to expectations of future higher inflation but, for countries such as Italy, the situation may be exacerbated by large government debt/GDP ratios. Nevertheless, if long rates do not converge it is a clear sign that markets are not expecting a union to be formed. The convergence criteria on long rates in the Maastricht Treaty seem loose, but even so long rates strongly suggest that Portugal and Greece are not expected to participate in a monetary union in the near future.

Government debt

In recent years, government primary balances have switched from deficit to surplus in France, Ireland, Denmark, Belgium and the United Kingdom. In contrast, primary deficits have been consistently recorded over the past decade for Italy, Greece and the Netherlands with Germany joining this group only recently. The sustainability of these positions depends upon whether the net government debt to GDP ratio is stable (although

Chart 1.12   *Gross government debt to GDP ratios for the UK,*
Ireland and Denmark

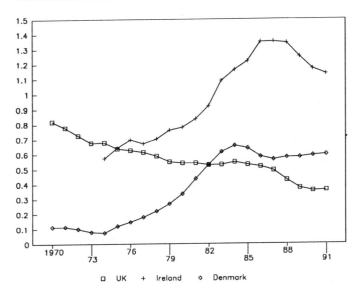

Source: NIESR database, Datastream.

Chart 1.13   *Gross government debt to GDP ratios for Italy, the Netherlands and Belgium*

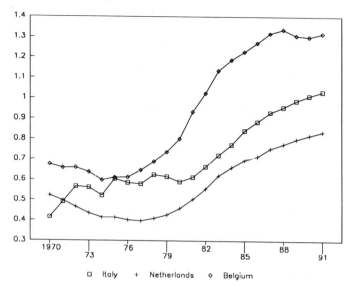

Source: NIESR database, Datastream

Chart 1.14   *Gross government debt to GDP ratios for Germany, France, Spain and Austria*

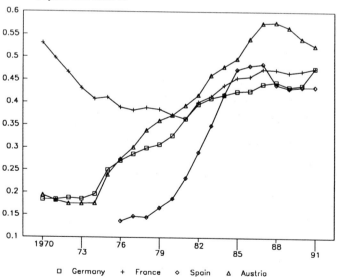

Source: NIESR database, Datastream

consideration should also be given to the absolute size of the net debt to GDP ratio). The Maastricht Treaty stresses the role of gross debt, in part because this is more easily measurable, although special consideration will be given to countries such as the Netherlands, where the funded public sector scheme drives a considerable wedge between the gross and net debt ratios.

Chart 1.12 shows that, although very high, Ireland's gross debt ratio is decreasing as are the smaller debt ratios of Denmark and the United Kingdom. Chart 1.13 reveals that the Netherlands, Belgium and Italy have substantial debt ratios, although Belgium seems to have halted the deterioration whereas Italy and the Netherlands seem to be on a less stable path.

As can be seen from chart 1.14, sustainable gross government debt positions seem to have been achieved by Germany, France, Spain and Austria. Consequently, taking into account both the absolute size and trajectory of debt ratios, convergence conditions require corrective fiscal action in Italy, Belgium, Ireland, Greece, Portugal and, perhaps to a lesser degree, the Netherlands.[9] However, the link between 'unsustainable' debt positions and real interest rates is somewhat tenuous – Italy and France have had very similar real interest rates over the past five years even though their fiscal positions have diverged substantially.[10] The high debt countries have seen their position deteriorate considerably in the 1980s, and face some risk of having an unstable debt position if real interest rates rise or growth rates fall.

External balance

From the viewpoint of external balance, charts 1.15–1.17 show that Belgium, Denmark, Germany, France, Ireland, Italy, Austria and the Netherlands seem to be in sustainable positions. However, this external equilibrium has been a fairly recent phenomenon for some countries and provides some tentative evidence of convergence; Denmark and Belgium registered current account deficits of over 5 per cent of GDP in the 1980s and Ireland began the decade with a 14 per cent deficit. Italy may be in a less favourable position than the chart suggests, as she has a small but deteriorating overseas deficit which may worsen due to the high Italian real exchange rate and narrowing of export profit margins. Germany has recently moved into current balance deficit and it should be remembered that the unusual temporary position of high demand for imports by Germany (because of reunification) has optimistically overstated the sustainability of the trading position of some ERM members.

Chart 1.17 shows that Spain and the United Kingdom may have structural trade problems which may only be solved by real devaluation or relatively slower growth.[11] However, capital flows are now more mobile

Chart 1.15   *Current balance to GDP ratios for Germany, France and the Netherlands (current balance as % of GDP)*

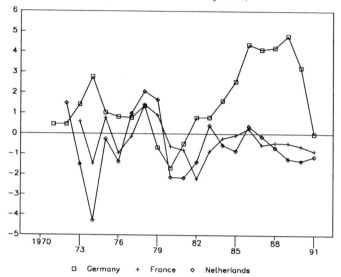

□   Germany   +   France   ◇   Netherlands

Source: NIESR database, Datastream

Chart 1.16   *Current balance to GDP ratios for Austria, Belgium, Denmark and Ireland (current balance as % of GDP)*

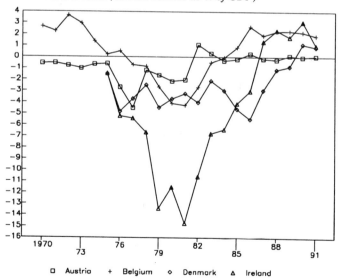

□   Austria   +   Belgium   ◇   Denmark   ▲   Ireland

Source: NIESR database, Datastream

Chart 1.17 *Current balance to GDP ratios for Italy, Spain and the UK (current balance as % of GDP)*

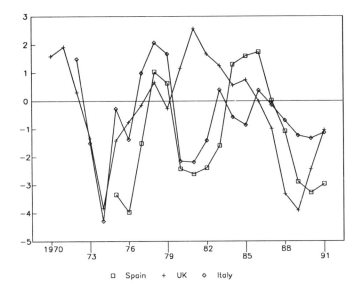

Source: NIESR database, Datastream

and substantial deficits relative to GDP can be sustained for long periods. Obviously, both fiscal and current balance deficits will be more easily sustained once monetary union occurs. Therefore, rapid convergence of these factors may not be as necessary as other macro-variables.

Unemployment

Both Italy and, in particular, Ireland currently have unemployment rates well above 10 per cent (and also reached higher levels in the process towards inflation convergence). But France, Belgium and Denmark also have high unemployment rates of around 9 per cent. The newcomers to the ERM, Spain and the United Kingdom, already have substantial unemployment rates of around 16 per cent and 9 per cent respectively (see table 1.5). The average unemployment rate within the ERM for 1990 of around 10.5 per cent compares unfavourably with the United States and Japan at 5.5 per cent and 2 per cent respectively. There is of course no reason to expect that all countries would have the same level of unemployment when they are at the NAIRU.

High unemployment rates seem to be partly the result of achieving nominal convergence with Germany via the implementation of deflationary packages.[12] The output/unemployment cost of these deflationary

Table 1.5 *Unemployment rates(a) (per cent of labour force)*

	Germany	Netherlands	Belgium	Austria	France	Denmark	Ireland	Italy	UK	Spain	Portugal	Greece
1978	3.15	3.43	7.24	1.71	5.34	7.29	8.19	7.29	4.92	6.96	7.92	1.83
1979	2.85	3.49	7.50	1.73	5.99	6.19	7.14	7.76	4.54	8.64	8.19	1.90
1980	2.52	4.13	7.89	1.54	6.33	7.00	7.30	7.66	6.10	11.46	7.98	2.75
1981	3.40	6.26	10.16	2.10	7.50	9.16	9.91	8.53	9.05	14.32	7.66	4.05
1982	5.02	8.82	11.89	3.11	8.15	9.79	11.42	9.19	10.43	16.41	7.50	5.78
1983	6.62	11.16	13.17	3.68	8.36	10.44	14.00	10.03	11.25	18.20	7.89	7.84
1984	7.08	11.18	13.21	3.79	9.80	10.06	15.53	10.14	11.40	20.15	8.55	8.15
1985	7.17	10.05	12.31	3.61	10.21	9.05	17.36	10.19	11.60	21.46	8.69	7.79
1986	6.44	9.18	11.63	3.11	10.39	7.82	17.36	11.24	11.76	21.03	8.59	7.38
1987	6.19	8.66	11.32	3.80	10.50	7.83	17.51	12.09	10.35	20.51	7.13	7.36
1988	6.16	8.28	10.28	3.58	9.99	8.59	16.72	12.17	8.18	19.49	5.75	7.68
1989	5.61	7.37	9.29	3.16	9.41	9.32	15.64	12.09	6.19	17.27	5.03	7.49
1990	5.07	6.47	8.79	3.30	9.01	9.58	14.05	11.04	5.52	16.25	4.63	7.74
1991(b)	4.99	6.46	8.84	3.54	9.43	9.79	14.72	11.30	8.22	15.92	4.50	9.00

(a) Commonly used definitions of unemployment rates.
(b) Includes forecast.

policies partly depends upon the credibility of the particular government's commitment to the exchange-rate parities of the ERM. By adopting credible policies consistent with the ERM exchange-rate bands, a government can 'borrow' the anti-inflation 'reputation' of Germany and reduce inflationary expectations. Studies such as Weber (1991) argue that reputation and credibility were not attained for the majority of the ERM countries until the later 1980s (around 1987) which may partly explain the high rates of unemployment prevalent in the last decade within the ERM.[13] Artis and Nachane (1990) claim that price expectations were shifted downward in the ERM period. They find that price expectations for ERM countries in the 1980s, relative to the 1970s, were more influenced by German inflation. Barrell (1990) shows that wage and price behaviour in some ERM member countries has undergone structural change in the past decade. However, although this change in structure has reduced the output costs of deflationary policies, it is possible that the fall in inflation has cost 700,000 and a million job losses in France and Italy respectively.[14]

The completion of the internal market programme in 1992 also has important implications for the labour market. Integration of the goods market in Europe should result in greater product price elasticity (as monopoly suppliers diminish) and hence a more price-elastic demand for labour. Either wage setters will become more responsive to the new conditions in the labour market or unemployment will rise further. It should be noted that the whole process of European integration, since the formation of the EC, has been associated with rising unemployment in Europe relative to outside the EC. One would expect the reduction of internal tariffs, greater cooperation and integration to actually decrease unemployment.

Longer-term prospects and convergence in Europe

We are presuming that a European Monetary Union will be formed some time around 1997 to include all member states except Greece and Portugal. The Maastricht Summit agreement defines, very precisely, what convergence criteria must be met for this to happen. However, interpretation may be much more liberal than the exhortation contained in the Treaty. We can, however, reasonably claim that monetary union will only take place if the following broad guidelines are met. First, interest rates must converge. Second, inflation rates (and price levels) must achieve some sort of long-term relationship. This long-term relationship is only likely to be possible if, thirdly, fiscal deficits are kept within bounds, and fourthly if the costs of convergence in terms of unemployment are not excessive.

We have used the National Institute global model, NIGEM, in order to produce a forecast of the medium term which assumes that governments in the Community are serious about their long-term commitment to union. We have assumed that interest rates in Europe converge by 1997. This alone will produce some degree of inflation convergence as the resulting system of fixed exchange rates will put pressure on wages and prices in the traded goods sector of the inflation-prone economies. Chart 1.18 plots our projections for inflation in the major four economies. We are anticipating that British and French inflation will be consistently below that in Germany over the next decade.

In Barrell and in't Veld (1991) we argued that the D-Mark was undervalued, and that this problem could only be ameliorated either by a revaluation or by faster inflation in Germany than in its partners. We believe that the second path is the more likely. The effects of German unification have loosened the German fiscal stance and have raised the rate of inflation in the Federal Republic. We expect that inflation will remain moderate in Germany, but that lower rates will be achieved in France and the United Kingdom. This is in part the effect of the initial small misalignment of the ERM system. If France and the United Kingdom are overvalued then exports will be lower than they otherwise would have been, imports will be higher, and the resulting balance of payments deficit will cause real wealth to drop increasingly far below its equilibrium trajectory. This will put downward pressure on demand in the overvalued countries, even if the deficit is easily financeable. Chart 1.19 plots our projections for the balance of payments of the four largest ERM members over the next decade. The pattern of deficits does not appear to be a potential source of stress in the Community.

The convergence of inflation will inevitably mean a gradual change in fiscal stance in some Community countries. The current version of NIGEM contains wealth effects in consumption, a full set of capital accounts and a set of public sector models for the major economies. This allows us to forecast public sector deficits in Europe over the next decade. Chart 1.20 plots the deficits in the major four economies. The public sector deficit in France is not currently excessive, and we expect consolidation to continue. Both the United Kingdom and West Germany have suffered recent deteriorations in their public sector balances and both might fail the Maastricht test next year. The deterioration in the United Kingdom is largely the result of the sudden downturn in activity, whilst that in Germany is the result of the costs of unification. Both countries can be expected to reduce their deficits in the medium term and to have no problems in meeting the Maastricht guidelines.

The Italian situation is somewhat different. We are assuming that the process of fiscal consolidation that has been under way since 1985 will continue. As a result the Italian deficit including interest payments (as a percentage of GDP) will fall from the current level of 9.5 per cent, and from its peak of 14 per cent in 1985 to the more manageable level

Chart 1.18   *Inflation rates in Europe*

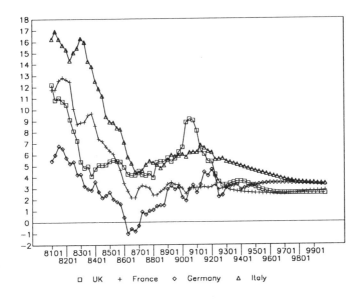

Note: Percentage change on a year previously.

Chart 1.19   *Current balances in Europe*

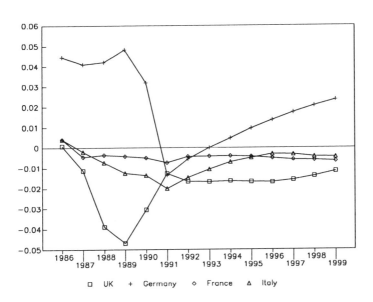

Note: Current account as a proportion of nominal GDP.

Chart 1.20 *Budget deficits in Europe*

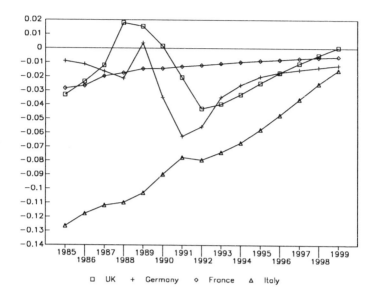

□ UK   + Germany   ◇ France   ▵ Italy

Note: Government sector net lending as a proportion of nominal GNP except the UK deficit is the Public Sector Financial Deficit as a per cent of nominal GDP.

of 2 per cent by 1999. This is a brave assumption, because we believe that this will only be possible if direct taxes are raised progressively. However the authorities are committed to reducing the deficit. In this forecast we are assuming that both public absorption of resources and public transfers will fall by 1½ per cent of GDP each whilst direct tax revenue rises from 25½ per cent of personal income in 1990 to 27 per cent in 1999.

Chart 1.21 plots our forecast of unemployment in Europe, and in some countries it stays stubbornly high throughout the decade. These economies may eventually return to full employment but the transition costs are not negligible. The Italian authorities believe that low inflation is a prize worth gaining, and high unemployment is a price worth paying. The National Institute's model, NIGEM, now has a complete model of the Italian personal and public sectors, and this allows us to quantify the effects. We have undertaken a simulation of our model in which we do not tighten fiscal policy. This would make union impossible, and inflation and interest rates would have to be higher. A looser fiscal stance in Italy would, over the medium term, raise growth by ½ per cent a year, inflation would be 1 per cent higher and unemployment would be slightly lower. In the long run, however, we believe that the real equilibrium of the economy may be little affected.

Chart 1.21   *Unemployment in Europe*

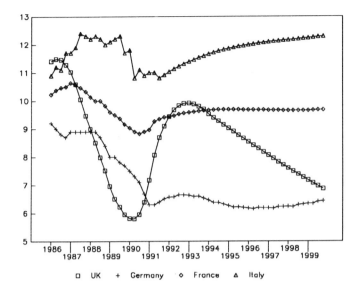

□ UK   + Germany   ◊ France   ▲ Italy

Note: Per cent of workforce

Conclusions

It is evident that substantial progress has been made towards nominal economic convergence among the ERM member countries. However, countries such as the United Kingdom, Spain and Italy are finding it more difficult to control price inflation and maintain competitiveness. Furthermore, countries such as France, Belgium, Denmark and Ireland have achieved inflation convergence *vis-à-vis* Germany only at the cost of substantially higher unemployment. Indeed, the ERM could be described as a low inflation–high unemployment regime. Conversely, the other members of the EC, Greece and Portugal, have not attained nominal convergence but have experienced relatively lower unemployment. It is worth noting that the best macroeconomic performance over the period analysed in this chapter was achieved by a non-ERM country, namely Austria.

Two major factors have had a favourable influence upon nominal convergence. First, most of the past decade has been associated with virtually worldwide macroeconomic stability. Convergence may have been more difficult to achieve if the ERM countries faced, for example, another substantial adverse oil price shock. Second, the inflationary impetus in Germany caused by reunification has given a flattering impression of convergence. However, compared with the past, German anti-inflation discipline is expected to be somewhat weaker for some time, therefore convergence may be further enhanced. But this does expose the fact that the ERM reputation of providing stable, and low, price inflation does depend on the ability of one nation to maintain control over price inflation.

The convergence of economic structures is an important factor influencing the sustainability of a monetary union once it has been formed. Inflation rates can be made to converge, and eventually it should even be possible for all economies in a union to operate at full employment with low inflation as long as no external shocks hit the system. Diversities in economic structures may well engender differing responses to external shocks, and differential experience of common events may make it politically impossible to hold a union together. Some differences in structure, such as those stemming from natural resources or from culture may be immutable. The United Kingdom, Norway and the Netherlands are energy producers and hence their response to an oil price shock will differ from that of the rest of the Community. Trading patterns, and in particular Britain's links with the United States, inevitably depend on culture. The effect on the Community of developments in the United States will depend on trade patterns, and shocks to the United States will feed through differentially. The effects of such shocks are inevitably asymmetric, and their implications are analysed in Barrell (1990a).

In Barrell (1990b) it is argued that other differences in structure such as those in labour markets may be more malleable. Labour market structures depend in part on the institutions that have been developed to deal with inflation and bargaining. Anderton, Barrell and McHugh extend this argument in Chapter 2. Some countries, such as Italy and the United Kingdom, appear to react rapidly to inflationary shocks, whilst others such as Germany respond only slowly. These differences will amplify the effects of common shocks. Even if a shock to the union is in the long run symmetric in its effects, differences in the dynamic patterns of response may make effects asymmetric in the short run. As Barrell, Gurney and in't Veld (1991) argue, these asymmetries may make a union difficult to sustain.

A successful union would be more likely if a shock had only small effects on the location of the new equilibrium for the exchange rate and unemployment in the economies of the union. This may require some convergence of structures and institutions. The mere existence of the union may help produce such convergence of structures. Labour market institutions will evolve in relation to the more stable environment. This process can be speeded up in various ways. The single market programme should increase competition within Europe, and this will produce pressures on wage bargainers to act in the same way throughout the Community. It will also increase the sensitivity of trade flows to competitiveness and, as Barrell and in't Veld (1991) show, this will reduce the effects of shocks on the location of the equilibrium exchange rate. However, institutional adaptation without political assistance can be very slow.

As Europe moves closer towards a full economic and monetary union the whole issue of convergence becomes more complicated. If the date for union is known, this opens up the possibility of devaluations immediately before exchange rates become rigidly fixed. This action would be beneficial for the devaluing countries in terms of short-term price competitiveness and reductions in the real value of government debt, but it might harm the anti-inflation reputation of the countries concerned. For this reason, some authors (for example, Froot and Rogoff, 1990) argue that convergence has peaked as expectations of the above scenario will cause prices and interest rates to diverge now. Conversely, the prospect of irrevocably fixed exchange rates may provide extra policy credibility and enhance the process of convergence.

Notes

1 For other studies of convergence in Europe see Ungerer *et al.* (1986, 1990), *European Economy* (1989, 1990), Froot and Rogoff (1991) and AMEX *Bank Review* (1991).

2 In Barrell, Gurney and in't Veld (1992) we demonstrate that the process of real exchange-rate adjustment may be very protracted and the adjustment costs are unequally shared, which could cause severe strains to be put on the union.

3 The requirement for a debt/GDP ratio to stabilise at its present level if $p = (i-g).d$ where p is the primary balance, i the nominal interest rate, g the nominal growth rate and d the desired or present debt/GDP ratio. This simply states that the non-interest surplus must be large enough to offset the increase in the debt/GDP ratio due to interest payments on debt. This condition can be modified to allow for taxation of interest payments on debt, valuation changes on existing debt and money-financed borrowing.

4 Chan-Lee *et al.* (1987) points out that the Netherlands 'reduced nominal minimum wages for workers under 23 by 10 per cent in 1983'.

5 See Mehta and Sneesens (1990) for further details.

6 Weber (1991) makes it clear that the French austerity programme really began in earnest after the March 1983 realignment of the French franc.

7 Barrell (1990) gives details of the *Scala Mobile* and shows that in 1983 the degree of wage indexation was reduced from 1 to 0.85. However, he states that the most significant reforms of the Italian indexation mechanism occurred in 1985.

8 The OECD report goes on to state that 'the level of wages for both private and public sector services (in Italy) has continued to exceed that in the exposed sector, suggesting that both employers and employees share the economic rent caused by the lack of competitive pressure'.

9 For calculations of the required primary surplus for debt sustainability for the ERM countries, see Commission of the European Communities (1990).

10 Barro (1990) estimates reduced-form models for expected real interest rates for ten OECD countries and generally finds fiscal variables to be an unimportant determinant of real interest rates.

11 Alogoskoufis *et al.* (1990) provides a thorough examination of external constraints for European economies.

12 In contrast, the failure of Greece and Portugal to achieve nominal convergence has been associated with relatively lower unemployment rates.

13 Opinions differ here as to the role of credibility. For example, Dornbusch (1989) argues that Irish inflation convergence was attained via old-fashioned deflationary policies with no extra credibility effect, whereas Kremers (1990) argues that extra ERM credibility may have decreased the unemployment cost of reducing inflation in Ireland.

14 The necessity for persistently high unemployment rates within the ERM in order to reduce inflation is a controversial issue. For example, in 1988 the long-term unemployed accounted for more than 60 per cent of the unemployed in Belgium, Ireland, Italy and Spain (see p. 51 of Layard, Nickell and Jackman, 1991). As the long-term unemployed are generally thought to contribute very little to the disinflationary process, the inflation cost of re-employing them may be negligible.

2

Nominal Convergence in European Wage Behaviour: Achievements and Explanations

Robert Anderton, Ray Barrell and James McHugh

Introduction

Monetary union in Europe both requires and will produce convergence in economic performance, at least in terms of inflation. A monetary union will force individual members to have similar rates of inflation, although the unemployment consequences in some countries could in the medium term be considerable. If a group of economies individually display no long-run trade-off between unemployment and inflation then it is always possible to fix their exchange rates together. However, the process is not without cost. A group of countries with different histories may well have different labour market institutions, and hence they may react very differently to shocks. Unless institutions also converge, the convergence of inflation in periods of external calm may not be sufficient for the successful maintenance of a monetary union in periods of external turbulence.

Labour market structures depend in part on the institutions that have developed to deal with inflation and bargaining. An obvious difference is the speed at which a shock to prices feeds into wages. There is a great deal of evidence available on this, but table 2.1 summarises a commonly held set of views. The Institute world model, NIGEM, contains wage relations for each of the four major European economies. In each case we have assumed that in the long run wages rise in line with prices. However the speed of reaction differs between countries with the longest lag (indicated by the mean lag) between wages and prices being seen in Germany, and the shortest in Italy. There is indeed some evidence that there is some overshooting of the response of wages to prices in Italy.

The ranking of the speed of reaction of wages to prices is in accordance with our prior beliefs. German inflation has been both low and constant over the last 35 years, and the authorities have built up a considerable anti-inflation reputation. Wage bargainers do not need to react quickly to changes in prices, because experience suggests that they do not signal a sustained acceleration in inflation. Italian experience has been very

Table 2.1   *Wage equations on NIGEM*

	Elasticity	Mean lag
	of wages with respect to consumer prices	
Germany	1.0	3.6
France	1.0	0.8
UK	1.0	−0.3
Italy	1.0	−1.0

different, and since the collapse of the Bretton Woods system inflation has been high and variable. Details of European experience can be found in Chapter 1 of this volume. Because the authorities lack credibility wage bargainers feed changes in prices into wages very quickly indeed. We have undertaken a number of studies (Barrell, 1990a, Barrell, Britton and Mayes, 1990, Barrell, Gurney and Dulake, 1990) that attempt to analyse the implications of dynamic asymmetries in Europe.

We can follow the EC study 'One Market, One Money' (Commission of the European Communities, 1990) and make a distinction between the effects of symmetric and asymmetric shocks, with the latter causing more severe coordination problems. Even if a shock to the union is symmetric, if differences in labour markets persist, then the effects of a shock would, in the short to medium term, be asymmetric. This chapter discusses the reasons for differences in labour market structure between countries, and it attempts to assess whether or not a union would aid the process of structural change. To that end we discuss the evidence of the effect of the ERM (and of other policy initiatives) on the structure of labour markets. We also investigate the effects of increasing competition within the Community in order to analyse the changing environment within which labour market bargains are struck.

The first section of this chapter discusses our approach to bargaining in the labour market and enumerates the factors that should affect the bargain. The second section assesses the effects of the ERM on wage bargaining in Europe and reports on our work on structural changes in the processes determining wages in Europe. This is followed by an assessment of the evidence for changes in the nature of trade competitiveness and a discussion of its implications for the future of wage bargaining in Europe. Our conclusion discusses the relationship between one market and one money.

Labour markets and the ERM

There can be no doubt that membership of the ERM and a reduction in inflation have been statistically associated over the last twelve years.[1]

Inflation has tended to converge on German standards amongst ERM members, and this convergence has been most marked since around 1985. However, there are two possible explanations. Membership of the ERM could have increased the credibility of the authorities and hence changed the nature of wage bargaining, increasing the effects of deflationary policies. Alternatively, all we may be observing is that a commitment to a fixed exchange rate mechanism must be associated with loss of direct control over aggregate demand, and hence in a number of countries the effects of deflationary policies were enhanced by worsening competitiveness. These effects together may be sufficient to explain the nominal convergence so thoroughly documented by the Commission in its paper on 'Wage Adjustment' in *European Economy* no. 50.

If one country in a fixed exchange rate mechanism is the dominant player then it will tend to dictate the inflation rate in the long run. At minimum this will operate through a process of disequilibrium in other countries. If, for instance, France inflates faster than Germany then it will become increasingly uncompetitive, exports will fall increasingly below their constant competitiveness path, and imports will rise. Current account deficits will cause wealth to decumulate, and aggregate demand will become increasingly depressed. Inflation will, as a result, have to fall until the price level reaches some equilibrium relationship with that in Germany. Evidence to support recession-generated convergence is given by Artis and Ormerod (1991), and the bivariate causality tests reported by Artis and Nachane (1990) also suggest that German inflation has affected inflation elsewhere in the ERM.

Inflation reduction could be produced in other ways. It is argued that German leadership allows other countries to adopt the Bundesbank anti-inflationary mantle.[2] Increased credibility supposedly changes the sacrifice ratio by causing the structure of bargaining to change. The evidence on this hypothesis is mixed. Dornbusch (1991) provides a cautious assessment, and Artis and Ormerod (1991) suggest that after a period of deflationary turbulence labour market behaviour outside Germany has returned to its previous pattern. The work by Barrell, Darby and Donaldson (1991)[3] is slightly more optimistic about the possibility of change, but locates the change in the positive transformation of institutions rather than as a 'manna from heaven' break in behaviour.

In order to assess the process of structural change in labour markets we have to understand the process of wage determination, both in long-run equilibrium and also in terms of its dynamic evolution. As up to three-quarters of all workers in Europe are covered directly or indirectly by collective bargaining we feel that it is productive to work in the bargaining framework discussed in Layard, Nickell and Jackman (1991). This work is the latest in a series of papers[4] that have developed this approach. The bargaining framework produces a reduced form wage equation that encapsulates the demand for labour and the supply of labour as well as the role of trade unions. The most common approach assumes that firms have the 'right to manage'. The wage rate is determined by the bargain between employers, unions and workers, and then the employers have the right to choose the number of employees. Hence, given the wage, they are able to stay on their demand curve for labour.

The outcome of any bargaining process will depend upon the objectives of the bargainers, their relative strengths and the environment within which they find themselves. The obvious objective for the firm to consider is to maximise its profits, and the profit function will also depend upon the price of other inputs, on the production technology and on demand conditions. We will assume that the union is interested in the welfare of its members, both those who remain in the firm and those who are outside it. The Nash approach to bargaining derives the equilibrium as

$$\max_{W} \ (U\ (W) - \bar{U})^{\beta}(\pi(\ W) - \bar{\pi}\ )^{(1-\beta)}$$

where β is an indicator of union power, U is the utility of the union, W is the wage, $\bar{U}$ is the fall-back utility level that the union will not go below, π is the firms profits, and $\bar{\pi}$ is the fall-back level of profits (which should over the longer term not be negative).

The bargain should result in a wage above the competitive level, and as a result employment in the industries covered will fall. Not all workers remain 'insiders', some are outsiders, and receive either the non-unionised wage or the level of unemployment benefit. The 'outsiders' may also be of no importance to the union when striking its bargain. Layard, Nickell and Jackman (1991) derive a simple and revealing formula for the mark-up of the union wage over the free market wage. They assume that the union utility depends upon the difference between the insider and outsider wage (or benefit) and on the probability of members of the union receiving the insider's wage. In order to simplify their analysis they also assume that the production technology is Cobb Douglas. This gives them a simple formulae for the mark-up of the insider wage over the outsider wage.

$$M = (1-\alpha K)/(\varepsilon_{sn}+\alpha\ K/\beta)$$

where M is the mark up, α is the Cobb Douglas production parameter reflecting the labour intensity of production, K is the indicator of product market competitiveness that depends upon the elasticity of demand for the products produced by the unionised sector, β is an indicator of union power and ε_{sn} the elasticity of the probability of remaining an insider with respect to the level of employment. Layard, Nickell and Jackman argue that $\varepsilon_{sn} < 1$.

The mark-up, or rent, gained by unionised workers will be higher the stronger are trade unions, the less competitive are product markets and the lower is the labour intensity of production. The product market competitiveness indicator K ($=1-1/|\varepsilon^{d}|$) is of particular relevance to our analysis. As the elasticity of demand for the product becomes larger the potential mark-up will fall, and if the ERM is associated with increases in product market competitiveness then it will be associated with lower real wages.

The determination of the wage (or benefit) received by those not employed by the firm is clearly of considerable importance in the determination of the economy-wide real wage. It first of all determines the wage of some proportion of the workforce and, given the constancy of the mark-up, it will influence the aggregate wage in the economy. We would expect the reservation wage in the non-unionised sector, and hence the overall wage, to be positively related to the level of benefits available to the unemployed. Unemployment may also affect the reservation wage and it may affect the relative power of unions and employers. A large pool of unemployed may make union members more fearful for their jobs, and it may also make it easier for firms to find alternative sources of labour.

Taxation and the real exchange rate may also have a role in the determination of equilibrium wages. The real consumption wage R may be written as

$$R = W \, (1-t^{d})/PC$$
$$\text{where } PC = ((1-s_{i}) \, P + \, s_{i} \, PMA) \, (1+t^{i})$$

where W is the nominal wage, t^{d} is the rate of direct taxation, and PC is the price of consumer goods. Consumers buy both home produced goods and imported goods, and s_{i} is the proportion spent on imported goods priced at PMA and the rest of expenditure is on home produced goods priced at P. We assume that indirect taxes t^{i} are paid on all goods.

These tax and import price factors give us a wedge between the consumer goods and the producer goods wage. As both the unionised sector wage and the reservation wage and benefits are subject to the same taxes, and consumption bundles all contain imports, we can say as a first approximation that the mark-up of the unionised over the non-unionised wage is unaffected by this wedge. If the wedge affects the quantity of labour supplied, and hence the wage, in the secondary sector it should affect the overall level of wages. Of course the smaller the secondary sector and the less elastic the supply of labour the less important is the wedge in determining wages.

The equilibrium real wage will therefore potentially depend upon unemployment, the power of unions, the degree of product market competition, the production technology, and the wedge. We may write this schematically as

$$W/P = f(u, \beta, (Y/L), K, \alpha, \text{wedge})$$

where Y/L is the level of productivity implied by the production function. If union power, unemployment, the degree of product market power and the essential production technology all remain unchanged then we would expect real wages to grow in line with productivity.

We have spelled out the factors affecting the bargain in order to demonstrate that we would not expect them to be affected by the policy credibility of the authorities or by the exchange-rates regime it chooses. If the exchange-rate regime is to have an effect on the structure of the wage–price system we must look for it elsewhere. However, our analysis does allow us to bring out some institutional differences between the countries of the community. These affect both the structure of the bargain and the dynamics of the wage–price system, and it is in the dynamics of the wage–price system that we should see credibility effects from exchange-rate systems.

The dynamic responses we observe in wage equations are not the result of accidents but follow from the conscious construction of labour market institutions. Bargainers construct the institutions partly in the light of the policy credibility of the authorities. If the authorities have a poor anti-inflationary record then bargainers will not wish to have too long a period between renegotiating contracts. They will expect inflationary shocks to be validated and not reversed, and hence they will want short contracting periods. The shorter the contracting period the less nominal wage rigidity we would expect to observe. Shocks to prices will be quickly absorbed into wages, and as a result real wages are likely to be less flexible.

There are other ways in which the credibility of the authorities will affect the dynamics of the wage–price system. In countries such as Italy or even Belgium the low anti-inflationary credibility of the authorities led to widespread contract indexation in the 1970s. Indeed in Italy until 1983 money wages were uprated in line with inflation once a quarter. Indexation mechanisms of this sort produce considerable rigidities in real wages and rapid propagation of shocks. They imply that the effects of a series of leapfrogging wage demands, or the effects of an oil price shock, could easily lead to a rapid acceleration in inflation.

Contracting periods and indexation mechanisms are not the only factors affecting the process of dynamic adjustment of wages. Individuals have to form expectations about the future, and their expectations generating mechanisms will depend on the credibility of the authorities. If expectations are based in part on current and past data then history will affect the evolution of the wage bargain. The more credible the authorities' anti-inflation stance the less will bargainers change these expectations in response to current news. If the authorities' stance becomes more credible, or the optimal information set changes, then we would expect the expectations generating mechanism to change. Anderton, Barrell and McHugh (1991) and Artis and Nachane (1990) both demonstrate that the optimal (in the sense of minimising least squares errors) information set changed in the 1980s, with German inflation becoming an important predictor of inflation elsewhere. These changes are already well documented, and we wish to investigate whether or not a change in perceived credibility changes the structure of the wage bargaining process rather then just affecting one of the inputs into the bargain.

There are many other reasons for observing dynamic or nominal inertia in wage bargaining. Persistence in the number of insiders, even if unemployed, can affect the wage bargain for some period of time. There are also many reasons why there can be lags caused by inefficient access to information in standard bargaining frameworks. Some relatively centralised bargaining systems, such as that in Germany, may process information efficiently and hence speed up the wage–price process. Decentralisation may do the reverse. We might not expect these elements of the dynamics to be affected by a change in the credibility of the authorities.

This chapter reports on a series of tests for the stability of the wage bargaining process throughout the European Community. We would expect that there is the possibility that the dynamics of the wage–price process may change as a result of ERM membership. We do not expect that the long-run structure of the bargain should be much affected. However, there have been other processes at work over the last decade. There have been changes in unemployment benefit regimes and in the power of trade unions. These may have changed the sacrifice ratios facing ERM members. The gradual removal of trade barriers between Community countries could have increased the degree of product market competition and hence may have reduced the insider wage mark-up and have changed the evolution of real wages over time.

The mark-up of the insider wage depends upon the elasticity of demand for the product produced. The lower is the elasticity of demand for the product the larger the monopoly rent that is available to firms, and hence the larger the pie for firms and unions to bargain over. If product markets were perfectly competitive then there would be little room for a union mark-up however strong the bargaining position of unions. If competitiveness elasticities have risen within Europe as trade has become less restricted then there is less room for independent variation in prices within the Community.

The opening up of trade within the Community has probably been associated with increases in product market competition. This should be associated with increases in competitiveness elasticities. If price behaviour becomes coherent across the countries of the Community then we might expect this to impact on the dynamics of wage setting and push them towards common dynamics patterns.

As margins are cut, and the rent available for division shrinks, we would expect short-run changes in wages to be increasingly dictated by short-run variations in prices. Price changes cannot be so easily absorbed by rents when they are not large. Even if this process has not gathered momentum, we would expect it to become more important as the Community continues along the road to one market.

Wage behaviour

This section reports on the work undertaken by Barrell, Darby and Donaldson (1990) and especially on that undertaken by Anderton, Barrell and McHugh (1991). Both pieces of work have approached the problem of structural change by estimating wage equations for European countries and testing them for structural stability. The first study covered only the United Kingdom, Italy, France and Germany, whilst the latter study has extended both our analysis and our coverage. We have studied all of the countries in the Community[5] and have also included Austria because of the strong links with Germany and the fixity of the schilling–D-Mark parity.

Our general approach has been to estimate a wage equation that includes both the long-run factors affecting the wage and the bargain, and also the factors affecting the dynamic process of wage adjustment. Our approach can be schematically summarised. We assume:

$\log (W/P) = a + b_1 \log (Y/L) + b_2$ tax wedge
$+ b_3$ real exchange rate $+ b_4$ unemployment indicators
$+ b_5$ union power indicators $+ b_6$ product market indicators
$+ b_7$ expectations $+$ dynamics.

Where W is the nominal wage, P is the price level, Y/L is the long-run level of labour productivity. We have in general used compensation per person hour in our analysis, and the tax wedge was defined as direct taxes, indirect taxes and taxes on employment paid by employers.[6]

Our hypotheses on this relationship are then

(1) $b_1 = 1$ Wages rise in line with productivity in the long run as long as other factors are constant.
(2) $b_2 \geq 0$ The tax and real exchange rate wedges should have a
      $b_3 \geq 0$ positive or zero effect.
(3) $b_4 \leq 0$ Unemployment should have a non-positive effect on wages.
(4)   If expectations affect the quarterly change in wages then their effect is scaled by the period that bargainers look ahead.

$b_7 \leq 1$ for quarterly indicators.
$b_7 \leq .25$ for annual indicators.

If real product wages over our sample period have not risen in line with productivity then this suggests that other forces are at work, and we hope to capture these in our analysis. However we may not be able to do so. Real wages in France have not risen in line with productivity over the last two decades. This could reflect the changing relative power of unions and employers or it could reflect the increased product market competitiveness that has come from the formation of the Community. Neither have real wages risen in line with productivity in Germany and the Netherlands over the last twelve years. Again we would hope to capture the causes in our analysis. However, the cause may be the formation of the ERM. Both these countries have high wages and high productivity. The formation of the ERM has reduced exchange-rate uncertainty and this may have induced large outflows of direct investment to lower cost locations. Schatz, Scheide and Trapp (1988) explain the large German current account surpluses of the 1980s as in part the consequence of a higher rate of return available outside Germany.

There is of course a great deal of debate over the variables that we might use in studying wage relationships. The current level of unemployment may not be a good indicator of the effect of unemployment on the wage bargain. If there is large proportion of long-term unemployed who may have become deskilled and demotivated then their presence in our unemployment count may change its effect on the wage bargain. We have therefore included both the level and change of unemployment in our regressions. If unemployment is rising we would expect its negative effect upon wage inflation to be enhanced, and the reverse when it is falling. Union power often cycles with the state of the economy, and we presume that it changes in line with the business cycle indicators that we include. Expectations[7] are proxied by either the one-period or four-period ahead change in prices. The relevant lead for expectations depends upon the contract structure. The shorter the contracting period the shorter the lead on expectations. Indeed, if the wage bargaining system includes some automatic backward indexation then there are groups who will not be affected by expectations. This situation was clearly the case with quarterly backward indexation in Italy under the *Scala Mobile*, and it also holds for groups whose contracts are governed by law, such as civil servants and those on minimum wages.

If the ERM changes wage behaviour then we should expect to see systematic change in the pattern of dynamics in our equations. If back-ward indexation is removed then we should expect to see the role of expectations enhanced. If the ERM alters the effective contracting period then we would expect the mean lag in our equations to change. We will first of all assess the evidence for the major four economies. We will then look at the EC as a whole.

We have looked at the stability of our estimated equations in two ways. We have taken as our null hypothesis that there is no structural change and we have then tested for systematic change in the whole relationship starting in the period 1979Q1.[8] Although this test is statistically correct, it is weak, and we have used two other approaches. The first used Salkever style dummies.[9] Our relationship is estimated over the whole period, and then re-estimated with a dummy on each time period after 1979Q1. If there is no systematic structural change these dummies should vary around zero. If however a wage equation for the 1960s and 1970s begins to systematically overpredict wages in the 1980s then the pattern of Salkever dummies should be revealing. Our third approach is to look at the stability of individual parameters.

The major four economies
The diverse inflationary experience of the four large European economies is documented in Chapter 1. Both the United Kingdom and Italy have experienced two major inflationary episodes in the last twenty years, whilst consumer inflation in Germany has never risen above 7 per cent over this period. These differences in experience should, we believe, be

Table 2.2   *Wage equations in the major four economies*

	General characteristics			
	Germany	France	Italy	UK
Productivity	Unit coefficient	Unit coefficient	Unit coefficient	Unit coefficient
Tax wedge	Little	Little	Little	0.5
Unemployment	Lagged, and change lagged 3 periods (significant)	Lagged level (not sig- nificant)	Lagged plus change in hours	Lagged
Expectations	No role	One quarter ahead preferred	Both work	One year ahead
Speed of dynamics of pass-through of prices to wages (mean lag)	9.26 quarters	7.49 quarters	1.68 quarters	5.35 quarters
Structural stability	No change	A little evidence	Some indicators	None

Chart 2.1   *Germany Salkever dummies (prediction errors from a wage equation for the pre-ERM period)*

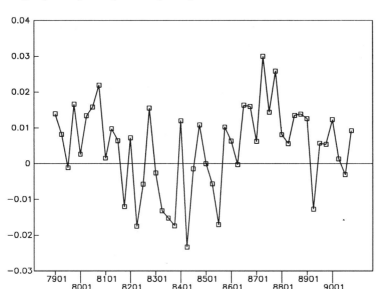

Note: No role was found for expectations in our German equations.

reflected in wage bargaining and hence in our estimated equations. Our equations for Italy, the United Kingdom and France all have a role for expectations, and hence differ somewhat from those described in table 2.1. However, there is no change in the ranking of the speeds of adjustment of wages to prices. Table 2.2 summarises our results.

Germany   All of our work on Germany suggests that there has been no systematic change in the structure of wage determination over the last twenty years. Inflation has been low, and collective bargaining has been relatively centralised. Contractual indexation of wages has been illegal in Germany over the period of our study. Our results suggest that unemployment has played a significant role in wage determination, and it is the short-term unemployed who have had more effect.

Neither price inflation expectations nor backward changes in prices appear to enter the German wage bargain. Wages rise in the long run in line with prices but in the short term acceleration effects from actual or expected changes in inflation are not built into wages. This in part reflects the long and stable contracting round in the German economy. Chart 2.1 plots the Salkever Dummies associated with our wage equation. These suggest that a wage equation based on 1960s and 1970s data does not produce biased forecasts of the rate of change in wages over the 1980s. There is some evidence of nominal rigidities in the late 1980s when price inflation fell below zero.

The United Kingdom   The United Kingdom economy saw a particularly severe period of deflation in the early 1980s. This was associated with a change in government, and the Thatcher administration clearly wanted to introduce a new regime into wage bargaining. The new administration's programme was essentially monetarist, anti-inflation policy was based upon targets for the growth rate of the money supply, and micro policies aimed at improving the supply-side of the economy were adopted. The tight monetary policy of the medium term financial strategy resulted in the minimum lending rate reaching a peak of 17 per cent in the early 1980s. During the Conservatives' first term in office, trade union reforms were introduced, credit markets were liberalised, government expenditure cutbacks were introduced and unemployment rose above three million. It was widely believed that these policies had transformed the behaviour of the labour market.

The second Conservative election victory in 1983 heralded the beginning of the government's privatisation programme and the continuation of income tax reductions. The government continued reducing the powers of trade unions and encouraging labour market flexibility by, for example, removing minimum wage council protection from half a million workers. The miners' strike ended in victory for the government in 1985 and enhanced the weakening of trade unions. By 1986 unemployment had peaked at 3.2 million but inflation had fallen to 2½ per cent in July of that year. In 1987 the government announced targets for the D-Mark and US dollar as sterling shadowed the D-Mark. By 1988, confidence in the British economy was at a peak; productivity was growing rapidly, inflation was low and unemployment was now decreasing fast. Unfortunately, substantial tax reductions, combined with financial and credit market liberalisation, resulted in an economic boom beyond the potential output capacity of the United Kingdom economy. The current balance began to move into substantial deficit (peaking at 4 per cent of GDP in 1989) and inflation rose to above 10 per cent in 1990. Skill shortages and supply-side bottlenecks tended to add to the inflationary impetus of the boom. The policy response was to raise interest rates (reaching a peak of 15 per cent in 1990) which eventually resulted in a recession during 1990–91. It was at this stage that the United Kingdom decided to join the ERM in 1990 with wide fluctuation bands of +/– 6 per cent.[10]

Our results suggest that there seems to have been no significant structural change in United Kingdom wage behaviour in the 1980s. However, the Salkever dummies for equation 1 (see chart 2.2) suggest that there may have been some downward shift in wage inflation in

Chart 2.2   *UK Salkever dummies (prediction errors for wage equations for the pre-Thatcher period)*

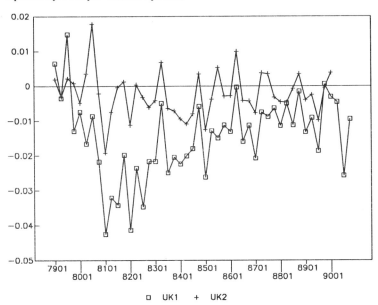

□ UK1   + UK2

Note: UK1 does not take account of expectations and is estimated by OLS; UK2 does take account of one-year ahead expectations.

response to the strong anti-inflation signals of the early 1980s. This effect is gradually eroded in the later years, even though trade union reform continued. This is congruent with the discussion of the late 1980s in *European Economy no. 50*. Perhaps the strong growth of demand over this period was inconsistent with a credible anti-inflationary policy. The forward-looking equation shows no discernible movement in the Salkever dummies.

Italy   After the rise in inflation during the early 1970s, many countries adopted either formal or informal wage indexation procedures. The reform of the indexation mechanism in Italy has been particularly instructive. In that country the process of wage indexation had become formalised in a set of agreements characterised as the *Scala Mobile*. Formal indexation agreements can be very informationally efficient if the authorities have a reputation for validating shocks. The Italian authorities' commitment to the ERM in 1979 was accompanied by a clear change in their anti-inflationary stance. However this shift and its sustainability were not obvious even in the early 1980s, and the process of removing the *Scala Mobile* was long and painful.

Wage bargaining in Italy has been structured as a three-tier process for some time. Negotiations take place at national, sectoral and firm level, and the state has often played an active role. Indexation and the effects of inflation have generally been handled at national level by union confederations, employers' associations and the government. The importance of the nationwide negotiations reached its peak in the early 1970s, but it was also significant in the debate over the reform of the indexation mechanism during the first half of the 1980s.

The debate on wage formation in Italy was for some time centred around the generalised price indexation of wages, the *Scala Mobile*. Reforms were introduced in 1977 and 1983, but the most significant changes were enacted in 1985. Automatic indexation had existed in Italy since the early 1950s, but price indexation was not particularly important in a period when real wages were growing rapidly. However during the 1970s real wage growth slowed considerably. In 1975 and 1977 the coverage of the *Scala Mobile* increased, and Bank of Italy estimates suggest that the proportion of wage changes 'caused' by the *Scala Mobile* rose from 60 per cent in 1975 to around 80 per cent by 1978. This centralisation and codification of wage indexation almost beyond doubt made the pass-through of price shocks to wages more automatic and more rapid.

It was only as the monetary stance of the Bank of Italy become more credible that it was possible to reform the *Scala Mobile*. In 1983 the mechanism was modified and the degree of indexation was reduced from 1.0 to 0.85. However, the most important reform took place in 1985. Firstly, the frequency of adjustments was reduced from quarterly to half-yearly, slowing down the speed of pass-through. Secondly, the indexation rules were modified so that only those on low wages were compensated fully. Wages above a rather low minimum were either partially indexed or not indexed at all. These changes in the *Scala Mobile* do appear to have had a significant effect on the wage–price spiral in Italy, and have contributed to observed changes in behaviour. However, it is fair to say that these changes were rather slow to come after the formation of the ERM, and they were painful to introduce. The authorities tried to remove the last vestiges of the *Scala Mobile* in the summer of 1990, but they were prevented from doing so by trade union pressure.

In our research it has proved difficult to find a permanent effect from unemployment upon wage inflation for Italy for the period 1970–90. The absence of short-run unemployment effects is also surprising. It is claimed that slack in the Italian labour market is frequently manifested in terms of reduced working hours rather than in increased unemployment. This may of course reflect a change in the structure of the market. Chart 2.3 plots the coefficient on unemployment on our wage equation when estimated

Chart 2.3   *The effects of unemployment on wages in Italy*
(coefficient of ITU(−1) and its two S.E. bands based on rolling IV)

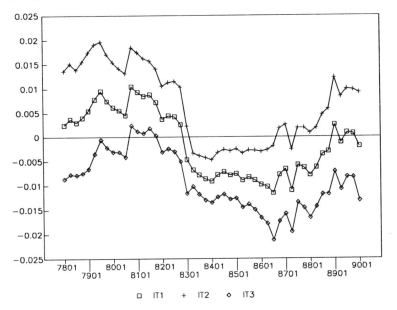

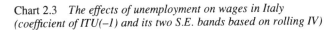

Note: Window size 30.

by rolling instrumental variables. We take our equation estimated over the whole period and re-estimate it over a moving time frame. If a parameter changes it should show up in the plot. The plot of the effect of Italian unemployment is instructive. During the 1970s unemployment had an insignificant effect on the determination of wages. However at some time in the early 1980s this changed, giving the authorities a greater degree of control. This parametric shift will have reduced the 'sacrifice ratio', cutting the unemployment cost of a given reduction in inflation. The change may have come either from a process of institutional change, or from an accession of credibility on the part of the authorities. The gradual erosion of the gain during the late 1980s may indicate that the re-emergence of an inflationary problem comes from more than an increase in demand. If labour market rigidities have increased as the public sector has increased wages then the costs of disinflation in the ERM may have risen.

Our results on overall structural change have been mixed. The study by Barrell, Darby and Donaldson (1990) found systematic evidence for change. Once we change our treatment of expectations then the evidence for structural change becomes weaker. However, the profile of the Salkever dummies in chart 2.4 indicates a downward shift in

Chart 2.4 *Italy Salkever dummies (forecast errors from wage equations based on pre-ERM data)*

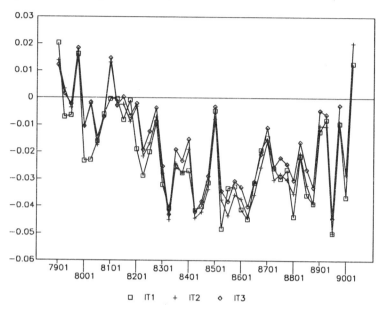

□ IT1   + IT2   ◇ IT3

Note: IT1 is estimated by OLS and does not take account of expectations; IT2 and IT3 take account of one-quarter ahead and one-year ahead expectations respectively.

wage behaviour beginning around the time of the initial dismantling of the *Scala Mobile*. The failure to find significant overall change in part reflects the weakness of full equation tests, and is in conflict with single parameter tests.

France   There have been a large number of labour market reforms in France over the last decade. The two that have been most discussed have been the gradual decentralisation of collective bargaining and the removal of stringent redundancy regulations. In the 1970s and early 1980s much of French bargaining was both national and industrial, a pattern similar to that seen in Germany. Many agreements had automatic backward-looking indexation included in them, reducing the degree of real wage flexibility. Over the 1980s bargaining moved increasingly to the firm and plant level, and has become much more like that in the United Kingdom. In 1986 there were major changes in redundancy regulations, making severance much easier. This deregulation has raised the degree of labour market flexibility. All redundancies previously had to be notified and approved. The effect appears to have been to reduce hirings for a given macro-environment and hence raise the NAIRU by extending the period of search between

Chart 2.5 *France Salkever dummies (forecast errors on wage equations based on the pre-ERM period)*

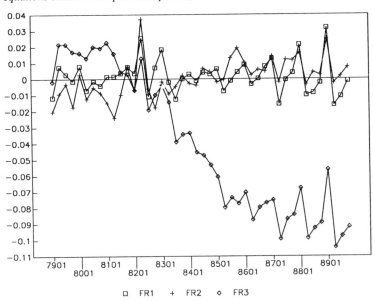

Note: FR1 is estimated without taking account of expectations; FR2 does take account of one-period ahead price expectations, but has no role for unemployment; FR3 takes account of one-year ahead expectations but has a positive and significant coefficient on unemployment and hence is implausible.

jobs. However, there is little evidence that the change in regulations on either redundancy or indexation has changed the speed of pass-through of shocks to prices and wages or of prices to wages and *vice versa*.[11]

French inflation has come down over the last ten years. The early years of the 1980s saw the failure of the Mitterand dash for growth. Wages and prices were frozen in 1982 and price controls were strengthened in 1983. These measures were accompanied by fiscal and monetary tightening which, along with increased exchange controls, reduced demand through the effects of higher interest rates and less government spending. These measures were a success, but they do not necessarily imply a change in the structure of wage and price behaviour. They could be associated with a change in the credibility of the authorities that would change the inflation expectations generating mechanism. Without observed expectations measures it is difficult to test this hypothesis, and their relevance may be low as French wage bargaining is still dominated by backward looking compensation for past inflation.

Once again there appears to be little evidence of systematic structural change in French labour markets. This conclusion strengthens that in

Table 2.3   *Results for smaller countries*

	Product-ivity	Tax wedge	Unemploy-ment	Expect-ations	Speed of dynamics of prices to wages (mean lag)	Structural stability
Austria	Unit imposed	Signifi-cant	Level and change effects	No role	2.74 quarters	Significant break
Belgium	Unit	Some role	Level	Signi-ficant	7.38 quarters	Clear pattern of change in the 1980s
Denmark	Unit co-efficient	Little role	Level and change effects	Some role	4.27 quarters	Clear pattern of change in the late 1980s
Ireland	Unit imposed	Signifi-cant	Weak level and change effects	Good evid-ence	4.4 quarters	Clear pattern of change
Spain	Unit imposed	Little role	Small level effect	Built into Moncloa	2.55 quarters	Clear pattern after 1986
Nether-lands	Unit imposed	Little role	Level effect	Little role	1.98 quarters	Little evidence
Greece	Unit imposed in the long run	Some role	Level and change	Little role	9.5 quarters	No change

Source: Anderton, Barrell and McHugh (1991).

Barrell (1990b). Even the Salkever dummies indicate little emerging change, with the only exception being a relationship with a positive effect from unemployment. It appears that the whole of the reduction in French inflation over the last decade has been driven by demand management policies and the direct effects of the fixed exchange rate policy on demand. As we presume that expectations are not systematically wrong, part of the reduction must have come from changing expectations, but there is no evidence that this has been associated with an increase in real wage flexibility and a fall in the sacrifice ratio.

Wage developments in other countries
Our analysis has extended to the smaller countries of Europe, and table 2.3 gives a synopsis of our results. As is stressed in Chapter 1, we can divide these countries into three groups. Austria, Denmark and the Netherlands

Chart 2.6 *Belgium Salkever dummies (prediction errors from a wage equation for the pre-ERM period)*

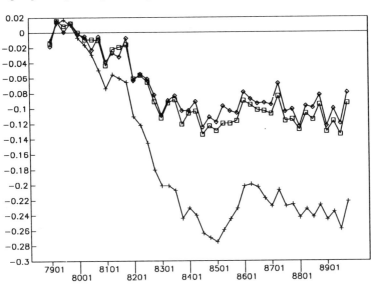

□ BG1   + BG2   ◇ BG3

Note: BG1 has no role for expectations in the wage equation; BG2 takes account of inflation one quarter ahead; BG3 takes account of inflation one year ahead.

are closely tied to the German economy, and their wage behaviour shows many of the same characteristics. The Belgian and Irish labour markets may have gone through a process of structural adjustment, whilst there is little evidence of any change in Greece.

Our results for Austria do not suggest that wage behaviour has become less inflationary in the 1980s, and there is even some evidence of the reverse. Indeed, as Anderton, Barrell and in't Veld (1991) show, a small interest differential opened up between Germany and Austria in the mid 1980s. We can find no role for price expectations in our Austrian wage equation. This suggests that the contracting structure is already rather long term, with compensation for increases in prices, but no effects from actual or expected increases in inflation. This is very similar to our results for Germany. Our results for Denmark and the Netherlands are similar to those for Germany, although there is some evidence that there may have been some structural change in Denmark in recent years.[12]

Developments in Belgium and Ireland have been more interesting. The Belgians undertook strong fiscal action in 1982 and the Belgian Franc was realigned. At the same time wage indexation was suspended (or eliminated) and some prices were frozen. In 1983 an 'external competitiveness norm' was implemented that limited wage growth. Wage control was supplemented by measures to improve labour market flexibility, and unemployment benefit qualifications were tightened. Our test for overall wage equation stability was passed, but our plot of the prediction errors over the 1980s in chart 2.6 is very revealing. Our 1970s wage equation progressively overpredicts during the 1980s, and there is clear evidence that the effect of unemployment rose during the 1980s.

The evidence on Ireland is perhaps more mixed. Dornbusch (1989) has argued that the apparent success of stabilising Irish inflation has exacted a terrible cost in terms of employment and poor economic performance. The main burden of fiscal readjustment fell on the taxpayer and employment, with a substantial increase in the tax wedge and a 20 per cent increase in real labour costs. The weakening of international competitiveness following EMS membership, high real interest rates, the large increase in the tax wedge and a fiscal contraction have resulted in a significant increase in unemployment and migration. In 1986, an unemployment rate of almost 20 per cent was recorded with a further 5 per cent of the labour force emigrating, mainly to the United Kingdom or United States. The significant labour migration during the 1980s may have weakened the impact of rising unemployment upon wage growth.

Some researchers have found some tentative evidence of a structural break in Irish price expectations formation, favouring the interpretation that Irish policymakers have been able to gain greater anti-inflation credibility after joining the ERM. Giavazzi and Giovannini (1988) found that the inflation VAR for Ireland starts to overpredict after two years of ERM membership. Kremers (1990) estimated a price expectations equation for Ireland which exhibited a structural break after ERM membership. Prior to 1979, expected movements in United Kingdom prices and international price competitiveness were the two most important variables in the Irish price expectations equation. After 1979, price expectations of Ireland's ERM partners began to play an increasingly important role. However, Dornbusch (1989) has argued that any policy credibility gains resulting from Irish ERM membership did not significantly reduce the costs of disinflation in terms of output and employment loss.

Our Irish wage equations reflect the results discussed above. We have estimated relationships that exclude expectations and, as chart 2.7 shows, they suggest that there has been no change in wage behaviour in the 1980s. This supports Dornbusch's conclusion, but when we take account of expectations our equations progressively overpredict, suggesting that there is a possibility that labour market behaviour may have changed.

Spanish experience is also enlightening. The significant fall in Spanish inflation during the 1980s has been associated with one of the fastest growing unemployment rates in Western Europe. Unemployment, which had averaged just 1 per cent during the 1960s, started its ascent in 1975, and peaked at 21.5 per cent in 1985 after ten years of rising continuously. Total employment began to show signs of recovery after 1985. However, increasing employment has made little impact upon the unemployment rate, due to an increasing participation rate. Unemployment is concentrated amongst women, who experience a rate 12 per cent higher than males and the young.

After joining the EC in 1986, Spain waited until June 1989 before it joined the ERM, entering with wide fluctuation bands of +/– 6 per cent. In terms of economic fundamentals, Spain has made progress towards convergence with the other ERM countries. By the beginning of the 1990s Spain had a short-term interest rate and inflation rate similar to those prevailing in Italy and in the United Kingdom. Spanish net accumulated public sector debt has stabilised over the past few years at around 30 per cent of GDP. The current account deficit was above 3 per cent of GDP in 1990 but this seems a fairly cyclical phenomenon.

The relationships we estimated for Spain do not show any statistically significant structural instability with a breakpoint at 1979Q1. This is not surprising given that Spain did not join the ERM until 1990. However, the Salkever dummies (chart 2.8) suggest a very small downard shift in wage

Chart 2.7   *Ireland Salkever dummies (prediction errors from a wage equation for the pre-ERM data)*

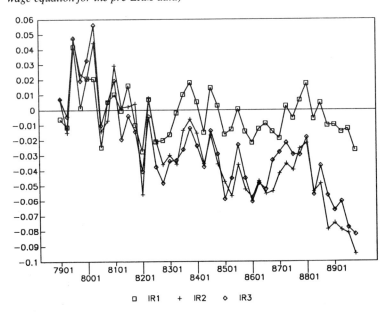

Note: IR1 has no role for expectations in the wage equation; IR2 has one-quarter ahead expectations in the wage equation; IR3 has one-year ahead expectations in the wage equation.

Chart 2.8   *Spain Salkever dummies (prediction errors from a wage equation for the pre-ERM data)*

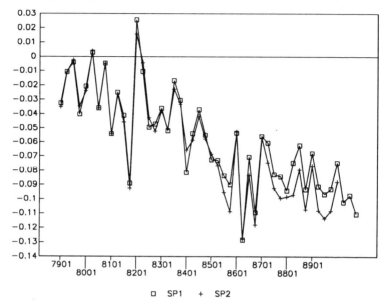

□ SP1   +   SP2

Note: SP1 has no role for expectations; SP2 has one-year ahead expectations.

behaviour in the early 1980s followed by a more substantial downward movement around 1986. The first movement may be associated with the successive Moncloa agreements on wage growth beginning in 1977, whereas the second shift may be a response to the need for economic convergence given Spanish integration into the EC in 1986. We tested for a structural break from 1986 onwards and indeed discovered that there is evidence of a change in behaviour if we take account of forward looking expectations. This may well have been driven by the removal of trade barriers on entry into the Community.

Conclusions on wage behaviour
We have discovered systematic evidence of structural change in European labour markets, but it is by no means universal. German, Austrian and Dutch labour market behaviour appears to be constant throughout the 1970s and 1980s. The same can be said of France, where institutional developments do not appear to have changed the process of wage setting. Where it has happened structural change appears to be from one of three sources. There is clear evidence that Spanish wage behaviour changed in 1986 when that country joined the Community. The forces at work were

driven by competition and the removal of trade barriers rather than by a change in the credibility of the authorities. A strong policy stance in the United Kingdom, and the gradual dismantling of the *Scala Mobile* in Italy helped to cause changes in the structure of the labur market, and unemployment may have become a more potent anti-inflationary tool. However the gains of the early 1980s in both countries appear to have been disappearing later in the decade. Failure to continue to put downward pressure on inflation may have led to a loss of credibility.

Institutions affect the inflation process, and changes in the United Kingdom and Italy were associated with major changes in economic structures. Trade union powers were reduced and indexation of wages declined. However, by the late 1980s and early 1990s, in both countries it proved difficult to remove indexation completely, and wages accelerated rapidly as demand increased. Among ERM members only Belgium and Denmark displayed systematic and sustained structural change. Tightened unemployment benefit regulations, first in Belgium and then in Denmark, helped reduce wages and the Belgians have also introduced indexation on competitors' wages. It appears that the costs of inflation reductions can be made lower by institutional change, but the process is not widespread, and it is costly.

Trade and competition

As noted above, the degree of competition in the product market has a direct impact upon the level of equilibrium wages. Since its formation the European Community has, by gradually reducing barriers to trade between community members, reduced the extent of monopoly power within European product markets. In terms of total visible exports, intra-EC exports have increased as a share of total EC exports (from around 53 per cent in 1970 to around 61 per cent in 1990).[13] Nevertheless the growth in intra-EC export share varies widely between countries. In the period from 1970–90 the United Kingdom's intra-EC export share increased from 33 per cent to 55 per cent. In contrast, for example, the share has not discernibly trended upwards for either Belgium or the Netherlands. (However, the absolute intra-EC export share of the latter two countries is greater than that of the United Kingdom.)[14]

This increase in European economic integration should promote competition within Europe, thereby reducing the degree of quasi-monopoly power and creating a more price-elastic product market. This should increase the elasticity of relative prices in both import and export volume functions for European countries and also reduce the degree of divergence of individual European import and export prices from the prices of other European competitors.

Any increase in European trade from further integration may also have been enhanced by the creation of the exchange rate mechanism. A reduction in exchange-rate uncertainty resulting from ERM membership may have increased intra-ERM members' trade.[15] In particular, changes in real exchange rates between ERM members in the post-ERM period may be perceived as being more permanent, and therefore containing a smaller transitory component, compared with the past. This may have contributed extra upward pressure on some within-Europe trade price elasticities.

Export pricing (manufactured goods)
Our hypothesis is that greater European integration may have been associated with a larger correlation between individual European export prices and European competitors' prices. That is, the pro-competition forces of increased integration may encourage a greater degree of movement towards the law of one price within the European market. Any such movement may be at the cost of a lower weight given to domestic prices (that is, a squeezing of export profit margins) and/or non-European export prices.

We test our hypothesis by estimating manufacturing export price equations for European countries and then see if there is any evidence that the weights on domestic prices, non-European prices or European prices are time varying. We do this in two ways: first, by adding to each of these components a second term multiplied by a time trend; second, we repeat the procedure above but multiply by the average intra-EC exports share (thereby relating any change in weights to the degree of integration). The significance and sign of these extra terms provide evidence as to whether the weights are changing over time. The results are shown in table 2.4. In general, the results show that an increasing weight given to European competitors' prices is offset by a declining weight on domestic costs and/or non-European prices.

Table 2.4   *Manufacturing export price equations component weights*

	PEUR	PNEUR	PDOM
Italy	↑	↑	↓
France	stable	stable	stable
Germany	↓	↑	↑
UK	↑	↓	↓
Netherlands	↑	↓	↓
Belgium	↑	↓	↓

Note: PEUR = European competitors export prices; PNEUR = Non-European competitors' export prices; and PDOM = Domestic manufacturing prices. An arrow indicates whether weight of component in export price is increasing or decreasing over time.

Export volumes (total visible exports)

A similar experiment was performed for European individual country export volumes. Our theoretical specification explains movements in export volumes in terms of fluctuations in world trade and price competitiveness. However, we disaggregate the relative price into separate intra and extra-EC price competitiveness terms and then multiply these by the time trend and intra-EC export shares in a similar fashion to the price equations. Again, table 2.5 shows that in most cases price elasticities have indeed been increasing between European countries. Some of these increases seem to be at the expense of declining non-European elasticities although some countries display increasing elasticities over time for both trading regions.[16] However, in the latter case the EC price elasticity is usually increasing at a faster rate.

Conclusions

It is evident that a certain degree of nominal convergence has been achieved within Europe, particularly among the ERM members. We have argued that much of this convergence is related to factors affecting labour market behaviour. In particular, we have stressed the role of institutional change and the competitive structure of the product market, both of which are related to the degree of European economic integration.

There is some evidence from our results that there was a downward adjustment in European wage inflation processes in the last decade which was partly associated with structural changes that have followed on from distinct changes in policy. These were in part related to the constraints

Table 2.5   *Long-run relative price elasticities (export volumes)*

Country	Price measure(a)	Trend term(b)	1980	1985	1990
Italy	EUR	2	–0.21	–0.68	–1.4
UK	EUR	1	0	–0.014	–0.1
	EUR	3	0	–0.102	–0.27
Netherlands	EUR	1	–0.30	–0.54	–0.78
	NEUR	1	–0.15	–0.23	–0.30
Belgium	EUR	1	–0.34	–0.67	–1.0
	NEUR	1	–0.04	–0.11	–0.18

(a)   EUR = relative export price *vis-à-vis* European competitors
NEUR = relative export price *vis-à-vis* non-European competitors
(b)   1 = Time trend
2 = Average European intra-EC export share
3 = Country specific intra-EC export share

imposed by ERM membership. We largely reject the idea that wage adjustment costs, in terms of savings in lost output and employment, were substantially mitigated purely by extra credibility gains from membership of the ERM. Governments seemed to gain anti-inflation reputation not as a result of joining the ERM but by actually implementing institutional change in the labour market and adopting policies consistent with ERM objectives.[17] ERM membership alone did not engender belief, harsh policies actually had to be implemented to gain the reputation of anti-inflation resolve.

We also investigated whether the competitive structure of the product market within Europe had changed over time. There certainly seems to be some evidence of increasing intra-European competition as Europe progresses towards further economic integration. Price setting in European manufacturing export markets seems to be moving away from imperfect competition towards perfect competition. Fewer opportunities for quasi-monopoly rents will put downward pressure on equilibrium wages.[18] Additionally, we provided evidence that competitiveness elasticities in export markets within Europe have been increasing over time (and seem to be linked with increasing integration). This implies a more binding external constraint upon wage demands as integration increases.

It seems that the creation of 'one market' creates pressures for labour market reform and promotes competition in trade. Given our interpretation of the ERM in terms of encouraging 'discipline', these processes would be further enhanced by the adoption of 'one money'. The irrevocable nature of a single currency should harness any potential credibility gains more efficiently than the ERM, but only if the necessary institutional changes required for convergence are also implemented early enough.

Notes

1 Anderton, Barrell and in't Veld (1991) present evidence on inflation convergence in Europe, as does Weber (1991).
2 The most commonly cited studies are those by Giavazzi and Giovannini (1989) and Giovazzi and Pagano (1988).
3 This work is summarised in Barrell (1990b) and has been extended in Anderton, Barrell and McHugh (1991).
4 The best known are probably Nickell (1984) and Layard and Nickell (1985).
5 We have had to exclude Portugal because we have insufficient data for adequate statistical analysis.
6 We have adopted the Error Correction Mechanism approach as advocated by Hendry and others. This allows us to encapsulate long-run and dynamic factors in one regression.
7 If expectations are consistent, and therefore on average correct, then actual one-period-ahead inflation is a good proxy for expectations. However, following Pagan (1984), we have instrumented this variable.
8 Our relationships including expectations have to be estimated by Instrumental

Variables, and we have used the Wald variable deletion test advocate
Godfrey (1988). See especially pp. 200–3.

9 These are explained by Godfrey (1984).

10 Studies such as Wren-Lewis *et al* (1990) argue that the level at which sterling joined the ERM was substantially above the FEER.

11 The evidence on the role of minimum wages is mixed. It is discussed in Anderton, Barrell and McHugh (1991).

12 These results are discussed further in Chapter 8 of this volume.

13 Although there has been an underlying upward trend in the share of intra-EC exports there has only really been strong upward growth since the early 1980s. The 1970s and early 1980s were characterised by volatility in intra-EC trade as the two major oil price shocks caused a transfer of income away from Europe towards the OPEC countries. This increased the importance of the latter as an export market relative to Europe.

14 For further details of intra and extra-EC trade for different categories of product see Commission of the European Communities (1989).

15 For example, Perée and Steinherr (1989) claim that exchange rate uncertainty adversely affects international trade flows.

16 This is contrary to the general perception that export price elasticities have been declining over time as non-price competitiveness factors began to play an increasingly important role.

17 Institutional convergence plays an important role in establishing nominal convergence. The adoption of a social charter by all EC members should enhance these processes.

18 This link between international competition and the labour market was particularly evident in Belgian policy. In 1983 Belgium implemented an external competitiveness norm which limited wage growth to that of Belgium's main trading partner countries.

3

European Monetary Union: Design and Implementation

Enno Langfeldt

Introduction

Currently, the members of the European Community are engaged in intensive negotiations about the design and implementation of Economic and Monetary Union (EMU). This chapter addresses some key issues of the introduction of a common currency. The purpose of this chapter is not to discuss in detail the proposals which have emerged from the Maastricht Summit of the heads of government; instead it focuses on broad issues which nevertheless include the major elements of the current debate.

The chapter is organised along the following lines. The first section specifies the necessary institutional framework which would allow the European central bank (ECB) to achieve the goal of price stability. The second section deals with the question of whether fiscal restraint is a precondition for the implementation of a common currency, and whether EMU creates the need for higher transfers, a harmonisation of national tax rates or a stronger coordination of fiscal policy to improve overall macroeconomic stability. Finally, the speed of the transition process and its nature is discussed.

Institutional monetary framework and monetary goals

Whether a common European currency will be desirable or not depends on whether it will be able to assure price stability. Past and recent experience in several countries has shown that inflation generates a great variety of welfare-reducing distortions.[1] Uncertainty over future price increases cuts the contract length in labour and credit markets and puts a risk premium on interest rates and wages, thereby negatively affecting long-term capital formation. Resources are absorbed into transactions and investments in order to avoid an inflation-generated loss of real wealth. In addition, by creating uncertainty about the extent to which actual price changes are relative or aggregate, inflation also hampers the working of the market system. Furthermore, inflation tends to raise the tax burden of private households and enterprises, as in many countries income taxes are progressive and not indexed. Finally, inflation increases the opportunity costs for money holders, thus leading to suboptimal cash balances.

Despite this, central banks and governments in most countries have allowed inflation to markedly exceed 2 per cent, a rate which would indicate the upper margin for possible measurement errors in price index numbers. There are several reasons why politicians take recourse to inflation. Firstly, it facilitates the financing of current budget deficits and can reduce the real value of outstanding government debt. Secondly, a discretionary use of monetary policy enables governments to manipulate the business cycle in such a way as to best fit the electoral cycle. Despite the evidence against a permanent trade-off between inflation and unemployment governments still try to achieve transitory employment gains by stimulating monetary expansion. Since the above-mentioned welfare costs of inflation are difficult to measure and sometimes show up only in the long run, the electorate is not likely to blame the government for its misuse of monetary policy.

Given the importance of price level stability and the not very favourable record of central banks in the European Community, it would be useful if some guarantees could be offered that the ECB would indeed deliver a stable price level. Up to now, proposals made for the statute of the ECB merely state that the bank 'would be committed to the objective of price stability'. However, such a statement of content alone does not ensure that price stability would actually be achieved, especially as at the same time monetary policy is to be geared to a wide range of other objectives, for example, 'balanced growth, converging standard of living, high employment and external equilibrium' (Delors Committee, 1989, p. 8). Thus, in the statute of the ECB it should be laid down that the objective of price stability has absolute priority relative to other objectives. In addition, governments should not be allowed to influence monetary policy in a discretionary way. Therefore, either binding rules for the conduct of monetary policy or sanctions in the case of missing the price stability target have to be introduced into the statutes of the ECB.

According to the recently published draft statute of the ECB there seems to be a consensus that price stability should be the primary objective of monetary policy, that the ECB should be independent from instructions by national governments or Community bodies and that the public sector should not be allowed to directly finance its budget deficits via central bank credits. Binding rules or sanctions are not usually in the interest of either central banks or politicians, who do not like to have their hands tied. Therefore, they have not shown up yet in the statutes of currently existing monetary authorities. Even in the Bundesbank law, which has a model character for the statute of the ECB, there are no special limitations for the conduct of monetary policy. But this does not mean that they are not necessary. In West Germany, consumer prices have more than doubled in the past two decades. The relatively favourable inflation record of the Bundesbank as compared to other central banks cannot be attributed to the autonomy of the Bundesbank alone. It also reflects that price stability is highly ranked in public opinion in Germany. In the European Community a similar ranking of price stability has not so far been observed. Binding rules or sanctions are therefore necessary to guarantee price level stability.

Opponents of monetary rules usually argue that the private sector lacks the necessary flexibility to cope with economic shocks. Economic policy therefore has to have the means to prevent or to counteract unsatisfactory conditions and to react to unexpected situations. However, there are many examples that, on the contrary, a discretionary pursuit of monetary and fiscal policy has increased cyclical fluctuations instead of dampening them. One reason is that a change in monetary policy affects economic activity only with a time lag. Another reason is that often the underlying problems of the economy have been analysed in the wrong way. In addition, actual wage and price rigidities are large because private agents rely on government intervention. A most recent example for the misuse of monetary policy is the massive reduction in interest rates in Great Britain after the 1987 stock market crash. This created an artificial boom with all its negative consequences, including the deep recession which followed.

The adoption of a monetary rule which would, for example, fix the growth rate of some monetary aggregate to a predetermined level would decrease the variability of monetary policy. It therefore decreases uncertainty and fosters stable economic growth. The specific type of the rule need not be agreed upon in advance, it could be improved over time as knowledge progresses.[2] There is empirical evidence that even rules with limited flexibility would have dampened cyclical fluctuations of domestic demand (Scheide, 1989). In addition, a recent empirical study shows that a stable aggregate demand for narrow money (which is a precondition for the usefulness of money supply rules) can be identified for the group of countries participating in the European exchange-rate mechanism (Kremers and Lane, 1990).

An alternative to a monetary rule would consist of severe sanctions which the members of the Central Bank Council would face in the case of a predetermined inflation rate being exceeded. As an upper limit, an average yearly inflation rate of 2 or 3 per cent over a time span of three years could be chosen.[3] This period would be long enough to ensure that the central bank is not made responsible for short-term price increases (for example, through higher consumption taxes or oil prices) which cannot be directly attributed to monetary policy. A similar limitation could be introduced with respect to deflation. The sanctions could mean that council members would lose their jobs, including the accumulated pensions. The income loss would be more pronounced if the duration of council members' contracts were at least ten years.

Another crucial issue is the responsibility for exchange-rate policy. German monetary history gives several examples that suggest that monetary policy must be safeguarded from external constraints if it is to be able to stick to its price stability target. In particular, the experience with the Bretton Woods system indicates that sticking to an exchange-rate target might lead to the importing of inflation from abroad. Because the government was strongly influenced by pressure groups (export industry and agriculture), necessary appreciations of the D-Mark were postponed or were not large enough. The Bundesbank tried to sterilise the additional money created by its obligation to undertake exchange market interventions. Empirical evidence, however, has shown that sterilised interventions take away the pressure on the exchange rate only for a short time. In the end the Bundesbank has had to expand the money supply more rapidly than intended. A separation of the responsibilities for monetary and exchange-rate policy in the EMU could lead to similar conflicts. Since the expenses for European agricultural policy depend directly on the dollar exchange rate, an appreciation of Ecu against the dollar increases the amount of export subsidies the Community has to pay, thereby creating a strong incentive for the Community bodies to put pressure on the ECB to depreciate *vis-à-vis* the dollar or at least to keep the exchange rate stable. So there are strong reasons to give the ECB full exchange-rate sovereignty, in particular since only then could the ECB be made fully responsible for a deviation from price level stability. This implies that only the ECB should have the right to intervene in the foreign exchange market in support of the European currency *vis-à-vis* third currencies like the dollar or the yen. It also means that the political authorities of the European Community should not be allowed to decide upon the exchange-rate regime (fixed or flexible) *vis-à-vis* third currencies without approval of the ECB.

The statutes of the Bundesbank include the obligation for the bank to support the government's general economic policy. If such an obligation is included in the ECB's statute it might easily impair its independence. A steady monetary policy oriented at the goal of price level stability is the best way to support the economic policy of the government.

A final prerequisite for the autonomy of the ECB is to give its statute a constitutional ranking. This means that a qualified and not just a simple majority is needed to change the statute of the ECB. This would prevent political authorities of the European Community or groups of countries from threatening the central bank with a change in its statutes if it does not comply with certain demands.

Despite its great independence from the actual political decision process, the ECB, as it is described here, is not free of control. It is obliged to preserve price stability and faces sanctions if its goal is not achieved.

The role of fiscal policy in a monetary union

In connection with the creation of the ECB there is an ongoing debate as to whether this will have to be linked with the harmonisation of fiscal policy. Two lines of argument can be distinguished. Firstly, there is the argument that binding rules limiting the size of national governments' budget deficits are necessary since otherwise the financing of excessive public deficits would create pressure on monetary policy to pursue a less price stability oriented stance. Secondly, it is often said that if monetary policy and exchange-rate policy can no longer be used as an active policy instrument, more coordination of fiscal policy is necessary. This includes a harmonisation of tax rates and the enlargement of transfer payments within the EC.

Binding rules for national fiscal deficits?
The Delors Report and the recent Maastricht Treaty call for effective limits on budget deficits. The Treaty proposal suggests that only countries whose current budget deficit does not exceed 3 per cent of GNP and whose total amount of gross public debt does not exceed 60 per cent of GNP shall be allowed to participate in the third stage of EMU when the common currency is created. In general, there are good reasons to have a constitutional limitation for public debt. However, reality has proved that it is difficult to enforce existing rules. Often governments take recourse to escape clauses like the bad state of the economy due to a recession or severe structural adjustment problems. In addition, there are many ways to circumvent rules. One example is that of the creation of so-called shadow households. In 1991, the German Treuhand Agency, whose purpose is to privatise former state-owned companies, will run a deficit of about DM25 billion. This corresponds to almost 1 per cent of total German GNP. The Treuhand Agency's deficit is fully guaranteed by the government but not included in the official budget deficit. An even more important objection is that it is not the size of the budget deficit but its origin that matters. Budget deficits can have different causes. They can either result from additional expenditures for infrastructure and from lower taxes or they can reflect increasing subsidies and transfer payments. In the first case, economic growth is usually stimulated, thus inducing higher tax revenues in the medium term which allow servicing of the higher public debt. A budget deficit created for investment purposes may therefore not harm but even benefit the economy. It is only in the second case that budget deficits create a problem.

It would therefore not only be difficult to define precisely a reasonable upper limit for the budget deficits in the individual countries; it would also be difficult to enforce such rules and to prevent them being circumvented. This poses the question of whether a budget deficit limitation for the member countries is really necessary. The main reasoning for fiscal restraint on a national level, in the view of its supporters, is that until now governments that borrow heavily face the risk that their currency will depreciate. This risk is also a major argument for financial markets to demand higher interest rates. After EMU, however, there can be no more exchange-rate risks between European countries. According to this argument, governments will therefore increase their borrowing, thus driving up real interest rates, not only for themselves but for the EC as a whole. In addition, monetary union is said to create a moral hazard problem. Countries raising their debt beyond levels which are considered to be sustainable could expect that the common monetary authorities will come to their aid. Such rescue operations would tax citizens in all EMU member countries with a higher inflation rate.

There are several flaws in this reasoning. Firstly, there is no unanimous relation between the development of budget deficits and the exchange rate. At the beginning of the 1980s, both France and the United States showed a strong rise in budget deficits. However, while the dollar appreciated strongly, there was downward pressure on the French franc within the EMS. Obviously, the financial markets expected tax reductions in the United States to increase the marginal rate of return on investment while the massive rise in minimum wages and in social transfer payments in France were assessed to have negative impacts on growth. Because of rising market pressure, France had to pursue a fundamental shift in its economic policy. Even within a fixed exchange rate system, therefore, markets can discipline governments.

The move towards a single European currency with a central bank committed to price stability is likely to further strengthen market discipline on expansionary governments. National governments will then no longer be able to reduce their real debt burden by inflating their currencies. The total liberalisation of financial markets and the fact that capital controls are no longer possible will intensify competition from other borrowers, especially those from abroad. Under these conditions it will be easier for the suppliers of capital to demand higher risk premiums if the debt burden of the borrower is high. As the market's attention shifts from inflation, current account imbalances and exchange-rate changes to the mere problem of the solvency of the debtors, budget deficits will receive the focus of attention. This would result in higher interest rates for high-risk debtors. In principle, governments would then be treated like enterprises, eventually further loans would be given only if the national government announced a credible and promising programme to reduce its debt. However, to let the credit-risk discipline work, rules which would imply a direct or indirect bail-out must be prevented from being introduced into the statutes of the European Central Bank. This would leave lenders with the risk that national governments might even default. The moral hazard problem which might otherwise exist would be a consequence not of the exchange-rate regime but of closer coordination and integration within the European Community (von Hagen and Fratianni, 1991). The fact that real interest-rate differences between industrial countries and some highly indebted Eastern European countries or LDCs do not fully reflect the default risks can be referred to the solidarity which the governments of industrial countries have often shown when they agreed to reschedule and cancel the debts of those countries.

However, even in the case of bail-out because of solidarity this does not mean that there is no pressure to adjust. During the last financial crisis of the city of New York the federal government was only ready to guarantee New York city's loans on condition that the city committed itself to limit its expenditure and to accept stronger federal supervision. Thus, even in the case where a bail-out can be expected a public authority may be very hesitant to risk a default. With increasing integration among the member countries of the European Community, rising public debt can make the country less attractive as a location of production. A higher debt burden would mean either higher taxes or a lower supply of public goods (Scheide and Trapp, 1991).

Stabilisation policy, transfers and taxes in a monetary union
A common currency does not imply that fiscal discipline is worsening. However, further arguments have been put forward as to why, as a consequence of EMU, national sovereignty with respect to fiscal policy would be diminished. It is argued that with monetary policy geared towards the achievement of price level stability, fiscal policy will have to play a more important role with respect to macroeconomic stabilisation, especially with respect to absorbing regional economic shocks. In this respect, additional income redistribution within the union is often called for. In addition, a harmonisation of national tax laws is frequently considered a precondition of monetary unification.

According to standard arguments, different rates among countries for taxes on goods, services and factors of production undermine the sustainability of the union as inconsistent tax rates could easily lead to persistent trade imbalances. However, the level of tax rates and the supply of public goods are important determinants of the competitiveness of a country. They will therefore affect the level of real exchange rates.[4] Thus, given the country-of-origin principle, an increase in the rate of VAT might lead to a current account surplus since lower public deficits *ceteris paribus* increase net capital exports. To a certain degree differences among countries with respect to the tax structure as well as the level of tax rates are not only compatible with the principles of the internal market but are also efficient (Vaubel, 1991). The optimal tax structure of a country depends strongly on demand and supply elasticities, which are likely to differ among EC member countries. There are also differences with respect to the amount of immobile factors of production and the importance of tax evasion. In cases where differences in tax rates tend to have a negative effect on economic growth and tax revenues, the national tax authorities will be forced by the market to adjust their tax rates. As compared to an *ex ante* harmonisation of tax rates by the cartel of finance ministers the market solution is likely to bring about a lower tax level for the Community as a whole.

With respect to macroeconomic stabilisation there are good arguments that monetary and fiscal policy should be based on stable rules rather than on fine-tuning the economy by discretionary policy actions. Very often international coordination of monetary and fiscal policy has had negative effects on growth and employment in the medium term. In the context of the so-called locomotive approach, Germany in 1978 vigorously agreed with international pressure for a stronger coordination of fiscal policy and increased government expenditure. This led to an overheating of the German economy, thus preparing the ground for the recession which followed. Therefore, for the purpose of international coordination of macroeconomic policy, it is not useful to provide the EC authorities with higher tax revenues or to oblige national governments to coordinate their fiscal policies.

Traditional literature on optimal currency areas stresses the role of fiscal policy as a shock absorber. In a monetary union nominal exchange rates are fixed and monetary policy is determined at a central level; thus in the absence of sufficient labour mobility or sufficient price and wage flexibility budgetary transfers may be necessary to equilibrate fluctuations in regional income and employment. Otherwise severe shocks would lead to defections (Sachs and Sala-i-Martin, 1989). Actually, labour mobility within the EC is lower than within the United States and Canada; real wage flexibility is also estimated to be substantially lower in the EC than in North America (Bruno and Sachs, 1985). In addition, the recent changes in the political landscape in Europe are likely to affect EC member countries in an asymmetric way. Thus, there seem to be good arguments in favour of either an increase in the Community's expenditures for regional and structural policy, which would allow a redistribution of incomes in a discretionary way, or the introduction of an EC-wide income tax and social security system, which would automatically cushion income fluctuations between member countries.

However, in the foreseeable future there is little chance that national authorities will be ready to substantially increase the revenue base of the European Community to allow for a larger redistribution of incomes.

There is also doubt as to whether this really is a precondition for monetary union. In the case of a permanent shock, countries or regions which are negatively affected can restore their competitiveness only if real incomes fall; this holds regardless of the exchange-rate system. The only difference is that in a monetary union wages and prices of other immobile factors cannot be reduced by a currency devaluation. It is, however, to be expected that wage and price flexibility will be higher in the individual member countries after the common currency has been introduced. With the commitment of the ECB to price stability and the introduction of a no-bail-out clause with respect to budget deficits those who are responsible for fixing wages and prices will also have to bear the consequences if the prices are not market-clearing. The supply side of the EC economies could be further strengthened if, for example, the labour market were included in the deregulation efforts of the EC. The introduction of a European Social Charter would lead in the wrong direction. In cases where the shock is only temporary there is also no need for transfers from the EC. National transfer payments could smooth economic development, especially as the enlargement of the capital market makes borrowing easier.

In general, a cushioning of shocks by an increase in transfer payments often delays unnecessarily the adjustment of households and enterprises. Moreover, shocks which are considered to be only temporary may turn out to be permanent. Transfer payments always include a moral hazard problem which is difficult to control. The main impetus for transfers is solidarity and not the creation of a monetary union. In connection with German unification, the massive transfers from the west to the east reflect the political aim of rapidly adjusting incomes in the east to those of the west. The actual problems in creating a self-sustaining upswing in the five new states indicate that large-scale transfer payments do not improve but rather hamper the convergence of market incomes. The strong rise in transfer payments to households and enterprises is an important reason for wage increases in Eastern Germany having been much higher than productivity gains. Within the EC solidarity is not as pronounced as within Germany. If an increase in transfer payments is seen as a precondition of EMU, a common currency is not very likely to be introduced.

To sum up, it is not to be expected that EMU will create an incentive to increase national budget deficits. So the introduction of a limit on budget deficits in the member countries is not necessary. Competition with respect to the optimal level and structure of public expenditure as well as with respect to the level and structure of taxes and social security contributions should not be prevented. Competition not only imposes a discipline on national governments and allows them to find out what the optimum levels for expenditure and taxes are, it also allows for a more rapid economic convergence between countries. Transfer payments among EC member countries should be limited instead of being increased. Apart from ruling out or strictly limiting borrowing by national governments and by Community authorities from the ECB, no changes in the pursuit of fiscal policy seem to be necessary as a precondition for the introduction of a common currency.

The transition process

In addition to the debate about the future constitution of the ECB and the future role of fiscal policy there is an ongoing discussion about what the transition towards a common currency should look like. First it has to be decided whether the transition process should be rapid or slow. In general, there are good arguments why a common currency, which is safeguarded with respect to price stability, should be introduced as quickly as possible. Historical evidence suggests that it is less costly in terms of output and employment losses to overcome inflationary expectations by a credible and well-understood regime change. The introduction of a European currency is likely to stabilise inflationary expectations more rapidly than efforts by national governments to stabilise their old currencies, even if currencies are pegged to other stable currencies. The higher credibility is due to the fact that a common currency means an irrevocable fixing of the exchange rate while otherwise there is always a possibility left that in the case of conflict the government will take recourse to a currency devaluation. In particular people in high inflation countries in the European Community could benefit more quickly from the advantages of price stability. Moreover, the benefits in terms of lower transaction and information costs will accrue earlier to money users.[5] Finally, the rapid establishment of an ECB would avoid conflicts which are likely to occur in the so-called second stage of EMU if monetary cooperation among national central banks is agreed upon but without specifying clear responsibilities.

However, a rapid move to the final stage of EMU is not very likely. Up to now, there is in particular no full agreement on the goals and the constitutional framework of the ECB. As long as the full independence of the ECB and its strict commitment to price stability is not assured, countries with a strong orientation towards price stability (like, for example, Germany and the Netherlands) would be well advised to ask for convergence of national inflation rates as a precondition for the final stage of EMU. Convergence of inflation rates to a low level would signal that the member countries are ready to commit themselves to price level stability. A gradual approach to EMU would also provide countries with higher inflation rates with some scope for the necessary restructuring of their tax systems. Up to now, seignorage has been an important element of total revenue in some EC countries (Drazen, 1989). It will also take time to dissolve hidden reserves in the national central banks' accounts. For example, the gold reserves of the Bundesbank are still valued at 35 dollars per ounce; the actual market price is ten times as high. These hidden reserves amount to more than DM120 billion, which is almost 4.5 per cent of German GNP. Another problem is the selection of the appropriate exchange rate for the revaluation of assets, liabilities, prices and wages. The exchange rates of some countries, especially those where interest rates are high, seem to be overvalued. If inflation rates have converged and exchange rates between member countries have been stable for quite some time, the dangers of fixing a wrong exchange rate would be much lower. To sum up, the adjustment process will be smoother if a gradual move towards EMU is taken.

If the introduction of a thirteenth currency, which could replace national currencies in a competitive way, is excluded, two main alternative strategies remain.[6] The first is the centralised coordination of national monetary policy as sketched by the Delors Report for Stage II of the process towards EMU. The second would be a more competitive approach, namely the stabilisation of currencies by independent national central banks.

The main elements of Stage II in the Delors Report and in the Maastricht Treaty include increasing exchange-rate stability among the member countries by creating a European Monetary Institute (EMI). The main task of the EMI would be to intensify the coordination of monetary policy and to develop the instruments of monetary policy which could be used by the ECB in Stage III. However, up to now neither the statute nor the tasks of the EMI have been fixed. A group of countries (among them France, Italy and Spain) wants the EMI to participate actively in monetary policy. They want EMI to be endowed with sufficiently large capital and foreign currency reserves to intervene in exchange markets. This is likely to affect the supply of money in the individual countries. Other countries, like Germany and the Netherlands, want the responsibility for monetary policy in Stage II to remain with the national central banks.

There are good reasons to keep responsibility for monetary policy with the national central banks as long as no ECB has been created. The main argument is that an EMI which would have the right to interfere in national monetary policy would not help to create structures for a genuine and permanent Community of stability. It is very likely that an institution like the EMI would encourage collusion among central banks as each central bank's control over and responsibility for the expansion of its monetary base is weakened. The outcome is more likely to be a convergence of inflation rates at the average level, not the lowest level. There is also the risk that the EMI would try to use monetary policy to influence economic growth and employment. Past experience with the

EMS has shown that economic targets between member countries differ. If politicians of different countries had to agree on common interest rates or exchange rates *vis-à-vis* third countries, the different interests would lead to permanent conflicts. Together with higher inflation this might easily lead to a dissolution of the economic and monetary integration process.

As an alternative, it would be preferable to have a stabilisation by independent central banks. If governments give their central banks the autonomy which they are willing to give to the ECB, the individual central banks would be able to announce a path towards price stability which would be credible. If in addition capital controls are fully abolished and if the Ecu and the other currencies of the EC member countries are allowed to be used as legal tender, there would be competitive pressure on central banks to have inflation rates converging at a low level. In the past, the D-Mark has had the function of an anchor currency. This, however, is not the result of German hegemony but of the fact that the Bundesbank operated a monetary policy which was oriented at the goal of price stability. The Bundesbank might lose its leading role if it became less stability oriented. The recent development of inflation rates suggests that other currencies are now more stable than the D-Mark. While in September, 1991, consumer prices in Germany increased by 3.9 per cent, inflation rates in Denmark and France only amounted to 1.8 per cent and 2.6 per cent respectively. Although these figures have been distorted by indirect tax changes in Germany, recent developments suggest that the German economy is not guaranteed to remain the nominal anchor of the existing ERM, and pressures from unification may keep inflation above that in France for some time.

Notes

1 For a more detailed analysis compare Neumann (1991, p. 79).
2 Langfeldt, Scheide and Trapp (1989, p. 43) have advocated that the rule might be changed under the condition that a group of independent experts change their estimates about trend growth of potential output and/or the trend of velocity.
3 For a similar proposal compare Vaubel (1989).
4 In a common currency area only nominal exchange rates are fixed. Real exchange rates will continue to change as prices will not move in line.
5 For a description of the benefits of a common currency compare Gros and Thygesen (1991).
6 The parallel currency approach is not neglected in this chapter because it seems to be unworkable. However, discussing the pros and cons would need a chapter of its own. In addition the political decision process has progressed in such a way that the thirteenth currency solution is no longer a viable option (Schlesinger, 1991).

4

France and Italy: a Tale of Two Adjustments

Paolo Onofri and Stefania Tomasini

In the first half of the 1980s, once the dates for the complete liberalisation of the movements of both production factors and goods between countries in Europe had been fixed, attention was rapidly concentrated on the many difficulties paving the road to monetary union. Studies appeared on currency substitution, on the centralisation of monetary policy and the degree of freedom to be left to individual fiscal policy as a shock absorber, and on the amount of international reserves required to guarantee that fixed exchange rates be credibly fixed in a context of perfect capital mobility, not to mention all the material produced on the institutional subject of the European Central Bank. Relatively few questions were raised as to the real impact of learning to live within a disciplined monetary union or the possibility of keeping the socio-political effects under control.

Should countries resist possible long-term pressures to redefine industrial specialisations across borders? Nobody seems to take serious account of the need for substantial income transfers to compensate for deeper regional specialisations in the future, as happens today inside individual countries. As a consequence, each economy will try to grow (as it did in the past) in a manner similar to the others; intra-industry trade will go on growing and will require very smart industrial policies to stay in the markets, but in such a competitive environment the loser risks losing a lot.

One cannot deny that in recent years the performances of the nominal variables in the main European economies have converged. As can be seen from charts 4.1 and 4.2, the variance of nominal variables has declined more than the variance of real ones. It is precisely for this reason that what matters now is the competitiveness of the economic system as a whole, the level of global productivity, and the convergence in the trade-offs the economies are experiencing.

In our opinion, the European Big Four have already achieved as much as can be achieved in terms of nominal convergence (chart 4.1). Now that we are approaching the final stage of EMU, we are entering the more

Chart 4.1 *EMS exchange rates changes and inflation variances*

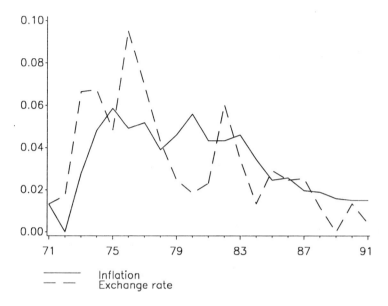

Chart 4.2 *Variance of domestic demand changes in EMS countries*

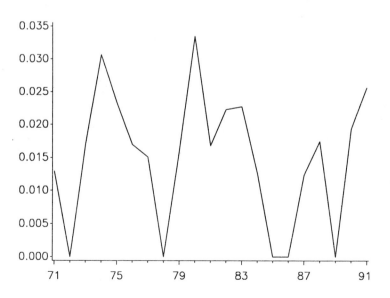

turbulent phase in which the path of real variables is brought into line with the dynamics of such nominal variables.

The temporary (albeit prolonged) effect of the EMS on expectations, mainly based on the strong reputation of the monetary authorities, must give place to a full credibility based on the long-term sustainability of the exchange rate (Williamson, 1991). Such sustainability in turn requires structural changes in the sheltered sectors of the economies, not just expectation effects on the nominal variables. Given the size of the service sector, this might be even more painful from a social point of view than the process experienced at the beginning of the 1980s in the manufacturing sector.

The single anchor of German monetary policy is no longer enough to help further disinflation in the higher inflation countries: domestic incomes and fiscal policies are to be the national anchors while, at the same time, labour markets and home goods and services markets must become more reactive to macroeconomic conditions. As a result, the variance of growth within EC countries might widen in the near future (chart 4.2); several countries still have real costs to pay, and their delay in paying has worsened the situation.

In the past the credibility impact of EMS seems to have been heightened by domestic demand recessions; hence, countries like Italy, which previously relied mainly on the exchange rate to disinflate, are likely to have to face a specific differential recession in the future in order to complete the disinflation process. In the next few years public opinion might perceive the goal of EMU as a negative-sum game, thus producing the possibility of rejection as it gets closer.

For several years now the EMS countries have been considered an almost ideal laboratory in which to observe different experiments designed to bring down moderate inflations. Denmark and Ireland have been widely studied (Dornbusch, 1989, Giavazzi and Pagano, 1990, and Kremers, 1989), as, by way of contrast, has the United Kingdom. As far as this chapter is concerned, we focus on the comparison of how France was successful in her adjustment to German inflation and how Italy began to diverge again just as nominal exchange rates were stabilised. All this might be instructive of the effects both of structural differences and of inconsistent policies on the process of convergence.

Following an overview of the problem of the disinflationary impact of EMS in the first section, we shall classify stabilisation policies according to the weight given either to the money supply target or to the exchange rate target.

In the second section, we shall distinguish between the first half of the 1980s when policies were aimed at real adjustments to the oil price shock, and the second quinquennium when the target of convergence (as a nominal adjustment) emerged. We shall reach the conclusion that France was successful in the first adjustment, pursuing a money-targeted policy and allowing the exchange rate to compensate for the deterioration of competitiveness, and that in so doing she paved the road for an easily successful nominal adjustment in the second half of the 1980s. Italy did not pursue a consistent set of policies in the first quinquennium and relied, to a larger extent than France, on the effect of EMS constraints and acccumulated losses in price competitiveness; moreover, when the years of the almost fixed exchange rate began, fiscal and wage policies were relaxed and inflation paths diverged again.

In the third section we shall take into account more structural differences that econometric evidence can reveal about the behaviour of the labour and the goods markets in France and Italy. In France, a labour market more prone to policy control has more efficiently transmitted the consistent determination of the French government to produce convergence, whereas Italian wage dynamics seem to reflect an aspiration to real wage growth incompatible with the comparative efficiency of the overall production system. Such relative supply inefficiency is mainly located in the Italian non-tradeable sector. Italy has not diverged much in the most recent years because of the constraint the EMS has exerted on manufacturing price formation. Our econometric investigation reveals that manufacturing prices in Italy are much more tied to the prices of competitors than French manufacturing prices seem to have been. In the final section, we shall draw the conclusion that for Italy the credibility of the exchange rate based on the reputation of the monetary authorities has already done all it could, and that what remains to be done in order to found credibility on sustainability does not seem to be so great; the problem is that, by taking all the normal steps to monetary union as if adjustment were complete, while at the same time trying to gain time before completing it, Italy has undermined the effectiveness of most macroeconomic policy tools. Thus a considerable effort seems to be required for the final small steps.

Some preliminary remarks

At the beginning of the 1980s the European economies had been facing the adjustment policies required by the second oil shock. Different countries had reacted to the shock to different degrees, but the basic aim was the same: to change relative prices in order to allow the transfer required by the deterioration of the terms of trade. In other words, the level of real wages had to be changed and the possible reduction of the inflation rate was merely a by-product of such a real adjustment.

The policies enacted in all industrial countries faced inflexible markets for goods and labour; the recession effect was exported to the producers of basic commodities and reimported by the industrial countries as disinflationary impulses. On these processes, the EMS superimposed a stimulus to enact contractionary stabilisation policies designed to reduce the inflation differential with Germany and to make such a lower inflation rate sustainable.

Much has been written about the importance of belonging to an exchange rate agreement that binds the parties to a regime of quasi-fixed exchange rates, a strategy for governments to render credible their will to pursue disinflationary policies (Giavazzi and Spaventa, 1990, and Giovannini, 1990). In addition, the importance of episodes in which parity has been successfully defended from attacks by agents has been emphasised for its part in building up the anti-inflationary reputation of individual governments (or in some cases, as in Italy, of the monetary authorities). It is suggested that this reduces the cost of disinflation in terms of GDP loss by modifying the expectations of agents, thus speeding up the process of adjusting the economy to a lower rate of inflation.

The empirical evidence as to the expectation effect of the EMS is uncertain, as is the fact that the real costs of disinflation with quasi-fixed exchange rates are low (Artis and Nachane, 1990, Barrell, Darby and Donaldson, 1990, Collins, 1988, and Giavazzi and Giovannini, 1988). It would seem legitimate to suggest that the exchange rate agreement has been effective not so much as a result of the expectation effect it generates, but when accompanied by traditional policies to limit demand (Dornbusch, 1991), and to the extent to which it has acted on the formation of profit margins. In any case, the flexibility of prices and wages is clearly of substantial importance.

Not surprisingly the credibility and the expectation effect of the EMS could not easily be distinguished from the other disinflationary effects exerted on all industrial countries. Both the countries of the observed sample (EMS countries) and those of the control sample (non-EMS countries) experienced common disinflationary policies (De Grauwe, 1990); on the other hand, in some of the observed countries disinflationary policies, more determined than in the past, may have produced proportionate reactions in the goods and labour markets which can easily be confused with structural changes either in the trade-off or in the formation of expectations.

The conclusion that the EMS was neither a necessary nor a sufficient condition for stabilising inflation seems too strong as such, mainly because it is impossible to prove that the stronger determination to disinflate is not the result of the constraint of the exchange rate agreement.

When, in the middle of the 1980s, the third oil shock restored the previous, more favourable terms of trade for the industrial countries, the phase of real adjustment seemed to be over, and a new phase began in which further disinflation in the EC countries could be pursued independently of the reabsorption of an external shock. This new phase coincided with the so-called New EMS. The awareness of the disinflationary effects of the exchange rate agreement was now more widespread; and, since then, a quasi-fixed exchange rate experiment has been isolated. Such an experiment appears much more significant as it is coupled with the completion of full capital mobility across the borders. This is the true period of possible price stabilisation through the exchange rate without any interference or other adjustments requiring a permanent reduction of real wages; nevertheless a few countries still retain large inflation differentials with Germany, of which the main ones are Italy and Spain.

We shall focus on Italy, a country which had still to reduce its inflation, and France, which had already achieved German inflation and we shall compare the stabilisation policies implemented during this period to those of the first five years of the 1980s.

Two adjustment policies: France and Italy in the 1980s

The stabilisation policies of the first and second half of the 1980s may be traced back to the more general debate about inflation stabilisation policies in hyperinflation countries. In very general terms, such a debate refers to two options: inflation can be fought by trying to anchor price dynamics either to a newly announced low and stable growth of the money supply or to a newly announced stable path for the nominal exchange rate (Fischer, 1986, 1988).

It has been shown (Calvo and Vegh, 1990) that the first option (money-based stabilisation policy with flexible exchange rates) implies a front loaded recession, the extent of which is related to the degree of credibility of the policy. The second option (exchange-based stabilisation policy) might give rise, under full credibility, to an expansionary effect due to the expectation effect (possibly supported also by an inflow of capital) which reduces nominal interest rates, while current home inflation remains sticky; later, the real appreciation of the exchange rate starts to offset the expansionary effect and a potential recession lies ahead. Not only might the real appreciation of the exchange rate reduce the growth of real net exports, it might also undermine the credibility of the policy.

In our opinion, *mutatis mutandis*, this might be a convenient schema with which to deal with inflation stabilisation policies in the EMS countries. (Indeed, it has been used in Giavazzi and Spaventa, 1990.)

Up to 1982, France and Italy, together with the majority of other industrialised countries, shared double-digit inflation and unemployment, current account deficits and strong pressure for restructuring the industrial sector. Germany's performance, on the other hand, was already showing opposing trends: two years of real decline in domestic demand (almost 5 per cent in cumulative terms) was driving inflation back to 5 per cent, while in France demand was still growing and in Italy it had just stopped growing, and French inflation was 6.7 points higher than in Germany and Italian inflation 11.2 points higher.

In 1987 French inflation was 3 points higher than German inflation; in the same year, the Italian inflation differential with Germany was reduced to 4.5 points. The current account deficit was almost nil for both countries; they seemed to have been running on the same track, with the advantage for Italy – emphasised in Giavazzi and Spaventa (1990) – of lower costs in terms of output losses.

Since 1987, inflation has again been growing in Italy, albeit to a moderate extent, while France has been reducing her differential inflation with Germany to zero (and currently to below zero). At the same time, the Italian current account has deteriorated to a greater extent than the French, while domestic demand has, in the most recent years (1989–91), been growing at a slower rate in Italy.

In the light of this it seems legitimate to ask whether the roots of the worsening performance in Italy in the last five years are to be found in unsound adjustment policy in the previous five years or in the specific policy pursued in the final years of the 1980s.

The oil shock adjustment

The deterioration of the terms of trade of the European countries implies a higher unemployment rate in order to keep inflation on a stable path. Germany reacted quite quickly: its current account was already negative in 1979, but returned to a surplus in 1982. Italy and France delayed their adjustment policies, so they added to the oil shock another shock, the worsening of their competitiveness with respect to other industrial countries. This increased the total cost to be paid in order to restore the balance of payments equilibrium. Once the two countries started adjusting (France's delay was longer than Italy's), France set up a fully fledged set of consistent policy tools, while Italy seemed unable to take such a consistent position.

The French policies
The sharp increase in the gap with Germany, the result of expansion conducted in one country alone in 1981–2, led to a sudden reversal of emphasis in economic policy. As early as June 1982 this became more restrictive, a temporary wages and prices freeze preparing the way for a realignment of the French Franc exchange rate within the EMS. At the same time negotiations got under way which led in March of the following year to the definition of a strategy of full economic readjustment.

This strategy was designed in the following manner. First of all a more restrictive fiscal policy which, as from 1984, led to a reduction in public spending, coupled with a tighter monetary policy. The target for 1983, set initially at 10 per cent, was revised during the year to 9 per cent (nominal GDP grew by 10.4 per cent in that year), while the measures taken to limit credit growth were particularly restrictive (the growth in bank lending fell from 17.6 per cent in 1982 to 12.7 per cent the following year).

The decision to set a nominal limit to the growth of monetary aggregates was accompanied by a wages and prices policy which shifted the horizon used as a basis for index-linking further into the future. Wage rises were tied to the planned rate of inflation for the two years under consideration (8 per cent and 5 per cent respectively in 1983 and 1984), and applied to all workers in those sectors over which the government could exercise control (public administration and companies wholly or partially state-controlled), thus affecting some 38 per cent of the workforce. Even the policy of raising the minimum wage (SMIC, accounting for 10 per cent of the workforce) in line with inflation was temporarily suspended. The agreement itself on one hand, and the credibility resulting from the application in the public sector of the measures announced, on the other, had the effect of subjecting wages in the private sector to the same kind of discipline, so that settlements here also came into line with planned inflation targets. France thus saw a swift reduction in the growth of wages in 1983 and 1984, a fall shared by the public and the private sectors alike.

This wages policy was accompanied by a policy of controlled price rises in all those companies having some kind of state participation as well as in those linked to them in some way, amounting to around 60 per cent of the nation's industry. The same was done for the prices of services. By means of various agreements and contracts around 70 per cent of prices were brought under control between the beginning of 1984 and June of the same year. The disinflationary effects of these measures were initially stronger on wages than on prices; the less rapid slowdown of the latter allowed companies to enjoy a rise in profit margins, which had been particularly squeezed over the previous years.

The exchange rate matched this process with the principal goal of restoring the competitiveness that had been lost as a result of the high inflation differentials. By the beginning of 1984 the FF/DM exchange rate had depreciated by around 35 per cent with respect to the beginning of 1979; in the same period the inflation differential had been 39.5 percentage points. As can be seen, belonging to the EMS had not prevented the substantial preservation of price competitiveness between France and Germany. Indeed in general, after the losses suffered in the early 1980s, as from 1984 the French currency depreciated in real terms, thus gaining increased price competitiveness.

The Italian policies

The second oil shock hit the Italian economy during a very strong economic expansion, at a time when both the reform of the National Health Service and rises in civil servants' wages and salaries (which had fallen behind those of the private sector in the 1970s) were engines of public spending which could not be stopped. In the following years budget policies tried to curb the growth of expenditure and to mitigate growth in the deficit. This went on until 1985, when primary PSBR, having reached 7.1 per cent of GDP, began to decline; unfortunately, by this time interest payments had reached such a level that the reduction of the primary PSBR did not show up in a significant reduction of total PSBR.

The most radical change in Italian policies was the well known 'divorce' between the Treasury and the Bank of Italy in 1981. The monetary financing of the PSBR began to decline but, given that fiscal policy was still loose, the ratio of debt to GDP started to increase rapidly. The realisation of the necessity to move away from exchange rate adjustment in response to the first oil shock towards a domestic quantities adjustment in response to the second one was slow to permeate all sectors of the economy. The more internationally oriented sectors faced financial stringency and this produced a reshaping of the industrial production processes, with the adoption of labour saving techniques and productivity increases. However, the primary PSBR continued to increase as did nominal wages. As a result the nominal exchange rate underwent several realignments and the real exchange rate in terms of unit labour costs depreciated by 1.6 per cent between 1979 and 1983. In 1983 the long and continuing process of dismantling the full indexation system began and during the three years 1983–5 the timing of indexation changed from quarterly to half-yearly and the degree of indexation was reduced from over 80 per cent to about 55–60 per cent; 1984 saw a temporary freeze of the indexation mechanism. After 1983 the exchange rate appreciated in real terms, even if at a relatively slow rate, as a result of the less frequent changes of parity within the EMS. The new exchange rate policy was backed by interest rate levels which were the highest for almost all the decade.

Costs and outcomes

The first impact of restrictive monetary policy in Italy was to reduce domestic demand growth to almost zero for three years (1981–3), after growth of almost 7 per cent a year in 1979 and in 1980. When in 1984 indexation was reduced and the mechanism frozen for a year, recovery of investment was quite sharp and the current account turned again into deficit. The costs of the French policy in terms of growth were far from negligible. In 1983 French GDP grew by only 0.7 per cent (compared to a European average of 2.4 per cent), the effect of this being felt mainly

Table 4.1 *Costs and gains of the adjustment*

	Δi	$\Sigma \Delta i$	ΔU	$\Sigma \Delta U$	Δd	Σb	$\Sigma \Delta i / \Sigma \Delta U$
1981–6							
Italy	−12.0	−6.4	3.1	1.9	28.3	−1.5	−3.3
France	−10.8	−5.8	3.2	2.0	11.3	−2.2	−2.9
Germany	−6.4	−3.7	3.3	3.2	4.2	3.5	−1.2
1987–91							
Italy	1.6	1.3	−1.1	−0.5	9.5	−5.9	−2.6
France	−0.2	−0.1	−1.2	−1.1	0.9	−3.1	0.1
Germany	3.3	2.3	−2.5	−1.3	4.3	4.1	−1.8

Source: Figures from IMF and OECD.
Note: $\Delta x = x_T - x_t$ and $\Sigma \Delta x = 1/(n+1) \sum_k (x_T - x_{t+k})$ with $T = 1986$ or 1991; $t = 1981$ or 1987; $k = 0,...,n$; $n = 3$ or 4, where x: i = consumer price inflation; U = unemployment rate; d = government net debt/GDP; b = net foreign assets/GDP.

on domestic demand. The improvement in the state of company finances and the increased competitiveness gained as a result of the reduction in the unit labour costs, however, paved the way for a new investment cycle after years of stagnation. During those years Italian policy seems to have produced a lower sacrifice in terms of domestic demand growth and a higher gain in terms of percentage points reduction in the inflation rate. Table 4.1 shows that this is apparent also in terms of additional unemployment: every percentage point increase in unemployment was associated with a 3.3 percentage point reduction in inflation in Italy and 2.9 per cent in France. This would appear to show that by waiting longer and being less tough the sacrifice is smaller – although contractionary policies elsewhere reduced imported inflation. If we take into account the fifth column of the table we observe that the debt to GDP ratio increased in Italy by seventeen points more than in France; this was the outcome of unbalanced policies, hence it represents the size of the disequilibrium that has not yet been corrected. Moreover, in France the convergence towards German inflation was almost over in 1986, while Italy was still far from the target.

During this phase French stabilisation policy seems to have followed relatively traditional procedures of restrictive monetary and fiscal policies, relatively concentrated in time, and supported by a social consensus on incomes policy. These policies were designed in the context of adjustable exchange rates, and followed and validated nominal exchange movements. The effectiveness of the full manoeuvre, in spite of gaining from the EMS, gained mainly from incomes policy, a consistent fiscal policy and the shift from backward to forward looking expectations associated with the change in policy regime from a higher emphasis on employment to a higher emphasis on low inflation rates, the costs being faced almost simultaneously with the adoption of the policies.

This shift in expectations allowed a certain degree of freedom to economic policy, rendering as it did the labour market and the price structure more reactive to the fiscal and monetary policies adopted. That this was possible would appear to have been the result of the signals given to the private sector by the restraints imposed on wage settlements in the public sector, a sure sign that left no doubt as to the government's real intention to pursue a policy of rapid readjustment.

It should be noted that the relative speed and ease with which the readjustment was achieved are to be partly attributed to the fact that the manoeuvre was adopted at a time when both the loss in competitiveness and the imbalances in the national budget and in the balance of payments were only just beginning to appear. Moreover, as it was not necessary for prices and incomes to grow more slowly in France than in Germany in order for France to recover the competitiveness that she had lost over the years, the whole manoeuvre was rendered considerably easier.

Compared with the French adjustment, Italian policy has been the more determined on the monetary side and the more relaxed on the fiscal side; as a consequence Italian policy has had to rely more on the impact of the EMS agreement as such. In fact, the slope of the time path of the exchange rates *vis-à-vis* the D-Mark is the same for France and Italy, but with different inflation rates; thus Italian policy started quite early on to signal that the exchange rate was not going to correct the whole differential of inflation quickly. Can we therefore argue that Italian policy, by relying more on the EMS, paid a slightly lower cost in terms of unemployment and output? It is really difficult to separate the effects of EMS and of the growing reputation of the Bank of Italy on the one side from the effects of general disinflation and of the social consensus reached in 1984–5 (visible in the result of a referendum supporting the temporary freeze of the indexation mechanism) on the other.

The nominal adjustment
In 1986 the drop in the price of oil cancelled out what still remained to be adjusted. The current account turned into the black for both France and Italy and inflation rates took another step downward. At the same time, the new goal of 'One Market, One Money' following the Single European Act entered the expectations of economic agents and deadlines were fixed for within a few years for the full liberalisation of capital movements.

Italy The financial integration of the Italian economy with the European economies is witnessed by the huge increase in both foreign assets and foreign liabilities, by the drop to almost nil of the differential between the interest rate on the Euro-market for Lira-denominated assets and

Table 4.2 *Government budget (Italy): changes in revenues and*
expenditures (1987–1990)

	Revenue	Expenditure
Total	3.0	2.6
– Interest payments		1.8
– Salaries		0.7
– Other items		0.1

domestic interest rates, and by the decline of interest rate differentials
with Germany and France.

The financing of the PSBR was eased by the growth of the share of
public debt in the hands of non-residents from zero to about 5 per cent.
The renewed expectations from day to day of the short-term stability of
the exchange rate *vis-à-vis* EMS currencies was the driving force of this
process. The Bank of Italy tried to resist the pressure of the market,
but nonetheless short-term interest differentials were reduced from the
order of magnitude consistent with the wider fluctuation band (6 per
cent) to that consistent with the narrow band. On a short-term basis,
the credibility of exchange rate stability seemed to have been increasing.
However, long-term differentials with France declined until 1987 but then
started increasing again. Long-term differentials with Germany imply a
much higher depreciation of the Lira in the long term than the current
band would allow. This weakens the case for increased credibility.

On the whole it seems reasonably sound to say that monetary policy
has been aimed mainly at stabilising the exchange rate, with periodic
concern not to allow it to appreciate too much, while on the other hand
budget policy has been directed towards an extremely gradual reduction
of the PSBR. This reduction becomes more substantial if we consider
the primary PSBR, but the speed of improvement has been so slow that
it has not been able to prevent the further deterioration of public debt
(table 4.2).

France In France the second half of the 1980s saw a period of consolidation of the country's anti-inflationary policy. The budget deficit reached
its lowest point in 1989 (a surplus of 0.2 per cent of GDP) whilst monetary
policy kept upward pressure on nominal interest rates. Stable inflation
allowed France to profit from the liberalisation of capital movements
by reducing her interest differential with Germany, thus limiting inflows
of capital.

Initial differentials with Germany have been completely ironed out
as regards short-term rates and systematically reduced for long-term
maturities. Long-term credibility of the current exchange rate, as

Chart 4.3   *Real exchange rates (in terms of unit labour costs)*

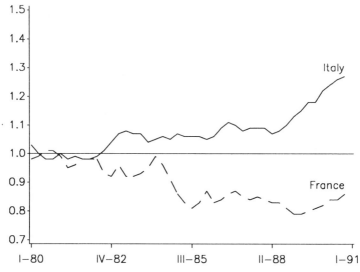

Source: OECD.

expressed by the expected depreciation implied by the differentials between French and German long-term rates, is not yet fully achieved, but the gap is closing.

Nominal adjustment to German inflation was completed by keeping the economy under control through both fiscal and monetary policy. In terms of labour costs, no backlog of losses in competitiveness had been accumulated in the past and, moreover, the real exchange rate continued to depreciate even with respect to 1984–5 levels. Nonetheless, the current account of the balance of payments moved into deficit, but it only averaged –0.6 per cent of GDP between 1987 and 1990.

Costs and outcomes

In the second half of the 1980s France pursued tighter monetary and fiscal policy and experienced higher growth and a further reduction of inflation. Her target of nominal adjustment was achieved; unemployment was reduced without any increase in inflation, and with an increase of a mere 3.1 percentage points in the ratio of foreign net liabilities to GDP (see table 4.1).

Italy, not having completed the real adjustment, did not succeed in the nominal one. She paid very low immediate costs, but just managed to keep inflation under control, relying on the reputation of the Bank of Italy, and turned the inconsistency between monetary, fiscal and wage policies into an increase in the public debt equal to 9.5 points of GDP and a ratio of foreign net liabilities to GDP that increased by 5.9 points.

Chart 4.4   *Relative price of services versus industrial goods*

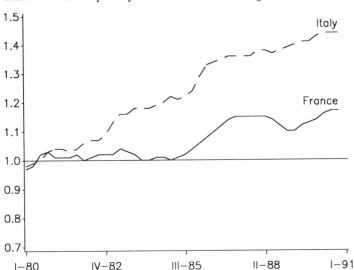

Source: OECD.

At this point the question at issue is to establish what brought about the inversion of the inflation rate in Italy? Or, to put it another way, what caused the appreciation of the real exchange rate of the Lira to speed up at a time when the Franc was still depreciating? First of all, how are we to document the real appreciation? Figures produced by the IMF for real effective exchange rates based on unit labour costs show a very sharp contrast between France and Italy (chart 4.3). Another description of the same phenomenon (one, however, that cannot provide a precise order of magnitude for it) might be the behaviour of the ratio of the price of home goods to the price of manufactured goods, the price of which is assumed to be internationally determined. The latter indicator shows that France and Italy followed a very divergent path (chart 4.4).

In any case, there is no doubt that we are dealing here with a substantial appreciation. At first sight, the answer to the initial question seems quite simple. Since 1987 (table 4.3) Italian wages in the private sector have been growing on average at 7.8 per cent a year, while French wage growth has been more than three points lower (4.6 per cent) and productivity has grown at very similar rates in both countries.

Was this the result of stronger growth in Italy than in France during that period? It has been argued that in Italy the liberalisation of capital movements brought about a reduction of real interest rates, thus stimulating a domestic expansion which might have given rise to an increase in domestic prices relative to international ones. Or, to put it another way, liberalisation eased the problems of financing the PSBR, thus

Table 4.3   *Average rates 1987–90*

	France	Italy
Inflation	3.2	5.6
Wages		
private sector	4.6	7.8
industry	3.7	7.9
Productivity (private sector)	2.5	2.4
Internal demand	3.6	3.6
GDP	3.3	3.0
Contribution of net exports		
to GDP growth	–0.4	–0.7

undermining the already low political will for its reduction, and keeping aggregate demand growing at a rate inconsistent with the equilibrium of the current account.

If we take into account economic activity, the picture is far from clear: only by 1987 was GDP growth higher in Italy than in France, but liberalisation did not start until 1988. If we consider domestic demand, this grew more rapidly in Italy in both 1987 and 1988, but not thereafter (chart 4.5). The investment cycle is of the same magnitude in both countries, but with slightly different timing; this was so in spite of the fact that monetary policy in France was able to keep real interest

Chart 4.5   *Domestic demand – deviations from a variable trend*

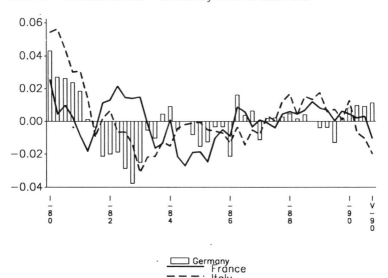

Germany
France
Italy

Source: OECD

Table 4.4   *Real wages (1980=100)*

	1980	1990	Average
Italy	100	111.4	104.3
France	100	111.2	104.6
Germany	100	111.4	102.7

rates on an increasing path, whereas Italian real rates have been declining slightly.

There does not seem to be any clear evidence of higher demand growth in Italy to explain the acceleration of inflation *vis-à-vis* further deceleration in France. During the two years 1987–8, the symmetric disinflationary shock due to the drop in the price of oil and the realignment of January 1987 produced a general expectation of exchange rate stability (with even backward looking expectations). This development favoured Italy because of her higher nominal interest rates and induced higher surpluses in the Italian capital account. These surpluses became higher and higher when liberalisation became effective, and went hand in hand with a deteriorating current account. However, at that time the differential growth in domestic demand had already turned negative for Italy.

We have, therefore, to look directly at the labour market to explain the differential wage dynamics. This is not much more helpful; in the period 1987–91 unemployment in France was on average 1.1 percentage points lower than in 1987, while in Italy it was 0.5 percentage points lower. Higher growth in France produced a stronger effect on unemployment, but the latter, in its turn, showed up in lower wage increases. On the other hand, Italian real wage rates experienced a larger decline during the first half of the 1980s, a fact which might explain the stronger push afterwards.

So, reference has to be made to the inheritance of the first quinquennium and other structural components. The very fact that the service sector is more prone to inflation in Italy is one of such components. Let us assume that we can describe the behaviour of France and Italy in the second half of the 1980s by means of a tradeables–non tradeables model. During that period both countries were hit by two different exogenous shocks: the improvement in the terms of trade following the drop in the price of oil, and the possible fall in manufacturing price trends due to the stabilisation of the nominal exchange rate. As such, the first shock implies a change in the tradeables–non tradeables frontier which reduces the relative price of tradeables versus non tradeables. The substitution effect feeds a higher demand for tradeables, while the income effect supports both demands, possibly most strongly for services. Given the inertia of wage and price

Chart 4.6   *Relative value-added: services versus industry*

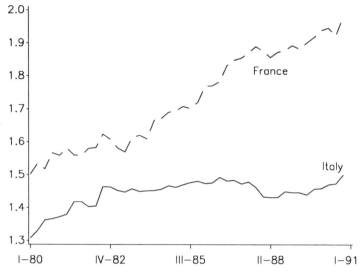

Source: OECD.

movements, the second shock (the stabilisation of the exchange rate) strengthens the reduction of the relative price of tradeables. Taking into account the previous history of inflation in France and Italy, it seems reasonable to assume that the impact of the second shock was stronger in Italy than in France.

Charts 4.4 and 4.6 show the different behaviour in each country of the relative prices of services and manufacturing on the one hand, and of the relative activity of services and industry on the other. We could summarise the two by saying that in France the relative price of tradeables–non tradeables is constant and the relative activity of the service sector increases, whereas in Italy the relative price of tradeables declines and the relative activity of services is constant.

These observations can be interpreted as meaning that the total relative price effect was lower in France and the exogenous long-term effect of the growing demand for services could show its impact particularly in the face of an elastic supply of services. In Italy, the stronger relative price effect and the associated income effect pushed up demand for services, but supply did not prove to be elastic.

Summing up this whole section, we think it apparent that French stabilisation after 1982–3 may be closer to a money-based policy than to exchange rate stabilisation. Restrictive monetary and fiscal policy plus an effective incomes policy brought about the desired reduction of inflation. The exchange rate had previously fully accommodated the inflation differential with Germany, no announcement was made at the

Chart 4.7 *Italy: capital movements balance and interest rates differentials (versus Germany)*

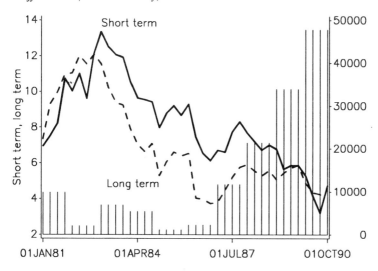

Source: IMF.

Chart 4.8 *France: capital movements balance and interest rates differentials (versus Germany)*

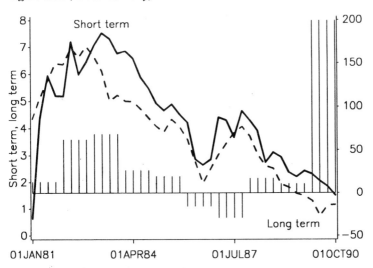

Source: IMF.

time to fix the exchange rate, and no significant real appreciation was experienced. Finally, when the New EMS started working, France had already reduced her inflationary gap with Germany to zero. On the other hand, no country, except Italy, has relied so heavily on the stabilisation effect of the nominal exchange rate alone to disinflate the economy. During the first phase of EMS the exchange rate was adjusted frequently, but not enough to compensate for inflation differentials. The main domestic support for the exchange policy was an episode of incomes policy in 1984–5. During the period of quasi-fixed exchange rates Italy had still to adjust both her inflation and her current account. Nonetheless she experienced a long honeymoon effect on interest rates supported by the liberalisation of capital movements (charts 4.7 and 4.8).

A comparison of the performances of goods and labour markets

It is clear from our comparison of France and Italy that both the policies adopted and the results achieved in the two countries have been different. Now we must consider whether it is possible to identify other factors more closely linked to the 'structural' characteristics of the two economies to help us understand the different results.

We shall not dwell on the attempts to identify changes in the formation of expectations, partly because we believe that the period of true exchange rate stability and of widespread awareness of the phenomenon is as yet too short for its effects to be seen in any reliable manner in the available data. We shall pursue a less direct line of enquiry, attempting to determine whether the traditional channels of transmitting a disinflationary thrust can account for what has happened in the two countries.

The labour market

There would seem to be a peculiar difference between the two countries in terms of the labour market and wage trends. Many studies of the French economy reveal that the usual econometric specifications of the wage functions are not completely satisfying. This is attributed to the weight a number of institutional factors (such as the existence of a minimum wage) have in the income structure in France, and even to the suggestion that the government's economic policy itself here has greater clout (Horn, 1991). Such a claim is in line with the success of the 1982–3 incomes policy.

Other studies have attempted to see whether there have been modifications in the structure of wage agreements, and the answers here are varied (Barrell, Darby and Donaldson 1990, Blanchard and Sevestre, 1989, Poret, 1990, and Ralle and Toujas Bernate, 1990). The studies seem, however, to agree with the fact that emerges from econometric analysis, that there appears to have been a shift in the horizon of wage indexation towards planned inflation targets, and an increase in the role played by the unemployment rate. In general, productivity is seen as not playing an important role.

With regard to Italy, the characteristics of the three-yearly rounds of wage bargaining with their emphasis on absolute rather than proportional increases have called for an efficient indexation system to defend purchasing power over the duration of the contract. Between 1983 and 1986 two agreements led to the reduction of the degree of indexation, but the pay bargaining of the years 1987–90 has reflected both a lack of belief in further disinflation and a nominal stickiness in the face of the necessary reduction in the demands for absolute wage increases.

Let us assume that $w(t)$ is the rate of change of the nominal wage rate, $pe(t)$ the rate of change of the consumer price index expected for time t, $g(0)$ a constant target real wage growth, $U(t)$ the unemployment rate and $U(0)$ an average of $U(t)$ over the sample to represent a 'normal' rate. We can write a very simple wage equation to take into account the overlapping contracts assumption:

$$w(t) = g(0) + a_1.pe(t) + (1-a_1).w(t-1) + a_3.(\ln U(t) - \ln U(0))$$

We have estimated the parameters of this equation without imposing the absence of the long-run trade-off between unemployment and wage inflation and we have taken the realisation of inflation in the previous quarter as the expectation of inflation for the current quarter.

The estimated parameters are the following:

$a_0 = g(0) - a_3.U(0)$;

$a_2 = $ free estimation of $(1-a_1)$.

Table 4.5 shows the results we have obtained for the different sample periods. These confirm that for France no significant change can be detected in the 1980s *vis-à-vis* the previous decade: they show no money illusion in the overall sample (even though estimation was not constrained), no changes in the importance of unemployment, and a slight reduction of the target real wage growth.

Table 4.5 *Wage equations: estimated coefficients*

	$g(0)$		a_1		a_2		a_3	
	I	F	I	F	I	F	I	F
72–80	5.6	1.8	0.44	0.45	0.41	0.62	–8.5	–3.3
			(2.5)	(4.5)	(1.6)	(5.2)	(1.1)	(5.7)
72–86	3.6	1.4	0.47	0.41	0.41	0.60	–6.5	–3.0
			(3.8)	(4.8)	(2.5)	(6.5)	(2.5)	(7.6)
72–90	3.4	1.2	0.47	0.41	0.37	0.59	–5.9	–3.0
			(4.4)	(5.6)	(2.8)	(7.3)	(2.8)	(8.4)

For Italy, the results reveal some degree of money illusion for the whole sample, in spite of the high degree of indexation, the emerging of the importance of unemployment in the 1980s, and a declining target real wage growth, but still about three times the target for French employees (we should not forget that the level of Italian wages still has some catching up to do with respect to the European Big Three).

As the sample moves on through the 1980s, the measure adopted for $g(0)$ reflects the unemployment hysteresis of that decade through the increase of $U(0)$. Such an increase is exactly the same for the two countries (2.5 points) with a stronger impact on the Italian target real wage growth, which shrinks by 2.2 points (0.6 for France). French wages seem to have reacted to the drop in demand for labour following the same pattern as in the past. The real shocks seem to have brought Italian wages back to a pattern more dependent on market conditions. Nonetheless, the aspirations of Italian wage earners still seem incompatible with the general efficiency of the economic system as a whole. Moreover, we could argue that after 1987 money illusion might have worked in a negative direction at a time when disinflation had to be completed. The government itself misperceived the systemic constraints when it allowed wages in the public sector to behave in a manner incompatible with the disinflationary target pursued by the monetary authorities through the fully stable exchange rate.

While in Italy wages in the 1980s grew faster in the public sector than in the private sector, in both France and Germany the opposite was true, particularly at the end of the decade, in the years 1987–90 (chart 4.9).

Chart 4.9   *Private and public sector wages in 1991, 1986=100*

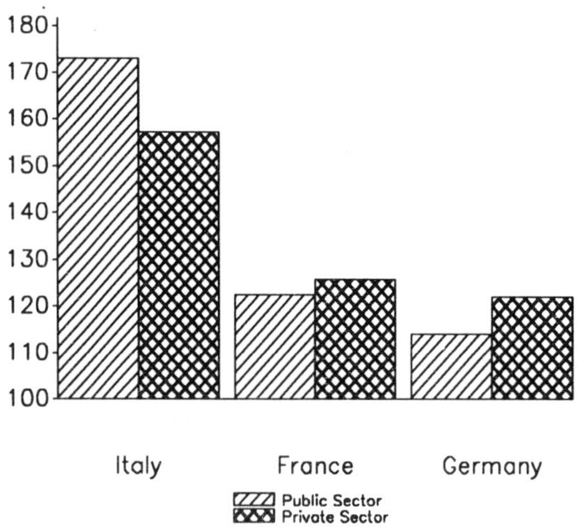

Source: OECD.

The goods market

In both countries the labour market was able to effect the real adjustment required in the first half of the decade. Differences emerged in the second half, however, when nominal adjustment was required. In the case of France, further disinflation put no particular sqeeze on profit margins, whilst in Italy margins came under more pressure, thus making it more difficult to sustain the inflation differential already achieved (table 4.6).

Let us define an equation for the percentage change in the price of manufactured goods (*pm*) in terms of the percentage change in unit labour costs (*ulc*), of the change in the price competitiveness (*c=pmf/pm*) of imported foreign goods (*pmf*) *vis-à-vis* domestic tradeable goods (*pm*), of the international terms of trade (*q=pmf/prm*) of manufactured goods versus raw material and energy prices and, finally, of a demand factor (*k*), the degree of capacity utilisation in the industrial sector:

$$pm(t) = a_0 + ulc(t) + \lambda. \, c(t) + \lambda.(1-\mu). \, q(t) + a_1.\mathrm{ln}k(t)$$

where $\lambda = \beta/(1-\beta)$ and β is the weight of overall imported goods on the gross industrial product; μ is the weight of imported manufactured goods over total imports of goods. The non-linearly estimated equation is the following:

$$pm(t) = a_0 + (1-\beta). \, ulc(t) + \beta. \, pmf(t) + \beta.(1-\mu). \, q(t) + (1-\beta). \, a_1.\mathrm{ln}k(t)$$

Right across the sample (table 4.7) the unit labour cost appears three times more important in French manufactured goods prices, while imported raw material and energy prices had slightly less weight in French final prices; finally, prices of foreign goods had a much stronger impact on the domestic Italian market of manufactured goods than in France. Such an impact may be the result of a larger inter-industry trade, of higher dependence on foreign intermediate products, and of the possible effect on the formation of mark-up. Moreover, whilst in France the weight of foreign goods decreased strongly in the 1980s, it increased in Italy during the same period. The increase in the impact of labour costs was greater in France than in Italy.

On the whole we might risk the conclusion that, in the French case,

Table 4.6 *Labour costs and prices: average rates*

	80–86		87–90	
	I	F	I	F
Wages	14.0	10.1	7.8	4.6
Productivity	1.4	1.9	1.9	2.0
Consumer prices	13.7	9.2	5.6	3.2
Producer prices	11.1	7.3	4.6	2.4

Source: OECD.

Table 4.7   *Estimated parameters of equation for pm(t)*

	$(1-\beta)$ (a)	$\beta\mu$ (b)	$\beta(1-\mu)$ (c)
Italy			
1970–90	0.20	0.68	0.12
1970–80	0.17	0.62	0.13
France			
1970–90	0.63	0.28	0.09
1970–80	0.49	0.43	0.07

(a) Unit labour cost weight.
(b) Competitors' prices weight.
(c) Raw material and energy prices weights.

on the one hand, the labour market was more efficient in turning the negative impulses on domestic demand into lower real wages and, on the other, lower wages played a more important role in disinflation. Foreign prices seem to have been of greater importance for Italian disinflation where the unit labour cost appears to carry less weight. More generally, the French labour and goods markets seem to allow stronger price effectiveness to restrictive policies and lower quantity effectiveness to expansionary policies. The opposite could be said for Italy, where the quantity effectiveness of expansionary policies seems to be stronger and the price effectiveness of restrictive policies weaker. However, the transmission channels seem to have been quite traditional. Econometric evidence confirms that it was the intensity of the effects of the new anchor adopted that reduced inflation, rather than an autonomous change in expectations based on the EMS credibility effects. This conclusion does not allow us to reject the statement that the EMS was uninfluential in the process of disinflation. In France, it corroborated the process mainly through the determination of the French government to pursue the required policies. We might say that it was the government that was credible rather than the exchange rate. Italian prices reflected the constraints imposed by the exchange rate, but the aspirations to real wage increases in both industrial and service sectors remained high and did not reflect the nominal adjustment required by EMS discipline. Moreover, the lack of determination shown by Italian policymakers raises a question as to what extent the short-term credibility of the exchange rate can be effective if it is not coupled with long-term sustainability.

From credibility to sustainability

An exogenous impulse of credibility (a change of regime) can allow a reputation to be built up, and this, in turn, can help to strengthen credibility. If this is not supported by sustainability, however, there is the possibility of financial instability. Having failed to adjust in terms of nominal variables, Italy is facing this risk.

As we have noted above, the partial adjustment of Italian inflation is reflected in the rise in both the public and foreign debt. The policy orientation required to stabilise both in Italy is still absent. This is no longer only a question of nominal adjustment. If Italy is to achieve a net export position sufficient to pay off the burden of her accumulated net foreign debt, a change in real wages is required. Only after reaching a sustainable position can the convergence requirements be taken seriously into account. In this final section we shall focus on Italy and the steps she has to take to achieve convergence.

From a theoretical point of view, sustainability refers to the possibility that the intertemporal constraint both for the public sector and the foreign sector be effective. If we look at the long-term time series for the surpluses of the private, public and foreign sectors (chart 4.10) we see that in the past the intertemporal constraint on the current account has been working and that the private and public sector surpluses are obviously integrated (see Basevi, Ferrari, Onofri and Poli, 1991).

The simple fact that in the past they have been sustained does not mean that they will be so in the future. In very recent years the current account deficit has kept on accumulating mainly as a result of an interest–debt circle; should this go on at this rate in the coming years, given the current condition of the government budget, how far should the private

Chart 4.10   *Italy: private, foreign and public surpluses*

surplus go in order to make up for both the foreign and the public disequilibria? Focusing attention on the government deficit and debt, as the Maastricht Treaty does, means trying to guarantee sustainability, leaving the distribution between private and foreign surpluses to the market.

To give an idea of the size of this possible phenomenon for Italy, let us consider that at the end of 1991 the ratio of public debt to GDP has reached 100.4 per cent and the ratio of the net foreign liabilities to GDP 11.1 per cent. The real burden of the public debt is 4.2 compared with a real growth of less than 1 per cent. We can define f^* as the primary PSBR required, *ceteris paribus*, to keep public debt constant at the current year level:

$$f^*=[ih/(1+g)]+[(g-i)/(1+g)]d$$

where i is the average interest rate paid on government bonds, h is the Treasury money stock in terms of GDP, g is the rate of growth of nominal GDP and d is the ratio of public debt to GDP.

This implies that in 1991 a primary PSBR of 1.9 points of GDP less would have been required, *ceteris paribus*, to keep the ratio of public debt to GDP constant at the 1990 level.

The same kind of computation can be made with reference to the external net debt. We can define m^* as the ratio of net imports, excluding the interest payments balance (let us call it primary net imports), to GDP that, *ceteris paribus*, would have left the ratio of net foreign debt to GDP unchanged:

$$m^*=[(g-i^* - e\,(1+i^*))\,/\,(1+g)]\,.b$$

where i^* is the international interest rate, e is the proportional change of the exchange rate, and b is the ratio of net foreign debt to GDP.

For 1991, this computation shows that net primary imports should have been 1.4 per cent lower in terms of GDP in order to stabilise the net foreign debt ratio. The formula for m^* could be complicated by showing the share of foreign debt denominated in the home currency (the debt on which the country could levy the inflation tax), but this is quite small for Italy.

The two figures for Italy are obviously higher than the analogous ones for France. They show, at least at first sight, that delaying the adjustment has not allowed Italy to avoid it. However, we should not forget that f^*, to a greater extent than m^*, is quite a volatile figure. It can change rapidly, according to some exogenous variables (seignorage, real growth and real interest rates) as it has done in the past.

Thus, if we are not worried about the level of the ratio of public debt to GDP (nobody knows where the instability point lies), things might become easier simply by waiting. Of course, the same statement does not apply to foreign debt to the same extent. The delay in the adjustment of both disequilibria produces an accumulation of debt, but this does not mean that it increases the effort required to stop debt growth. The adjustment costs increase with certainty only if the levels of the two debts are included in the loss function of the government. If not, if the Maastricht Treaty for monetary union allows countries joining to be in a non-increasing public debt condition (the consideration of the whole situation of the country) it might pay a risk-loving government to delay the adjustment to the final year. However, even now the further adjustment required for Italy does not seem out of reach.

The true question is whether the domestic or the foreign target has to have the priority. Pursuing government deficit correction does not guarantee that the external current account is corrected too. If we use the quarterly Prometeia model of the Italian economy to simulate the effect of a correction of budget policy equivalent to the amount required to stabilise the public debt to GDP ratio we get a result where domestic activity does not change in a dramatic manner (table 4.8a). The fact that a large share of government expenditure is made up of transfer payments, the high level of wealth–income ratio and the much stronger smoothing behaviour in consumption than in disposable income are the main reasons for the moderate reaction of consumption and the almost irrelevant effect on the current account. The more so, if we remember the experiences

Table 4.8   *Simulation of policy shocks with the Prometeia model*

	1 year	3 years	5 years
(a) Restrictive fiscal shock equivalent to the amount required to stabilise the public debt to GDP ratio			
GDP(a)	–1.1	–1.2	–1.5
Primary net imports/GDP(b)	–0.2	–0.3	–0.3
Current account/GDP(b)	0.2	0.3	0.4
Primary PSBR/GDP(b)	–2.6	–1.9	–1.6
PSBR/GDP(b)	–2.7	–2.4	–2.3
CPI(a)	–0.1	–0.4	–0.5
(b) Restrictive fiscal shock (as above) associated with a nominal devaluation of the parity of 13 per cent			
GDP(a)	0.9	0.3	0.4
Primary net imports/GDP(b)	0.2	–0.4	–0.5
Current account/GDP(b)	–0.3	0.4	0.5
Primary PSBR/GDP(b)	–3.1	–1.8	–1.6
PSBR/GDP(b)	–3.3	–2.4	–2.5
CPI(a)	1.4	2.7	2.7
WPI(a)	4.4	5.5	5.5

(a) Percentage differences from the levels of the baseline simulation.
(b) Absolute differences from the levels of the baseline simulation.

of Denmark, Ireland and the United Kingdom, when fiscal contraction produced an expansionary impact. Several different explanations can be suggested, but it is difficult to neglect the possibility that the size of the Italian public debt and deficit have reached such a level that the Italian consumer has become to some extent a 'Ricardian' consumer (Nicoletti, 1988). We cannot exclude the hypothesis that we have reached a point from which an improvement in the government deficit might be acknowledged as a confidence gain.

All this could be interpreted as if the costs of public finance austerity had been brought to zero. Indeed, this means simply that the costs will be paid under the item 'current account equilibrium'. How? Monetary policy is in European hands, fiscal policy (the only instrument of economic policy left to individual countries) has a reduced impact; what about an exchange rate devaluation?

The Prometeia model suggests that the correction required in net primary imports in order to stabilise the net foreign debt to GDP ratio could be the result of a real depreciation of the Lira of 7 per cent, if domestic activity may be taken as constant. Actually, given the high degree of import penetration, the absorption effect combines with the negative terms of trade effect to produce a slight deterioration of the current account even if associated with a higher level of activity (table 4.8b). The validation of the effects of a devaluation requires, of course, a restriction on domestic demand, but neither fiscal policy nor monetary policy seems able (for different reasons) to accomplish the task. Was Italy as precipitous in the full liberalisation of capital movements as it was lazy in adjusting her budget policy? In a sense, the answer should be yes. Actually, the loss of effectiveness of the policy tools is just another aspect of the cost of a delayed adjustment.

Italy, therefore, is not far from a sustainable position both in her public debt and in her foreign net debt. This position would allow her to rejuvenate her shrinking credibility and then to complete the adjustment. Nonetheless, the story we have told shows that those very few steps have become difficult to take.

Conclusion

Our argument is therefore that France, in taking EMS discipline seriously, was able to converge to German performance without the EMS exerting a crucial role, but that Italy was inconsistent in her attitude to EMS discipline, and reached partial convergence mainly because of the effect exerted by EMS. Of course, having one's hands tied is more useful for undisciplined people than for disciplined ones!

For a long time, in the 1970s and in the 1980s, Italy was unconsciously proud of what Keynes had said about her, when describing the deflationary policies enacted soon after World War I, '... [in] Italy ... an imprudent desire to deflate has been balanced by the intractability of the financial situation, with the happy result of comparatively stable prices' (Keynes, 1923).

Many Italian economists cherished the hope that being different would pay off in the end. We have told our tale of the two adjustments to show that, actually, this was not the case and that now Italy is facing the question of a possible deindustrialisation (or, more generally, of a reduction in real growth) with few macroeconomic tools left (a fiscal contraction, still necessary but no longer sufficient, and an incomes policy) and, as we mentioned at the very beginning of this chapter, the necessity to resort to industrial and supply-side policies with all the social conflicts that they imply.

5

The Achievements of the ERM and the Preconditions for Monetary Union: A French Perspective

Christian Bordes and Eric Girardin

Introduction

The EMS that was created in 1979 has been deeply transformed over time. It is now usual to distinguish between the old EMS (1979–87) – characterised by frequent parity realignments, capital controls and a sharp asymmetry between Germany and other members – and the new EMS, where realignments are the exception, capital market integration is very strong and inflation has generally converged towards German levels. Since June 1990, the new EMS has overlapped with the first stage of European Monetary Union. This should lead to the setting up of the European Monetary Institution in the second stage and the adoption of a single currency in the final stage.

Three questions must be raised à propos this process: what are the main achievements of the functioning of the old EMS? Have they been reinforced by the functioning of the new EMS? Are the preconditions for the setting up of a genuine monetary union being fulfilled? The answers to be given to these questions vary according to the point of view adopted. The EMS is an example of international monetary cooperation in which participating countries register gains and losses which are specific to them. In this chapter, it would be too ambitious to try to achieve an exhaustive balance sheet of the implications of the functioning of the EMS for all member countries and to consider their specific situation in the perspective of the formation and strengthening of monetary union. We will thus only endeavour to answer our three questions for France.

In the first section of the chapter, we will examine the main achievements stemming from French participation in the old EMS. The contribution of the EMS to disinflation is clearly central. In the second section, we will study the implications of the functioning of the new EMS. We will see that the positive effects of the competitive disinflation policy take a very long time to work themselves out and that in the present

context the authorities do not have any means to accelerate the adjustment
process of the economy, so that *ceteris paribus*, the unemployment rate
would remain at a high level. In the third section, we will endeavour to
show that the functioning of the European monetary union could give to
French economic policy a margin for manoeuvre which is not available
now. This margin for manoeuvre could be even wider if the authorities
immediately granted to the Bank of France the full independence it
now lacks.

France in the old EMS: 1979–87

*The franc–D-Mark exchange rate and the divergence of
nominal developments*
At its inception the objectives of the EMS were to reduce exchange-rate
related uncertainty, to increase anti-inflationary discipline and credibility,
to increase coordination of exchange-rate policy and to pave the way
for monetary union. The initial aim of the EMS was the stabilisation
of exchange rates and the harmonisation of economic developments in
member countries. The German authorities were worried more than any
other country by monetary stability.

The increasing solidification of the ERM is detailed in Chapter 1. In
the first years of the system realignments were frequent. The relative
weakness of the D-Mark at that time helped in the system's survival.
Between 1979 and 1987, the French franc was devalued six times.
Between the end of 1981 and early 1983, three successive realignments
generated a depreciation amounting to more than 23 per cent of the
franc–D-Mark central parity. In the end, after the last realignment of
the franc on 12 January 1987, this central parity was almost 30 per cent
lower than in 1980. Chapter 1 gives extensive detail of developments in
Europe. French and German experience has become less diverse. From
1971–3 inflation rates were similar in France and Germany. In 1974 there
was a wide gap of around 6 per cent. In Germany, inflation reached a
ceiling of only 6.3 per cent a year in 1981, but after an acceleration
of 3.6 per cent, a little smaller than that in France. In 1981 and 1982,
the inflation gap between the two countries was around 7 per cent.
World inflation peaked in 1980 (in the United States, Japan and in the
EC). Inflation was reduced almost everywhere in 1981. By contrast, it
remained almost unchanged in France and diminished only in 1982. The
inflation differential between France and Germany then became very
large. The disinflation process thus started later in France, the more
significantly so as the deceleration observed in 1982 is largely due to
a strict price freeze.

*Wage discipline policy, restrictive monetary and fiscal
policy*

The French authorities implemented a new wage policy in 1982 with the short-term objective of reducing the purchasing power of wages. The authorities were also preoccupied with the longer-term problem of a rate of inflation higher than that in its trading partners.

Traditionally, there existed profound differences between France and Germany in the process of wage formation, which are manifest in estimated wage equations (Chan-Lee, Coe and Prywes, 1987; Morin, 1988). In the French case, the wage rate was characterised by the following features: unitary elasticity with respect to the overall price level after one year; a small response to the unemployment rate; no direct link with the variations in labour productivity; and influence of increases in the minimum wage. In Germany the wage is influenced by unemployment, is directly and strongly affected by movements in labour productivity and its degree of indexation is more a subject of debate. Some studies indicate an under-indexation, some others agree on the existence of a unit price elasticity of the nominal wage. These differences give an advantage to Germany over France. If there were a negative shock on productivity, German wages would adjust immediately downwards while in France profits would bear the whole burden of adjustment in the short run. In case of an increase in the price of imports, French wages would adjust much more quickly than German wages.

In the middle of 1982, the French government implemented a wage freeze. Then immediately after the end of the freeze, the authorities wished to base wage settlements in both the civil service and the private sector on carefully discussed expectations. The government recommended to employers' associations that price and wage increases should not exceed official forecasts. Subsequently France, as other EMS countries, pursued a wage discipline policy aimed at transferring value-added to firms. The increase in the real wage rate remained smaller than the growth of labour productivity so that the growth in labour costs remained negative.

At the beginning of the 1980s, French fiscal policy was expansionary in order to stimulate economic activity. Subsequently, the government tried to reduce the PSBR. The weight of public debt (as a percentage of GDP) then increased while remaining smaller than in other European countries. Moreover, monetary growth slowed very markedly. The combination of the wage discipline policy and the demand restricting policy led to a slowdown in economic activity. While at the beginning of the 1980s the rate of economic growth was higher in France than in Germany, over the 1983–8 period the reverse was true every year.

*French disinflation, the role of wage discipline and of
the EMS*

The impact of wage discipline   Minczeles and Sicsic (1986) and Morin
(1988) evaluated the role of the wage discipline policy in disinflation
between 1981 and 1985. They suggested that the impact was small
and transitory. The slowdown in inflation which it caused would have
amounted to 1.1 per cent on average and around 2.5 per cent in 1982
alone. It had hardly any impact in 1983. The disinflationary effect
represented 1.5 per cent in 1984 and 1985 (table 5.1).

Even though a few studies point to the opposite (Ralle and Toujas-
Bernate, 1990), the consensus view is that the process of wage formation
has not been fundamentally altered in France in the 1980s: the long-term
degree of indexation is still unitary. This is confirmed by a Ministry
of Finance study using sectoral financial accounts (Cotis, 1991) which
shows that capital and not labour is still bearing most of the burden of
terms of trade changes. This was the case in the mid-1980s for the
positive oil shock as it was in the mid and end of the 1970s for the
negative ones.

Some studies examining wage contracts (Blanchard and Sevestre,
1989) find that whilst unitary ex-post indexation was common before
1982, thereafter expectations-oriented or ex-ante full indexation became
common. If such a change represents a durable phenomenon it would be
a significant improvement since the wage contracts literature (Fischer,
1986a) suggests that the output costs of disinflation are reduced (the
sacrifice ratio is lowered) inasmuch as the shift to ex-ante indexation
permits a more rapid response of wages to the reduced rate of price
increase. However, the evidence available does not enable us to determine
the effects of this change in indexation in accelerating the process of
disinflation.

The impact of EMS discipline   The role of exchange-rate appreciation in disinflation is sometimes emphasised. An appreciation of the

Table 5.1   *Role of economic policy in disinflation*

	1981	1982	1983	1984	1985
Inflation (year-on-year)	13.5	8.6	9.9	6.4	4.5
Disinflation/1981		−4.9	−3.6	−7.1	−9.0
Impact of economic policy					
Morin (1988)		−2.5	−0.1	−1.6	−1.3
Minczeles-Sicsic (1986)		−2.5	+0.3	−1.5	−1.5
of which wage disindexation		0.1	−0.4	−1.7	−1.6

real exchange rate exerts a direct disinflationary effect because a fall in competitiveness reduces net exports, and there is also an indirect disinflationary effect because the authorities of member countries have an incentive not to follow inflationary policies between realignments as they would wish to avoid the loss of competitiveness which would ensue (see for instance Russo and Tullio, 1988, Giavazzi and Giovannini, 1988, and Vinals, 1990). While the franc–D-Mark real exchange rate depreciated by 1.6 per cent a year over the 1980–82 period, it appreciated by 4.5 per cent a year from 1983–5.

However, the most popular explanation of the disinflationary effects of the EMS puts the emphasis on credibility. The central banks of member countries must follow the same monetary policy as the Bundesbank in order to stabilise the exchange rates of their currency *vis-à-vis* the D-Mark (Giavazzi and Pagano, 1988, and Giavazzi and Giovannini, 1989). The EMS is often characterised as being assymetric and being dependent on German leadership. The German authorities choose the monetary policy of the area, while the other countries adjust their own policy so as to stabilise the exchange rate of their currency *vis-à-vis* the D-Mark.

The interest-rate differential between a member country and Germany reflects expectations of devaluation of its currency *vis-à-vis* the D-Mark. Assuming uncovered interest parity, we can combine offshore Euromarket interest-rate differentials with current spot exchange rates to calculate expected exchange rates, in a way pioneered by Svensson (1990). Analysis of this differential indicates that over the period March 1979–August 1987, the one-year expected franc–D-Mark rate usually lay outside its ERM band, suggesting that realignments were continually anticipated over this period.

Short-term real interest rates have themselves remained higher in France than in Germany (5 per cent versus 3.2 per cent in 1987 for instance). The excess interest-rate differential enabled discipline to work. France witnessed high real interest rates, and these exerted a restrictive action on demand and favoured convergence towards the German situation.

Sharp variations in interest rates have been common in the EMS. A country wishing to stabilise the exchange rate of its currency *vis-à-vis* the D-Mark can trace speculative attacks against its currency (Wyplosz, 1988). The French authorities kept foreign exchange controls in place between 1981 and 1990 in order to reduce the effects of such an attack. The main component of these regulations was the security-currency mechanism according to which residents could only exchange between themselves the stock of foreign securities denominated in foreign currencies which they previously held. French residents could not buy foreign currencies with French francs in order to acquire foreign securities. These tight capital controls protected the franc from speculation and insulated

Chart 5.1   *Onshore and offshore French interest rates (one month)*

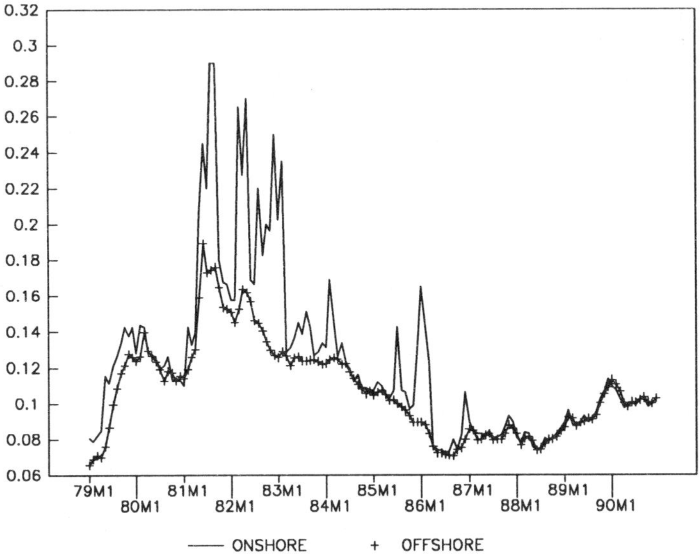

Source: Bank of France.

the onshore or domestic interest rate from movements on international money markets. During periods of speculative attacks, offshore French interest rates bore the whole burden of the adjustment (chart 5.1). Thus for a three-month maturity, while the volatility of this offshore interest rate was almost six times higher for France than for Germany over the 1979–87 period (that is, a standard deviation of 2.91 vs 0.61), this volatility was only one third higher for onshore rates in France than in Germany (0.81 vs 0.61). On the basis of such an insulation some have argued that capital controls brought some de facto symmetry in the EMS (de Grauwe, 1990).

The asymmetry implied by the German leadership hypothesis can also be questioned on the basis of causality tests. Gudin *et al.* (1991) found that over the period January 1981–December 1986 there is mutual causality between the French and German day-to-day interest rates. However, Artus *et al.* (1991) found that over the 1983–8 period, the German rate seems to play a major role in the French reaction functions.

Were capital controls an essential prerequisite of the viability of the EMS or were they an obstacle to the gain in credibility of French policies? They were probably both, in turn, protecting France from speculative attacks until the mid-1980s until French monetary policy gained credibility and then further gains in credibility may have been dependent on the lifting of capital controls.

France in the new EMS (from 1987 onwards)

The new EMS and its positive role

The new EMS can be characterised by freedom of capital movements, new rules of functioning and exchange-rate fixity. It remains an asymmetric system centred on the D-Mark, but expectations of central rates realignments have almost disappeared. Capital controls started to be lifted in France in Spring 1986 when their main symbol, the security currency mechanism, was abolished. The abolition went on gradually with measures taken almost every year (usually before or during the summer) until the complete lifting of capital controls in advance of stage 1 of the Delors programme in December 1989.

This gradual lifting of capital controls has not generated capital flight in the medium run. The balance of portfolio investment has persistently been positive even in the second half of the 1980s. It is true however that 1986 saw a sharp fall in net inflows but this was made up subsequently. There has not been a persistent flight to tax havens in Switzerland or Luxembourg. Gross flows have indeed occurred but the increase in the purchase of foreign securities by French residents was matched by the growth in the purchase of French securities, and especially government bonds, by non-residents. For private (bank and non-bank) short-term capital movements, the lifting of foreign-exchange regulations had a positive impact on net inflows. Recent developments have seen in turn net outflows and net inflows, but no general pattern has emerged. Free capital movements do not appear to have been destabilising.

Besides the lifting of capital controls, the new ERM is characterised by new rules of functioning. Under the Basle–Nyborg agreement of 12 September, 1987, EMS members undertook 'to lay emphasis on the use of interest rate differentials to defend the stability of the EMS parity grid, to use the permitted fluctuation margins flexibly in order to deter speculation and to avoid prolonged bouts of intramarginal interventions' (communiqué quoted in Ungerer *et al.*, 1990). Indeed, in the case of the French franc, actual exchange-rate behaviour was significantly different after the Basle–Nyborg agreement, as can be seen by an inspection of the change in the distributions of monthly exchange-rate deviations from central parity represented in chart 5.2. It is apparent that over the period following the agreement exchange-rate observations occupied the band more fully than before September 1987. The shift from a bimodal distribution, with the modes near the margins, to a central unimodal distribution is very significant, because it suggests crises and speculative attacks have become less common.

Chart 5.2   *Distributions of D-Mark–franc deviations from central
rates before and after the Basle–Nyborg agreement (monthly data)*

(a) March 1979 – August 1987 (% deviations)

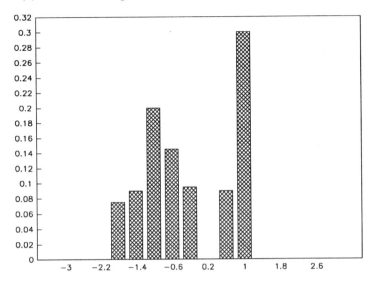

(b) September 1987 – July 1990 (% deviations)

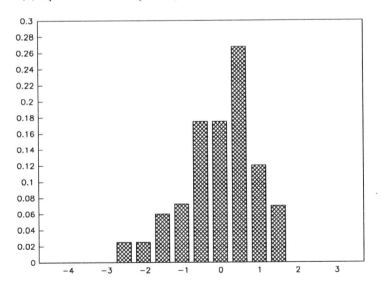

Source: Bank of France

The new EMS has indeed not been characterised by disruptions or by speculative crises. This can be explained by the fact that the gradual lifting of capital controls, helped initially by the reduction in the frequency of realignments, may have subsequently contributed to reduce the need for such realignments. The lifting of capital controls generated a greater fixity of exchange rates since, without the protection they represented for the reserves of central banks, the cost of realignments increased. Expectations were modified when markets realised this situation, and assigned a smaller probability to the occurrence of realignments. This has in turn reduced the frequency of devaluations.

The gain in credibility of the ERM in the French–German case can be documented by the same measure used above. The one-year expected exchange rate calculated using offshore interest rates to calculate uncovered interest parity, indicates that the one-year ahead expected franc–D-Mark rate has gradually tended to be confined to the ERM band over the September 1987–July 1990 period. The improvement in the credibility of the exchange-rate commitment has been gradual with several relapses but it seems that it is only since early 1990 that the target zone between the franc and the D-Mark has become fully credible.

Studying the credibility of the exchange-rate target by measuring the effect of parity announcements on exchange-rate expectations, Weber (1991a) finds that September, 1987, is the most likely time of policy switch in France, so that the latter may be partly attributed to the new control procedures in the ERM introduced by the Basle–Nyborg agreement. Such an early gain in credibility would mean that the weakening in confidence in the D-Mark linked to German reunification is not the main explanatory factor behind an increase in the 'apparent' credibility of the franc–D-Mark zone after early 1990.

A competitive disinflation policy
After the revaluation of the D-Mark in January 1987, the French authorities implemented a rigorous monetary policy in order to give a firm basis to the exchange-rate objective. This willingness was, for instance, manifest after the stock market crash of October 1987, when the Bank of France and the Bundesbank decided simultaneously to decrease German official rates and increase the French ones. At the end of 1987, the short-term interest differential thus reached 5 per cent. This competitive disinflation policy aimed at reinforcing the competitiveness of firms by means of a moderation of French price increases relative to those in Germany. This is a standard disinflation problem in an open economy with fixed exchange rates. A macroeconomic model with price inertia and inflationary expectations seems most appropriate to analyse the effects of such a policy (Bordes, Driscoll and Strauss-Kahn, 1989).[1] In this framework, the reduction of inflation and the restoration of competitiveness

are inevitably accompanied by a slowdown in economic activity and an increase in unemployment, since the threat of unemployment is a good means to discipline wage increases. The latter leads to a reduction in the rate of inflation or an increase in profit margins of firms and generally a combination of both. The improvement in profitability enables firms to invest and the moderation of their costs enables them to gain market share on export markets. Activity is then stimulated and in the long run the level of employment is improved. This strategy thus represents a virtuous substitute for a devaluation which would immediately generate the same effect but which sooner or later would see its effects on competitiveness countered by the rise of inflationary tensions.

Charts 5.3–5.6 plot the dynamic effects of a competitive disinflation policy for an economy where wages and prices are not perfectly flexible and where the initial situation corresponds to that of France in 1987.[2] The authorities determine monetary and fiscal policy so that they target the rate of increase of prices in the main trading partner. In the first stage, the unemployment rate increases because of the reduction in aggregate demand due to the decrease in real money balances and to the increase in the rate of interest. Then competitiveness improves and the unemployment rate diminishes. At some point the rate of price increase is below that abroad. The economy thus tends towards an equilibrium situation where competitiveness is restored. The return to equilibrium is faster when prices and wages adjust more rapidly.

The developments of the French economy since 1987 match this scheme well. First, competitiveness – as measured by the ratio of French to German prices – went on deteriorating until 1989 (chart 5.6b) before starting to improve in 1990. Second, the deviation between French and German nominal interest rates declined gradually. Between the beginning and the end of 1990, the short-term nominal interest rate differential was brought from 2.66 points to 1.2 points. A similar movement can be observed for long rates. After having declined until early 1990, the long-term interest rate differential reached a limit at around 1 per cent. All in all, the long-term differential went down from 1.86 per cent at the beginning of 1990 to 1.6 per cent at the end of this same year, and to 1.03 per cent in the middle of 1991. During the first semester of 1991, the short-term differential became on average smaller than 0.5 points. The reduction in the nominal interest-rate differential is well correlated with the reduction in the trend inflation differential. Third, the slowdown in inflation and the decrease in interest rates were accompanied by an increase in real money balances (chart 5.3b). Finally, the gap between effective and potential production decreased little by little (chart 5.4) and the level of unemployment improved gradually (chart 5.5).

The main problem faced by the competitive disinflation policy has to do with the slowness of adjustments. French price-competitiveness

Chart 5.3   *Path for real money supply*

   (a) Theoretical path

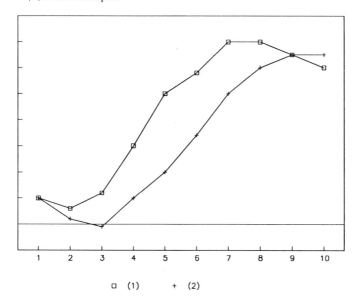

   □   (1)   +   (2)

   (b) French case

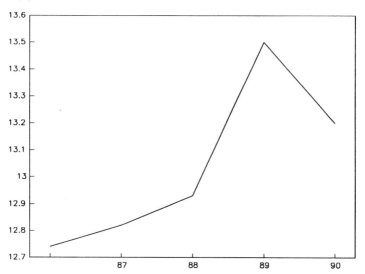

Notes: Real money supply = ratio of M1 to GDP deflator. In this and subsequent charts the following convention is adopted. (1) Quick adjustment of prices and wages to economic conditions. (2) Slow adjustment of prices and wages to economic conditions.

Chart 5.4 *Path for GNP gap*

(a) Theoretical path

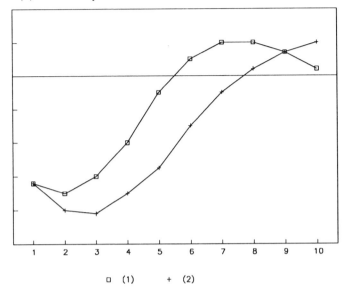

□ (1)   + (2)

(b) French case

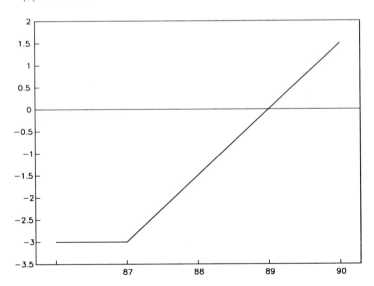

Note: $((Y-Y^*)/Y^*) \times 100$ where Y^* is potential GDP; for Y^* we have used estimates from the IMF, World Economic Outlook, May 1991, 44–45.

Chart 5.5   *Path for unemployment*

(a) *Theoretical path*

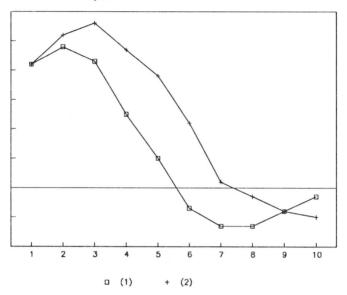

□   (1)   +   (2)

(b) *French*

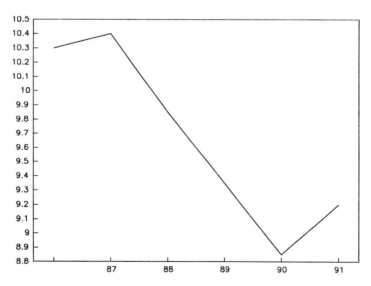

Source: OECD.

Note: French unemployment as % of labour force.

Chart 5.6   *Path for competitiveness*

(a) *Theoretical path*

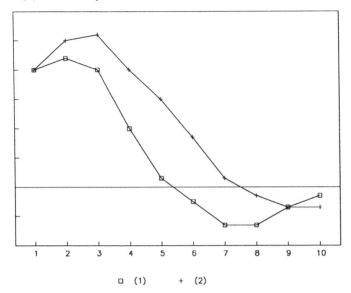

□   (1)   +   (2)

(b) *French case*

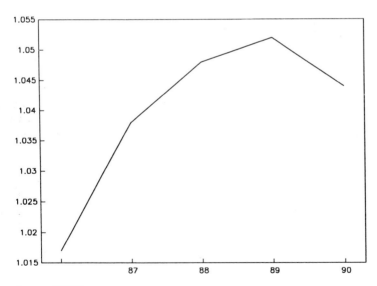

Source: OECD.

Note: Ratio of GDP deflator in France to GDP deflator in Germany,
1985 = 1.

remains worse than it was in 1987. It seems that the slope of the short-run Phillips curve did not change significantly. According to Atkinson *et al.* (1992): 'it does not seem that the moderating effect of unemployment on wage developments has been significantly different over the 1980s from what it was over the previous decade'. In such conditions, the gains of competitiveness are not as high as expected for firms. Indeed, firms have a tendency to favour the improvement in their margins over competitiveness on external markets. This choice in favour of profit increases does not seem to have generated an acceleration of investments which would have been favourable to future competitiveness. Capital expenditures of firms over the 1986–90 period remained similar to European averages. The competitive disinflation policy has been questioned partly because French growth has been below the European average and France has been losing export market share. Indeed, the competitive disinflation policy based on the stabilisation of the franc–D-Mark parity led to the appreciation of the franc *vis-à-vis* the currencies of the rest of the world in the context of an appreciation of the D-Mark *vis-à-vis* the dollar. This situation benefits both the United States, since it stimulates its exports, and Germany, which imports disinflation, but exerts a negative effect on French growth. In a recent study the forecasting division of the French Ministry of Finance estimated that the appreciation of the franc *vis-à-vis* the main non-EMS currencies (mainly the dollar and the yen) would have reduced growth by 0.5 points in 1990 and one point in 1991 (computations made on the basis of 5.5FF to a dollar).

All in all, if the competitive disinflation policy has indeed the expected beneficial effects, the latter take a substantially longer time to manifest themselves. Our appreciation is thus analogous to the one of Atkinson *et al.* (1992) whose 'evaluation of the competitive disinflation strategy is at most moderately optimistic. The reduction in unemployment to be expected from this strategy will be slow and ... if one had to rely only on that, the nineties would again be characterised by a high though decreasing unemployment rate'.

Alternative strategies
It is useful to explore the means available to improve French economic performance. One could imagine the abandonment of the present strategy because of the associated adjustment costs. A competitive devaluation strategy could be substituted for the competitive disinflation policy. Alternatively, in a less radical way, one could implement monetary or even fiscal policies accelerating the adjustment process of the economy inside the present strategy.

Competitive devaluation   Colbertist and interventionist views have developed a new popularity in France. Their advocates have not abandoned the idea of re-establishing the traditional instruments and orientations of French economic policy. According to them, for 'structural' reasons, economic growth in France requires some inflation. They suggest the implementation of an expansionary fiscal policy to sustain a high level of demand and the use of industrial policy and of competitive devaluations in order to improve the competitiveness of firms. Cotta (1991) is the main advocate of this type of view. He considers that only higher inflation could reduce real interest rates which are now 'killing' firms. 'To reinflate the economy is the first necessary condition for a resumption of growth and of full employment...Only the increase in inflation can regain calmly and painlessly the ground left to the 'rentiers' over the last ten years and thus give back to firms opportunities which now remain too limited'. The return of inflation would mean 'a recapture of autonomy of French economic policy' and that 'France sees its destiny differently from under the German wing'. Simultaneously, the State should 'reconstruct industrial policy with the aim of relocating, with specific industrial projects, our large groups in world oligopolies and for those which are already among them, to strengthen their position'. Since this strategy goes against the Rome Treaty, it would be necessary to modify it 'on crucial points such as the ability of the Commission to rule on the thickness of our European borders' (Cotta, 1991).

It is clear, however, that such a criticism does not hold up. The Bank of France has no power to control real interest rates in an environment of strong capital mobility. These are determined by overseas interest rates and inflation, in combination with exchange-rate expectations and the risk premium which has been reduced since the liberalisation of capital movements and financial deregulation. In case of an increase in prices aiming at reducing real interest rates, one could witness an increase in nominal interest rates under the pressure of capital movements. Nominal rates could even overshoot in reaction to the increase in inflation – as happened in the United Kingdom, where a rebound in inflationary tendencies translated itself into an increase in real interest rates. However, this type of criticism illustrates the dangers with which French authorities may be confronted. Faced with a deterioration of economic performance they may have difficulty in maintaining the objectives which they set themselves. In this context, it is important to find other means to give French policy the room for manoeuvre which it lacks at present.

Relaxation of demand-side policies   The willingness of France to affirm its monetary autonomy was publicised for the first time on 31 October 1990: the Bank of France reduced its intervention rate by 0.25 per cent (the tender rate was put down to 9.25 per cent) while the next day the Bundesbank raised its Lombard rate to 10 per cent and central banks of neighbouring countries (Belgium and the Netherlands) followed suit.

Until the end of 1990, any further reduction in leading French rates became impossible, but the differential between money market rates has kept on going down. The Bank of France declared anew its desire for autonomy in Spring, 1991, by reducing the tender rate from 9.25 to 9 per cent on 18 March, after the Bundesbank had raised its Lombard rate from 8.5 to 9 per cent on 31 January. The authorities did the same in autumn of the same year when they brought down the tender rate to 8.75 per cent. But very soon it was manifest that it was impossible to disconnect the French monetary stance further from the German. In spite of the French authorities' desire for autonomy, it is clear that the ERM remains an asymmetric system centred on the D-Mark. The only difference with the preceding period is that the expectations of realignments have, as we saw, almost disappeared. The movements of short-term French rates still mainly depend on the outlook for German monetary policy.

The recent experience is yet another illustration. After having announced on 17 October 1991, a quarter point reduction in its leading rates, the Bank of France had to raise them by 0.5 per cent for tenders as early as 18 November in order to support the franc, showing that its room for manoeuvre for reductions in rates has been used up and that contrary to the wishes of the French authorities, French monetary policy could not disconnect itself from German monetary policy. Today, the weakly based hope of some disconnection of French rates from German ones has vanished.

The relaxation of French monetary policy can only be considered in the framework of a strategy aiming at putting pressure on Germany. This can first be conceived of as a coordinated action by France, Italy, Spain and the United Kingdom which could form a common front against Germany by deciding simultaneously to implement a more accommodating monetary policy. It is mainly in the framework of the future European central bank that France will be able to weigh more efficiently on German monetary policy.

The French fiscal stance is often criticised as being overly restrictive. Over recent years, it only accompanied movements in economic activity. Moreover, the budget for 1992 also seems quite restrictive: according to OFCE (1991), the movement in taxes should weigh at the margin on economic growth (–0.05 points) and the macroeconomic impact of the reduction in expenditure – such as the fall in military expenditure in real terms – should exert a slight recessionary effect. In fact fiscal policy let automatic stabilisers play partly to support economic activity while using temporary measures to limit the budget deficit – such as taxes on the Caisse des Dépots et Consignations – which will not have negative macroeconomic effects. It is generally accepted that in the present context, expansionary measures going further than the free play of automatic stabilisers would face an external constraint.

In brief, it is in the framework of monetary union that French economic policy seems to be able to find, in both the monetary and fiscal fields, the room for manoeuvre which it now lacks.

France and European monetary union

In the negotiations for the building of European Monetary Union, the French authorities have always been in favour of the adoption of strict disciplinary rules in fiscal matters and have manifested some reservations, de facto if not openly, *vis-à-vis* a total independence of the Bank of France and of the future European Central Bank. This attitude can be easily explained by the consciousness on the part of the authorities, already mentioned, that they do not enjoy any room for manoeuvre in the fiscal field since any attempt aiming at adopting a more expansionary fiscal stance would be likely to face tensions on the foreign exchange markets. It is however possible to question this attitude as well as its foundations and to ask, in the perspective of EMU, whether it would not be more suitable to accept the principle of total independence of the central bank and to advocate the principle of some autonomy for fiscal policy.

Independence of the central bank

In terms of independence of the central bank, three criteria play a decisive role: the operational independence which consists in the freedom it enjoys to elaborate and implement monetary and exchange-rate policy; the independence of its board which depends on the say which governments have in its nomination; and financial independence which can be measured by the opportunity that the State has for a direct or indirect monetary financing of its expenditures by the central bank. For the time being the Bank of France does not enjoy operational independence, since internal as well as external monetary policy and credit policy are legally under the responsibility of the government of which the Bank of France is the executive arm, directly or indirectly through the 'Conseil National du Crédit'. Neither does it enjoy an independence of its managing board, since the Governor can at any time be dismissed, nor financial independence, since while there exists a ceiling for direct financing of the State, the indirect financing is left legally to the judgement of the Bank of France; de facto it is a government decision.

The existence of a negative correlation between central bank independence and inflation is usually accepted. But, in this field, it is necessary to be more specific. Bade and Parkin (1987) found that the statute of the central bank influences inflation only when the central bank enjoys complete independence – that is, operational as well as financial independence and independence of its managing board – analogous to the one enjoyed by the Bundesbank or the Swiss National Bank, and that partial independence has no significant effect on inflation. This result implies that the independence of the central bank is a factor of price stability if and only if this independence is complete.

The French government is still not enthusiastic about the idea of a completely independent central bank, for the Bank of France as well as for the future European central bank. It is not in favour of the operational independence of the bank, that is the freedom it would have to define and implement the directions of monetary policy. To substantiate this assertion, here are the terms used by the Minister for Economics and Finance on this matter: 'In a lawful society, power is based on universal ballot. The central bank must not be subject to the hazards of political life and this is why the principle of its independence is given. *But monetary independence does not mean ignorance of political necessities.* The central bank will have to manage in an independent way the Community's domestic policy, money creation and interest rates *inside economic directions which are the responsibility of a political authority emanating from the European Council. The community's external monetary policy – parities, exchange rates – will also be defined by public authorities'* (Beregovoy, 1990, our emphasis). And to the question whether he would be ready to have a completely independent Bank of France and to let some margin of initiative to the European System of Central Banks, he answers that: 'the Bank of France enjoys an acknowledged autonomy(!). We can very well participate in the European System of Central Banks without modifying the statute of the Bank of France. When we will reach the end of the second stage and the beginning of the third, at a time when the process will be irreversible, the problem of the statute of the Bank of France will become a matter of discussion' (Beregovoy, 1990).

However, there are some good reasons to think that the operational dependence of the Bank of France and the lack of independence of its managers contribute to the existence of a risk premium and to high real interest rates. In such conditions, to grant total independence to the Bank of France would only be beneficial: by reducing the risk premium, it would give French authorities the room for manoeuvre which they now lack and which could be used to accelerate the adjustment process of the competitive disinflation policy, the slowness of which we emphasised earlier.

Autonomy of fiscal policy
The present developments show that we are now heading towards a situation where EMU member countries will face strict rules limiting their fiscal independence. The Delors Report called for the setting up of 'a new process of coordination of fiscal policies including specific fiscal directives and medium-term orientations and opening the way to concerted fiscal actions by member countries. The Treaty signed

at Maastricht in December 1991 requires that the budget deficit of a country wanting to participate in EMU should not be greater than 3 per cent of GDP and that its public debt should be smaller than 60 per cent of GDP. The arguments supporting such disciplinary rules are well known: in fiscal matters, it will not be possible to rely on the disciplines stemming from the functioning of financial markets inasmuch as the credibility of rules of non-mutual assistance between member states cannot be ensured. French authorities are very much in favour of such rules (see appendix at the end of this chapter), probably because they think that for the time being they do not enjoy any autonomy in this matter.

However, one may examine the justifications for the preservation of the autonomy of national fiscal policies in the framework of the future European monetary union.

A first justification of fiscal policy autonomy is the existence of asymmetries in the effects of fiscal policy. The analysis of the effects of fiscal policy in a French multi-country macroeconometric model (MIMOSA) implemented by Aglietta and Coudert (1990) implies that these effects differ considerably between countries. In Germany or Italy, a fiscal expansion with fixed exchange rates generates an appreciation of the real exchange rate and a sharp deterioration of the current account but has a strong positive impact on growth. In France the same policy generates a slight improvement in competitiveness in the short run and a slight appreciation in the medium run with a more limited deterioration of the current account so that the effects of such a policy are quite favourable. This can be explained by the result that in this model at least an expansion in activity generates productivity gains which, as we saw earlier, do not translate into wage increases in France. In the United Kingdom, a similar fiscal policy generates a sharp deterioration of competitiveness and has only limited effects on growth. Thus, the effects of fiscal policies being potentially so different, it would be erroneous to submit these countries to identical EC rules and to a uniform management of their budget.

A second justification of the autonomy of fiscal policies concerns the existing asymmetries between national preferences and the differences in initial situations of member countries at the time of their entry into EMU. This thesis is put forward by Masson and Melitz (1990) on the basis of simulations with MULTIMOD. They consider the case where France would witness a deficit on current account due not to structural differences in productivity, the rate of time preference or demographic conditions, but to a smaller capital intensity and to a higher value of the marginal productivity of investment than the German ones. They reach the conclusion that inside EMU, France will have to worry less about its current account deficit since even with fixed exchange rates two adjustment mechanisms will naturally tend to bring the current account back to balance: first, there will be wealth transfers from France to Germany which will induce a fall in absorption in France and an increase in absorption in Germany; second, such a deficit will enable France to finance capital accumulation at home, and thus to improve its marginal productivity of labour and its competitiveness. However, these adjustment mechanisms may require a long time to work themselves out so that France may benefit, in the case in point, from accelerating them by restricting its fiscal stance.

A third justification lies in the transformation of economic structures generated by the implementation of monetary union. First, national government deficits will influence interest rates much less than in a non-integrated space. An expansionary fiscal policy in France would only generate a marginal increase in the Community's interest rate. Moreover, in an integrated space, the different countries should become more specialised. This may imply that shocks become more important. For instance, if an economy is strongly dependent on a specific industry, it can register specific shocks linked to the developments in this industry. An increase in the budget deficit can thus be justified, for instance during a period of restructuring (see Atkinson *et al.*, 1992). The removal of the external constraint inside the Union does not imply that the different countries should disregard their competitiveness. An excessive expansionary policy would result in a sharp increase in domestic prices and to a collapse of external demand from other members of the union, with some risk of relocation of firms. A competitiveness constraint would thus substitute for the present external constraint to limit the temptations for lax fiscal policies.

These justifications for some autonomy of fiscal policy in EMU seem quite robust. One may then wonder whether, by advocating the opposite view, French authorities do not make a mistake due to an error about the real reason why they are today unable to use this instrument because of worries of a speculative attack on the franc. This reason may be linked to the insufficient independence of the Bank of France which implies that there is always the risk of a monetary financing of the deficit. To get rid of this mortgage by modifying the statute of the central bank in the direction of total independence could give back some room for manoeuvre to fiscal policy (especially if this first measure is accompanied by fixing the franc–D-Mark parity immediately).

Conclusion

The old EMS has undoubtedly contributed to the good performance of the French economy in terms of disinflation. The gains France gathered from participating in the new EMS are much smaller. The effects of the competitive disinflation policy indeed matched expectations but they took a very long time to materialise because of the slowness of the dynamic adjustment of nominal variables to movements in economic activity and unemployment. The natural process of adjustment of the economy appears to be so long that we should expect, *ceteris paribus*, the persistence of a high unemployment rate in France.

In the present context, the French authorities do not have a margin for manoeuvre enabling them to accelerate this process. First, a devaluation of the franc could indeed have a favourable effect on competitiveness but this would not be long-lasting and the credibility accumulated at so high a cost over recent years would be jeopardised. Besides, there is a great risk that previous gains could also be jeopardised under the pressure of those who favour the return to the old Colbertist and interventionist French tradition and the adoption of an inflationary policy. Second, recent experience has confirmed that French monetary authorities do not enjoy any autonomy with respect to Germany on the level of interest rates. Moreover, fiscal policy, by letting automatic stabilisers play freely, uses the whole of the room for manoeuvre that is available without facing an external constraint.

The negative effects of the competitive disinflation policy can only be reduced as part of a transition to European Monetary Union. France has nothing to lose in the monetary field and there may be something to be gained from the formation of such a union. The functioning of the European Central Bank could enable France to weigh on German monetary policy while it does not have such an opportunity at present. Moreover, by granting the Bank of France total autonomy immediately, the authorities would lift all remaining worries concerning their willingness not to finance a budget deficit by money creation, which would give them some more room for manoeuvre. This margin for manoeuvre could be reinforced in the fiscal field by the softening of the external constraint, inasmuch as the numerous arguments in favour of fiscal autonomy in a monetary union are accepted.

Appendix

French proposal for EMU (28 January 1991) (From Notes bleues, Ministry of Finance, 1991)
The French proposal specifies the means at the disposal of ECOFIN to ensure convergence of economic policies of member states, including some disciplinary powers, notably in case of excessive budget deficits. It gives to the European System of Central Banks (ESCB) price stability as its foremost objective. Moreover, the ESCB must be independent, EMU must have an active exchange-rate policy *vis-à-vis* the outside world, which ECOFIN would direct after consulting the central bank, which

implements interventions on the foreign-exchange markets.

The Union should have an 'economic government'. In the French proposal, the European Council is in charge of the definition of broad orientations for EMU. The council ECOFIN is the centre of economic government; the EC Commission has the power of proposal and of advice; the Parliament and the Congress are in charge of the parliamentary control of the council and of the ESCB.

No country should be able to obstruct the passage to single currency, but no country should be *a priori* excluded. The French proposal suggests that the Treaty should include the exchange-rate agreement which links member countries in the EMS so that the opportunity of opting out would no longer exist. The ESCB, set up at the beginning of stage 2, will play a central role in coordinating national monetary policies and of the instruments of stage 3. Finally, the French proposal lays the principle according to which the Ecu should become, as soon as possible, a strong and stable currency. When the time comes, the council will be able to decide on passing to stage 3, with transitory arrangements for some countries. It is desirable that this time should come as soon as possible.

Notes

1   In this chapter, new evidence on price level inertia in France is reported. The results obtained confirm the findings of related studies, especially those of Demery (1984) on the United Kingdom; price level inertia seems to be present to a significant degree in France.

2   The simulations of the effects of a competitive disinflation policy represented in charts 5.3–5.6 were implemented with Macro-Solve (Hall and Taylor, 1991) by taking parameter values traditionally used in the French case: that is, a low sensitivity of investment to the rate of interest and a high propensity to import (see for instance Artus and Bismut, 1986). This leads to the following four equation model:

(1) $Y = 2.54(M/P) + 1.27G - 1.27(EP/P^*)$
(2) $\pi = \pi^e + 0.8$ GDP gap
(3) $u = u^* - 0.33$ GDP gap
(4) $\pi^e = 0.4\pi_{-1} + 0.2\pi_{-2}$

Equation (1) is a reduced form of a standard open-economy IS–LM model. It explains real income, Y, by government expenditures G, real money balances M/P, and competitiveness measured by the real exchange rate (where P and P^* are the domestic and the foreign price level and E is the foreign price of domestic currency); equation (2) describes price adjustment. The rate of inflation thus depends on inflationary expectations π^e and on capacity utilisation (GDP gap); equation (3) is Okun's relation, where u^* is the NAIRU; equation (4) explains inflationary expectations by past inflation.

6

Irish Experience of Monetary Linkages with the United Kingdom and Developments since joining the EMS

John Bradley and Karl Whelan

Introduction

In an essay on policymaking in the small open economy, McCormack (1979) identified two strategic choices made by Irish policymakers in the postwar period: the move from protection to free trade and EC membership, initiated in the 1950s; and the positive decision on EMS membership in 1979. To this list might be added two previous choices: the first none the less important for being essentially passive, of maintaining the link with sterling after independence in 1922; the second of erecting protective tariff barriers in the early 1930s. All these choices represented a redefinition of the nature of Ireland's participation in the world economy.

The decision by the Irish government to join the EMS from its inception in March 1979 made inevitable the termination of a monetary union with the United Kingdom which dated back as far as the beginning of the nineteenth century. Historians and economists have long debated whether this monetary union served the Irish regional economy well during the period of inclusion fully within the United Kingdom and during the following 56 years of 'voluntary' monetary linkage. Whether or not it did, the newly emerged Irish Free State felt that there were overwhelming reasons for maintaining the monetary status quo and decided to keep the fixed link with sterling after independence was achieved in 1922. The sterling link was not finally broken until 30 March 1979, when, with Ireland having committed itself to the EMS, the strength of sterling pushed it beyond the reach of the Irish pound, constrained as the latter now was within the narrow band of the ERM.

In the second section of this chapter, we consider the period of the fixed link between the Irish pound and sterling, which lasted from 1826 to 1979. The problems that arose and the debates that took place within the Irish Department of Finance during the period of voluntary linkage with sterling from 1922 to 1979 are interesting in the light of moves towards EMU. However, only towards the end of the period was the sterling link seriously called into question. In the third section we deal with the events leading up to the decision to break the sterling link, while in the fourth we discuss the period from 1979 to the present, during which Ireland participated fully within the narrow band of the EMS. The cutting of the umbilical cord with sterling was followed by a most dramatic period for Irish fiscal policy as the disequilibrating consequences of public spending and tax cutting initiatives of the post OPEC-I period came home to roost. We examine the official attitudes brought to bear on the question of whether or not to join the EMS, the *ex ante* expectations of the likely benefits of EMS membership, and the *ex post* reality. The fact that the first decade of EMS membership coincided with a time of forced fiscal adjustment and disinflation has complicated the task of evaluating the benefits of the new exchange rate regime. This is particularly seen in international research such as Dornbusch (1989) and Giavazzi and Pagano (1990).

Ireland's EMS experience may have a wider relevance for the other small peripheral EC member states and the newly liberalised Eastern European states. A better understanding of the extent of this relevance is facilitated by a structural framework of analysis. In the fifth section we use the familiar Scandinavian model framework to organise the empirical research that bears on Ireland's pre and post-EMS experience. Central elements include price determination in the exposed or tradeable sector, wage determination in the leading tradeable sector, links between tradeable and non-tradeable labour markets, and price determination in the non-tradeable sector. In our concluding section we draw on this framework to evaluate Ireland's EMS experience, interpreted in a fairly broad sense.

The sterling link: Ireland and the United Kingdom 1800–1979

The Act of Union in 1800 between Ireland and Great Britain established Ireland as a region within the United Kingdom, on much the same basis as Wales and Scotland, which had been incorporated in previous centuries. The financial provisions of the Act abolished all tariffs between the two regions and provided for the eventual abolition of the Irish currency. For most of the period to 1826 the Irish pound was at a discount with sterling, but thereafter was completely assimilated.

It has been claimed that this Union was the political context for the subsequent long-term economic decline of industry in most of Ireland and the diverging industrialisation of the northern region (O'Malley, 1989). In its basic form, the argument is the familiar Myrdal–Kaldor analysis of cumulative causation and underdevelopment. Although Irish industrialisation had made considerable progress by the end of the eighteenth century and local economic and social conditions were by no means inimical to growth, Ireland was still a relative latecomer and, from the start of the nineteenth century, found itself in a relationship of free trade with Great Britain, the pioneer of the industrial revolution. Much of the subsequent Irish industrial decline can be interpreted in terms of mainland British cumulative competitive advantage, where the weaker Irish competitors were eliminated and barriers to entry became very high.[1] Not surprisingly, the pre-independence rhetoric of Irish nationalists blamed the economic and monetary union with Britain for most of Ireland's woes and emphasised the protection of infant industries to promote industrial development.

At independence in 1922 the industrial sector of the Irish Free State had, relative to the rest of Britain, been reduced to very small dimensions and per capita income levels lagged substantially behind.[2] However, Britain was the most advanced economy in Europe at this point and any discussion of Irish failures must be tempered by the observation that being a backward region of the United Kingdom still meant Irish income levels were quite high by European standards: on gaining independence Ireland had higher living standards than such presently wealthier countries as Norway, Finland and Italy. Ireland's access to the prosperous British market was clearly the reason for this comparatively successful economic performance and the maintenance of the sterling link was seen as a vital element in retaining British demand for Irish agricultural exports.

Not surprisingly then, once the government of the new Irish Free State was established, it was in no hurry to alter the existing currency arrangements. In fact, it was not until three years later, in April 1925, that the Minister for Finance 'drew attention to the fact that, owing to the setting up of the Irish Free State and the passing of consequent legislation, apart from gold there is no legal tender in the Free State' (Fanning, 1978, p. 176). In 1926 Irish token coins were issued, and subsequently in 1927 there was an Irish note issue, backed one-to-one by gold and sterling assets, which circulated in Ireland alongside sterling, both being treated as perfect substitutes. Free trade was also maintained, despite the pre-independence nationalist stance. The attitude of the secretary of the Department of Finance was quite categorical: 'to revert to free trade from a protectionist regime is almost an economic impossibility; the reason being that protection tends to force trade and commerce into unnatural and uneconomic channels and the industry thereby created requires artificial conditions in which to prosper' (Fanning, p. 203).

The maintenance of free trade orthodoxy lasted until the early 1930s, when a change of government and a very different international climate ushered in a period of protection. Speaking in Dublin in April 1933, Keynes supported the move to protection and praised an Ireland 'which has lifted a lively foot out of its bogs to become a centre of economic experiment and stands almost as remote from English nineteenth century Liberalism as Communist Russia or Fascist Italy or the blond beasts in Germany .... I sympathise, therefore, with those who would minimise, rather than with those who would maximise, economic entanglement between nations' (Keynes, 1933). But this espousal of self-sufficiency was heavily qualified by Keynes, who questioned whether Ireland was a large enough geographical unit 'for more than a very modest measure of national self-sufficiency to be feasible without a disastrous reduction in a standard of life which is already none too high'. Indeed, he advocated that Ireland should 'enter into an economic arrangement with England which would, within appropriate limits, retain for Ireland her traditional British markets against mutual advantages for British producers'. However, it was not until much later that such an arrangement was eventually brought about (the Anglo-Irish Free Trade Agreement of 1965) and analysis has shown just how high a cost protective measures imposed (McAleese, 1971).

When, on 21 September 1931, the British government announced the departure of sterling from the gold standard, the Irish response was discussed within the Currency Commission (the precursor of an Irish Central Bank). The Chairman likened sterling to 'a raft, and the Irish pound as a swimmer who clings to it'. Indeed, the maintenance of the sterling link is hardly surprising given that, despite protectionism and the rhetoric of 'self-sufficiency' which permeated the depression and war years, the overall extent of Ireland's trade dependence on the United Kingdom was not reduced to any extent and furthermore, since the bulk of imports were used as inputs to production processes, dependence rather than self-sufficiency increased.

Official thinking on maintaining the sterling link was reflected in the 1938 report of the Banking Commission, which recommended a continuation of past currency arrangements on the grounds that, first, the maintenance of this link ensured to the Free State the advantage of exchange stability with the British market, which was of the greatest importance for its foreign trade and in which the bulk of its foreign investment was held. Second, the link with sterling enabled the Free State to participate in a monetary and credit policy which was in general conformity with Irish interests. Third, the link had the advantage of possessing the confidence of the Free State public and, conversely, any suggestion for relaxation of it would meet with distrust. Finally, any attempt to depreciate the Irish currency would lead to evils which 'no euphemisms could long disguise, and no exchange control could appreciably mitigate'! (Fanning, p. 376).

The tone of the Banking Commission Report implied that the sterling link was not only necessary on grounds of economic efficiency, but also for the very survival of the economy. In the later postwar years, the link came to be justified on the basis of more sophisticated economic analysis. For example, the aspects emphasised in 1973 by the Governor of the Central Bank of Ireland were, first, an open economy with trade dependence on the United Kingdom market; second, an open Irish–UK labour market, with free and easy migration; third, integration of financial and other economic institutions; and fourth, the continued ability of the Irish to use high tariff barriers, export subsidies, and investment grants (the latter two in the post-1958 period) in lieu of exchange rate variations (Whitaker, 1973).

Thus, the openness of the economy favoured the principle of a pegged exchange rate with the currency of a larger area, while economic dependence dictated that this would be the sterling area. Whitaker's defence of the sterling link policy explicitly invoked elements of the theory of 'optimum currency areas' which suggested that if a region's product, factor and other markets were sufficiently integrated with other regions, then the exchange rate would not be an efficient tool of adjustment and the optimum choice would be a shared currency. This remained the official position on the sterling link prior to the break in 1979. Even during the Second World War and the large devaluation of sterling in 1949, the policy went largely unchallenged. In June 1949, the Department of Finance, discussing the likely effects of devaluation on foreign trade, concluded that: 'In view of the closeness of our economic relations with Britain and the settled tendency towards a parallel structure of wages and prices, any exchange value between the Irish pound and sterling other than parity would be unreal'.

The maintenance of parity with sterling was not without cost. The state of the balance of payments was a constant policy preoccupation and the operation of the Irish monetary system was held to require large external reserves of sterling. In particular, a succession of balance-of-payments crises in the 1950s, both in Ireland and in the rest of the sterling area, resulted in severely deflationary Irish budgets which made an already bad economic performance worse. In addition, the high level of tariffs which was maintained up to the 1960s can be interpreted as an attempt to control Ireland's balance-of-payments problems in the absence of a variable exchange rate. McAleese (1971) has shown that by 1966 tariff and export incentives were jointly equivalent to a devaluation of 19 per cent and that their removal on a unilateral basis, without reciprocal concession from trading partners, would have required a devaluation of this magnitude to restore equilibrium in the balance of payments.

Moves towards breaking the sterling link

Although the actual break in the link with sterling did not come until 1979, there had previously been fundamental changes in the economy likely to force a re-evaluation of the balance of real and monetary advantages. The prolonged Irish experiment with protectionism had failed to create large, self-sustaining, domestic industries with diversified markets. The 1950s had been a decade of failure, with poor employment growth and large-scale emigration, an outturn that was all the more galling in the light of vigorous European reconstruction and growth. The Irish economy continued to be highly dependent on a poorly performing British market, implying that while Ireland was maintaining its position relative to its dominant trading partner, it was falling further behind the faster growing European economies.

This naturally led to reassessment of whether the degree of integration with Britain was harming Irish prospects and potential. In 1952 an interdepartmental committee examined the respects in which British policy had been detrimental to Irish economic interests and concluded that 'a corollary of the close trading and economic relations between Ireland and Britain was that practically every aspect of British economic and monetary policy impinged in some way or another on us'. While it concluded that some aspects had been advantageous, such as low interest rates and free access to the Sterling Area Pool for foreign exchange requirements, British policy in regard to social welfare, full employment and wages had set headlines which stimulated similar (presumably inappropriate) standards in Ireland and thus imposed serious strains on the economy.

The dismal experience of the 1950s led to a general loss of faith in protectionist policies and this was formally accepted by government with the publication of a seminal Department of Finance study entitled Economic Development (Stationery Office, 1958). The whole nature of Irish economic policy was gradually transformed after 1958, the main new features being a series of national plans and trade agreements which guided the Irish economy from protectionism towards free trade, culminating finally in membership of the EC in 1973, together with Denmark and the United Kingdom; and a new industrial policy which aimed at attracting direct foreign investment (DFI) from multinational companies. This policy explicitly marketed Ireland as an attractive industrial location, and incorporated incentives such as investment grants and low corporate taxation.

These developments had a profound strategic impact. The new industrial policy coincided with a worldwide expansion in direct foreign investment and many multinational companies located production subsidiaries in Ireland, with large-scale capital inflows significantly easing

Chart 6.1 *Exports by geographical destination (% of total)*

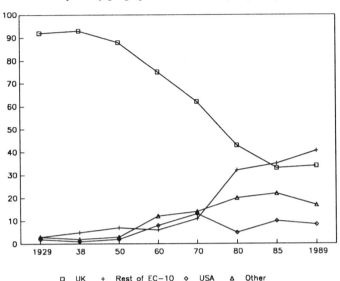

□ UK   + Rest of EC–10   ◇ USA   ▵ Other

the problem of financing growth out of domestic savings. Furthermore, these new foreign industries were primarily export-oriented and permitted a significant trade diversification which allowed Ireland to benefit from the unprecedented rates of economic growth which prevailed in the world economy during the 1960–73 period. Membership of the EC was seen as further facilitating the move towards trade diversification and the CAP had a major beneficial effect on Ireland's large agricultural sector, which had suffered in the past from low prices in the United Kingdom market.

Throughout all this innovative period, the sterling link was maintained. By the 1970s, however, the level of market integration between Ireland and the United Kingdom was declining, thus weakening the optimum currency area argument for the sterling link (chart 6.1). There was also acceptance by all analysts that the sterling link implied that United Kingdom inflationary trends were transmitted to Ireland rapidly and completely.[3] These inflationary trends in turn influenced wage bargaining, so *ceteris paribus* Irish price and wage inflation mirrored their United Kingdom counterparts. The high inflation performance of the United Kingdom economy during the 1970s thus left many in Ireland unhappy with the levels of imported inflation which the sterling link was forcing upon Ireland.

There was a general realisation that if the Irish pound was floated, a devaluation was unlikely to bring any lasting benefits, but could very likely introduce great uncertainty in the domestic economy. However, the converse was not accepted; to the extent that the economy was very open, a revaluation was held to be a powerful anti-inflationary weapon (Whitaker, 1973). There was an expectation that a permanent shift from a soft currency regime (sterling) to a hard currency one (the D-Mark dominated EMS) would bring these disinflationary benefits at limited real cost, provided sensible domestic fiscal and wage policies were adopted.

Active discussion of the appropriate currency link for Ireland took place from the mid-1970s in the context of the Snake and the EMS proposals. If the United Kingdom were to join the EMS, then the issue was effectively decided for Ireland. However, what if the United Kingdom stayed out? The governor of the central bank listed the following factors which were taken into account when the decision was taken to join the EMS in the absence of the United Kingdom (Murray, 1979): the limited alternatives to the sterling link open to us, effectively a floating pound or a trade-weighted exchange-rate objective; the benefits in terms of a reduction in inflation to be obtained from adherence to a hard currency regime; the *communautaire* enthusiasm arising from commitment to a major EC initiative, and the negative alternative if we opted out; and EC support in the form of resource transfers.

However, it was realised that there were going to be costs associated with foregoing absolute stability with the currency of the dominant trading partner and the need to impose exchange controls and incur other banking costs. While the governor's analysis of the issues was comprehensive, his predictions were naturally more circumspect. In effect he did anticipate that the EMS regime would be stronger than the previous sterling link and, with the active support of appropriate domestic fiscal and incomes policies, would bring down the rate of price inflation significantly. Other analysts were more dogmatic and assertive, and confidently predicted that after a decade of high inflation, 'we could now contemplate the prospect of an early and sustained return to inflation rates comfortably back in single figures' (McCarthy, 1979).

Ireland within the EMS: 1979–91

In the event, for Ireland the EMS regime proved very different from expected. Sterling initially appreciated dramatically with respect to the other EMS currencies under the influence of the oil price shocks of 1979 and the strict monetarist policies pursued by the new Conservative administration. Subsequently, the Irish pound–sterling rate had a much bumpier ride than the Irish pound–D-Mark rate (chart 6.2). In most of the EMS realignments the Irish pound central rate was unchanged as the D-Mark was revalued and the Franc devalued. In March 1983 and August 1986 the Irish pound was devalued, by 3.5 per cent and 8 per cent respectively.

Chart 6.2 *Exchange rates in Dublin market*

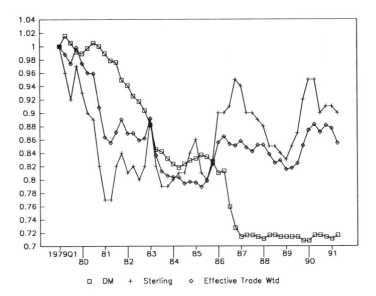

Chart 6.3 *Irish–German interest differential (% per annum)*

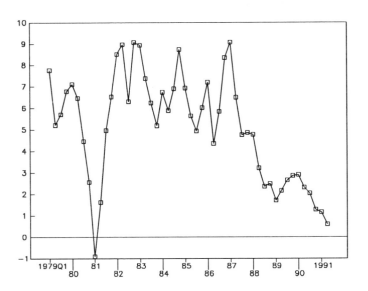

Chart 6.4　*Irish–UK interest differential (% per annum)*

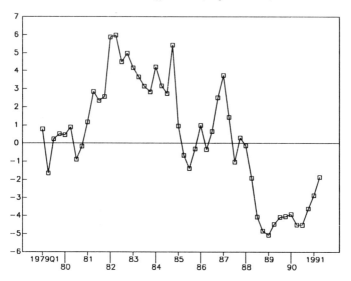

With the minor exception of the period at the end of 1981 and the start of 1982, Irish interest rates failed to converge to D-Mark rates until after 1987 (chart 6.3). From 1981–5, and again briefly in 1987–8, Irish rates moved above United Kingdom rates, and only fell below them after 1988 (chart 6.4). Far from immediately falling to German inflation rates, Irish inflation took until 1985 to converge to EMS average rates, and only moved below the United Kingdom after 1986 (chart 6.5). As a result, on the basis of relative hourly earnings in a common currency there was a systematic trade-weighted loss of competitiveness, the gain against the United Kingdom being outweighed by the loss against the EMS countries (chart 6.6, where a rise in the variables graphed indicates a loss in competitiveness). However, the same graph shows that on the basis of relative unit labour costs, Ireland gained competitiveness. This, however, was more the result of the gradual replacement of labour intensive traditional manufacturing firms by high technology modern ones and is somewhat misleading as an indicator. The truth probably lies somewhere between the two measures.

A comprehensive form of Murphy's law operated against Ireland: everything that could go wrong, did go wrong: political instability at a bad time (1980–2), followed by a somewhat fractious centre-left coalition from 1982–7 that was unable to agree on major cuts in expenditure; a period of low growth (chart 6.7); a level of inherited state expenditure that had ratcheted upwards sharply during the inflationary 1970s (chart 6.8) and was not reduced until after 1987; a sharply rising debt–GNP

Chart 6.5   *Inflation rates (annual percentage change)*

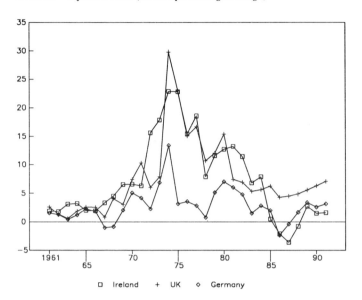

Chart 6.6   *Irish international competitiveness (Index 1980 = 100)*

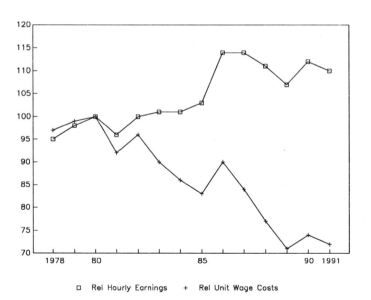

Chart 6.7   *GNP growth rates: 5-year averages (average annual growth)*

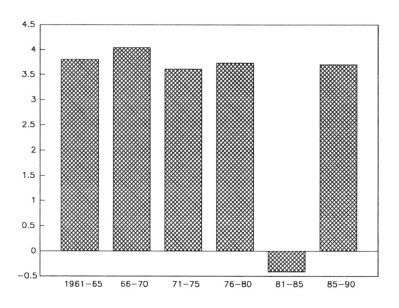

Chart 6.8   *Public expenditure/GNP ratios (% of GNP)*

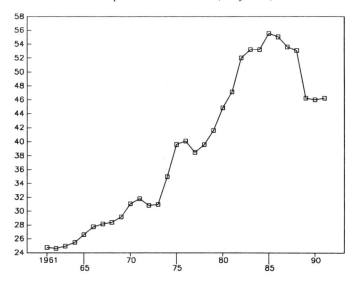

Chart 6.9 *Debt/GNP ratio (% of GNP)*

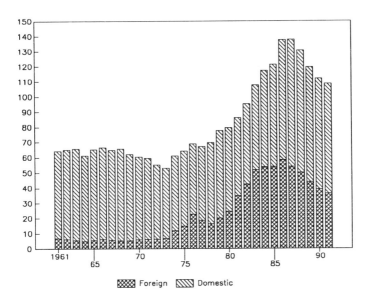

Chart 6.10 *Unemployment rate (% of labour force)*

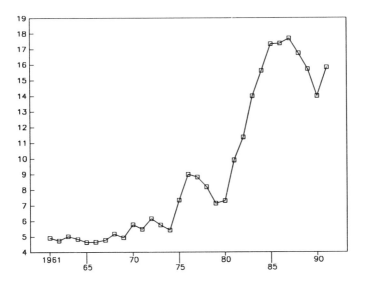

ratio (chart 6.9) and a massive rise in the rate of unemployment (chart 6.10), even at a time of high outmigration.

It was against this turbulent background that we must attempt to evaluate Ireland's experience within the EMS. Here, we have simply stated some of the stylised facts. We now outline our interpretative framework, and we attempt this evaluation in the last section.

The small open economy: an interpretative framework

In the previous sections we have outlined the historical context within which policy analysis of the Irish economy can be set. In order to examine the nature of the choices available to Irish policymakers and to marshal and evaluate empirical research findings on the Irish economy, it is also useful to have a suitable analytical framework which is rich enough to encompass a variety of features and not so narrow as to become bogged down in excessive country specific detail. The Scandinavian model has commanded much attention both in Ireland and elsewhere and serves as a useful organisational and expositional device (Lindbeck, 1979). Most of the relevant Irish theoretical and empirical work can be classified and evaluated within this framework, in terms of a two-sector model with tradeable and non-tradeable goods. The essential elements include price determination in both traded and non-traded sectors, wage determination, and the nature of the national labour market.

Output determination
The Scandinavian model considers a stylised economy consisting of two sectors: tradeable and non-tradeable. For the Irish case, production activity in the tradeable sector is driven by exogenous 'world' demand and cost competitiveness, which is affected by factors such as relative wage costs and corporate taxes (Bradley and Fitz Gerald, 1988). Activity in the non-tradeable sheltered sector is driven in Keynesian fashion by domestic demand (Bradley, Fitz Gerald and Kearney, 1991).

Tradeable sector price determination and PPP
The crucial starting point in Irish empirical work, and the lynch-pin for evaluation of exchange-rate changes, concerns the determination of producer prices in the tradeable sector of the economy (manufacturing, agriculture and some services). The stylised Scandinavian model assumes perfect commodity arbitrage for a homogeneous tradeable commodity, implying that

(1) $\hat{p}_T = \hat{e} + \hat{p}_W$

where $\hat{p}_T$ is the Irish price of tradeables, $\hat{p}_W$ the world price, e the exchange rate, and the hat denotes a relative rate of change. More generally, we can view Irish tradeable prices as being determined in the following manner:

(2) $\qquad \hat{p}_T = \beta(\hat{e}_{UK} + p_{UK}) + (1-\beta)(\hat{e}_{EMS} + \hat{p}_{EMS})$

where $\hat{e}_{UK}$, e_{EMS} are the Irish currency price of sterling and the Ecu, and $\hat{p}_{UK}$, $\hat{p}_{EMS}$ are the British and EMS rates of inflation. The definitive post-EMS study by Callan and Fitz Gerald (1989) confirmed previous results on the applicability of extended forms of this simple price-taking model for Irish manufacturing (including United Kingdom, German and United States prices), but found some novel features in the nature and timing of the foreign influences. For example, the effects of changes in exchange rates on prices are much slower to materialise than are the effects of changes in foreign currency prices. Thus, while PPP did not hold in the short run, it did hold in the long run for the period 1979–87, that is, the post-EMS period.

A decision to move from a sterling link ($\hat{e}_{UK} = 0$) to the EMS ($\hat{e}_{EMS} = 0$) means that tradeable price determination changes from

(3) $\qquad \hat{p}_T = \beta(\hat{p}_{UK}) + (1-\beta)(\hat{e}_{EMS} + \hat{p}_{EMS})$

to

(4) $\qquad \hat{p}_T = \beta(\hat{e}_{UK} + \hat{p}_{UK}) + (1-\beta)(\hat{p}_{EMS})$

In the latter case, movements between the Irish pound and sterling are determined by movements between sterling and the Ecu. If in the long run there is purchasing power parity (PPP) between the United Kingdom and the EMS zone, then we have

$$\hat{e}_{UK} = \hat{p}_{EMS} - \hat{p}_{UK}$$

which implies

$$\hat{p}_T = \hat{p}_{EMS}$$

So, if PPP were an adequate explanation of the behaviour of floating exchange rates, then an SOE would inherit its tradeable price inflation from the country to which its exchange rate is pegged. However, the fact that flexible exchange rates do exhibit large and often persistent deviations from PPP means that in the short to medium term this result may not obtain. Furthermore, how tradeable price inflation translates into domestic absorption inflation depends on other aspects, now considered.

Wage determination and labour market homogeneity
The simple Scandinavian model assumes that wages are determined in the leading tradeable sector in a bargaining process that results in roughly

constant factor income shares, that is, that wage inflation equals price inflation plus the exogenous growth of productivity (q_T) and a set 'Z' of other variables that may influence wage bargaining.

$$(5) \qquad \hat{w}_T = \hat{p}_T + \hat{q}_T + Z$$

In empirical models this is usually generalised to include a tax and/or terms-of-trade 'wedge', a proxy for bargaining power, and dynamics. Dreze and Bean (1990) have recently estimated such a model for a range of countries, and table 6.1 presents some summary results with Irish results added (Bradley and Fitz Gerald, 1991). In keeping with the other European countries, it is seen that Irish real wages incorporate measured productivity gains quite rapidly, in contrast to the United States. The coefficients on unemployment imply a short-run reduction in wage share, per percentage point of unemployment, ranging from 0.4 per cent in the high unemployment countries to 2.5 per cent in Austria: Ireland is about mid-way between the extremes, at 1.8 per cent. However, the long-run sensitivity of Irish real wages to unemployment, as portrayed by the wage equation in isolation, is exaggerated due to the extreme openness of the Irish labour market. Econometric evidence suggests that migration decisions are influenced by relative employment prospects in the alternative (mainly United Kingdom) labour market and relative real wages, in what is the developed economy version of the well-known Harris–Todaro rural–urban migration model (Walsh, 1974).[4] However, adding such migration equations into Irish labour market models is no trivial modification since the labour supply then becomes very sensitive to relative domestic–international economic conditions, with labour flows highly responsive to any changes. It effectively means that Irish real wages are determined by United Kingdom labour market conditions and. that a stable relationship exists between Irish and British unemployment rates, at least in the long run.

Unlike less developed countries, the Irish labour market is relatively

Table 6.1   *Elasticities of wages*

Variable	Austria	Belgium	Britain	Germany	Nether-lands	US	Ireland
Productivity elasticity (SR top, LR bottom)	0.412	0.882	0.100	0.660	0.562	0.0017	0.602
	1.060	0.821	1.0	1.0	0.839	0.017	1.0
Unemployment Semi-elasticity	−0.025	−0.004	−0.011	−0.004	0	−0.002	−0.018
	−0.028	−0.007	−0.110	−0.004	0	−0.013	−0.031

homogeneous. Both tradeable and non-tradeable workforces are highly unionised and pay deals struck in the leading traded sectors tend to be passed on to the non-traded sector, often through nationwide pay agreements. Hence, to a close approximation wage inflation in both sectors is the same, that is,

$$(6) \qquad\qquad \hat{w}_N = \hat{w}_T$$

We shall see that this property means that exchange rate changes will be unable to shift the relative prices of tradeable and non-tradeable goods. Were the Irish economy less open and the labour market to exhibit non-homogeneous behaviour, as perhaps is the case in Portugal and Greece, then a very different situation would prevail.

Non-traded sector and overall price determination
There is some evidence that prices in the non-tradeable sector are determined as a mark-up on unit labour costs (Bradley, Fitz Gerald and Kearney, 1991), although data inadequacies ensure that less is known about the behaviour of this sector than about the more data-rich tradeable sector. Hence,

$$(7) \qquad\qquad \hat{p}_N = \hat{w}_N = \hat{q}_N$$

so, using (1), (5) and (6),

$$(8) \qquad\qquad \hat{p}_N = \hat{p}_T + \hat{q}_T - \hat{q}_N + z$$

Thus aggregate domestic price inflation, defined as a weighted average of $\hat{p}_T$ and $\hat{p}_N$, is equal to

$$(9) \qquad\qquad \hat{p} = \hat{p}_W + e + (1-\alpha)(q_T - \hat{q}_N + z)$$

and so is determined, not just by foreign prices and the exchange rate but also by the productivity differential between tradeable and non-tradeable sectors, and any other factors which affect domestic wage bargaining.

These different elements of the Scandinavian model, augmented by other aspects of the supply and demand sides of the economy, can be assembled into complete models and serve to motivate much official policymaking and analysis in Ireland (Bradley and Fitz Gerald, 1991). Essentially such models provide a medium to long-term structural framework of the real economy within which likely deviations from the underlying assumptions can be discussed and evaluated. The most important characteristics of Irish models from this analysis are as follows. First, growth in Ireland is intimately related to world growth and the role of domestic demand works through non-tradeable sector channels.

Second, growth policy in Ireland should be viewed as competitiveness policy, in the sense that it should be focused on improving Ireland's position within the international division of labour. The magnitude and composition of output in Ireland will be heavily influenced by its attractiveness as a location of production relative to other world locations in a competitiveness process in which the spatial allocation of investment in the rest of the world is determined. Finally, Irish domestic policy will affect growth by altering those characteristics of the economy which determine its position in the spatial distribution of activity in the rest of the world.

This framework proves particularly useful in evaluating and interpreting Ireland's experience within the EMS over the decade of the 1980s.

Evaluating and interpreting Ireland's EMS experience

We can use the insights from a Scandinavian model-based analysis to discuss three aspects of Irish experience within the EMS: the process of inflation realignment as the currency link shifted from sterling to the EMS; how EMS membership affected the performance of the real economy in Ireland; and how the currency regime change influenced the manner of, and costs incurred by, the necessary process of fiscal correction of disequilibria that had originated during the previous sterling era.

Inflation and disinflation during the 1980s

It would be wrong to view Ireland's reduction of inflation during the 1980s as the result of a Latin American style stabilisation package aimed at reducing chronically high rates of inflation which were destroying economic activity. In fact there were two separate, but interrelated, processes at work: the Irish decision to join the EMS was mainly motivated by a desire to escape from the high imported inflation of the United Kingdom; the stabilisation programme had as its primary focus the restoration of control to the public finances.

The sharp appreciation of sterling in the early 1980s meant that for Ireland, at first, EMS membership was more inflationary than the sterling link. The sharp rises in the tax wedge and large pay awards to the public sector also helped fuel non-tradeable price inflation. Once these factors subsided, the inflation rate began to converge towards low German-style rates. The model of imported price inflation would appear to provide an adequate description of Ireland's long-run inflation performance during this period, although the adjustment of inflationary expectations was less well understood. We need more information on how Irish firms and trades unions handled the transition from the sterling to the EMS regime, particularly in the light of sterling's gyrations outside the ERM.

The EMS and the performance of the real economy

The Irish economy's performance during the first half of the 1980s was undoubtedly poor: GNP growth ceased (chart 6.7) while both unemployment and emigration rose to record levels (chart 6.10). Was EMS membership and the associated disinflation an important contributing factor? In the context of a critical discussion of the New Classical credibility theories, which state that a fully credible disinflation will be costless, Dornbusch (1989) has asserted that it was indeed an important factor: 'The triumph of low inflation has come at a cost (perhaps inevitable) of extraordinary high unemployment, massive emigration and a precarious debt overhang'. The principal failing was identified as being a lack of flexibility in the Irish labour market.

In the previous section we highlighted the crucial importance of the external economic environment and the competitiveness of the tradeable sector as keys to the performance of the Irish economy. The post OPEC-II recession was particularly severe in the United Kingdom and this drove many of Ireland's more traditional, labour intensive, UK-oriented firms out of business. Furthermore, the recession also saw a drying up of the high levels of DFI on which Ireland had been relying to sustain industrial expansion. This slowdown of DFI continued for some time after the recession ended elsewhere and meant that for much of the 1980s Ireland was losing more industrial output and employment through closures of traditional firms than it was gaining through new foreign investment. Overall, industrial employment continued to fall into the middle of the 1980s. In addition, high unemployment in the United Kingdom labour market, the traditional destination for Irish emigrants, combined with a large natural growth in the labour force to produce record levels of unemployment. Did this mean that the Irish labour market was particularly inflexible, as Dornbusch has asserted? Certainly, Ireland was not America, and in this sense the labour market was not flexible enough to offset the hostile external and domestic policy environments (Barry and Bradley, 1991). However, could the real wage have moved to bring the labour market closer to clearing? Hardly! In the light of the Dreze–Bean results quoted above, Ireland was merely exhibiting a European-wide pattern of behaviour, where wage formation is dominated by unions and governments who are greatly concerned about distributional fairness. To suggest that the Irish real wage could have been lower would be to expect the Irish labour market to behave in a radically different way from other European labour markets.

Turning to domestic policy, the precarious state of the public finances meant that instead of deploying expansionary or neutral fiscal policies to deal with the negative external factors, the government was obliged to run a primary budget surplus in order to arrest the growth of debt. Furthermore, as the worldwide fund of DFI dried up during the early 1980s, and the competitiveness driven battle for international, export-oriented, high value-added industries intensified, Irish cost competitiveness moved in the wrong direction (chart 6.6). In particular, the government's attempts to stabilise the state finances by massive increases in tax rates, combined with a freezing of public expenditure, led to large increases in the wedge between employers' wage costs and employees' take-home pay. This contributed both to wage inflation and industrial unrest and decreased Ireland's attractiveness as an industrial location.

Clearly, one interpretation of Ireland's experience in the 1980s is that the EMS quasi-fixed exchange rate regime was responsible for the loss in competitiveness since a possible response, in the context of floating outside the EMS, could have been to devalue and restore competitiveness (Leddin and Walsh, 1990, p. 284). However, any gains from such devaluations are likely to be very transitory, if they exist at all. In the long-run Scandanavian model outlined in the previous section, a devaluation of 10 per cent simply increases domestic currency tradeable prices also by 10 per cent which, in turn, increases sectoral wages, non-tradeable prices and aggregate price inflation by the same amount. The devaluation affects only nominal variables, leaving the real wage and competitiveness unaffected. Of course, such a model is highly simplified and has no dynamics. In reality, nominal wage rigidity may mean that a devaluation has a temporary effect in boosting competitiveness. Whether this temporary effect makes the nominal exchange rate a policy tool worth using is a point of controversy. Soft currencies imply high risk premia. Charts 6.3 and 6.4 show the sharp rises in interest rate differentials that followed Ireland's 8 per cent devaluation within the EMS in 1986.

It would appear to us that interpreting Ireland's poor economic performance during the 1980s as being intimately tied up with the disinflation that accompanied EMS membership is not particularly convincing. Rather, the poor performance can primarily be assigned to a worsening of the key world indicators affecting the Irish economy and domestic policy decisions which adversely affected both demand and international cost competitiveness. It is very doubtful whether economic performance would have been superior if the alternative option of keeping the sterling link had been chosen.

EMS and fiscal adjustment

The principal concern of Irish fiscal policy throughout the 1980s was the perilous state of the public finances. The fiscal problem, which began during the 1970s when successive governments operated Keynesian deficit-financed public expenditure programmes, turned particularly serious during the 1980s as the economy stagnated, public spending commitments were difficult to cut in real terms (chart 6.8), and the large rise in the interest rates exacerbated the debt problem (chart 6.9).

These high real interest rates were a world problem and not particularly confined to the EMS or Ireland. There was, however, an additional risk premium over German rates which had two main causes. Firstly, there were fears that the Irish debt position would become unsustainable and eventually lead to wholesale monetisation and a large depreciation. An unsolved issue is whether or not these premia would have been lower if the sterling link had been retained or the Irish pound had floated? On balance we think probably not: it is doubtful whether being linked to sterling would have decreased the fears of eventual monetisation. Secondly, the Irish commitment to a fixed exchange rate within the EMS was not entirely credible prior to 1987. It often appeared that Irish policymakers were also attempting to stay within a target range against sterling, an impression reinforced in 1986 by the 8 per cent devaluation of the Irish pound within the EMS, which the central bank felt was needed to provide a competitive boost to traditional Irish firms exporting to the United Kingdom. In recent years, large cuts in public expenditure have helped stabilise the debt–GNP ratio and, combined with the absence of a devaluation within the EMS and the recent British entry into the ERM, has established Irish credibility within the EMS. Risk premia have been reduced, but are still positive (chart 6.3); Irish enthusiasm for EMU certainly reflects the desire to remove them entirely.

Ireland's recent economic performance
What then of the recent performance of the Irish economy? The period after 1987 saw a dramatic upturn in Irish economic performance: growth rates turned strongly positive, the balance of payments moved strongly into surplus, unemployment and emigration were reduced, inflation stayed low and, simultaneously, the long-awaited fiscal stabilisation came about as the debt–GNP ratio began to fall.[5] The reasons for this turnround have been the subject of a certain amount of controversy. Giavazzi and Pagano (1990) and others claim that Ireland's experience was an example of an 'expansionary fiscal contraction', the Barro–Ricardo proposition being invoked to produce an explanation based on an expansion of private sector domestic demand which more than offsets the contractionary effects of the fiscal contraction.

Certainly, the post-1987 fiscal package was a far more successful effort than the previous attempts, in that it obtained broad cross-party political support, was seen as credible and was implemented largely through cuts in public expenditure rather than competitiveness-unfriendly tax increases. Thus, the package helped cut the risk premium component of domestic interest rates, did not hurt the competitiveness of Irish industry and may indeed have boosted the confidence of Irish consumers by convincing them of a likely superior future economic performance accompanied by tax cuts. In particular, the fiscal adjustment may indeed have been directly responsible for the fall in the savings ratio from 17 per cent to about 14 per cent. However, even if this increase in consumption was caused by the fiscal reforms, it is likely that the net effect of the fiscal contraction on domestic demand was still negative. In any case, since domestic demand constitutes such a small proportion of total demand for the Irish tradeable sector's goods, any argument for a domestic demand based expansion cannot explain the rapid expansion of the export-oriented tradeable sector during this period.

A more conventional explanation of Ireland's economic 'miracle' is that the period 1987–90 was one in which the external environment was very favourable for Ireland, with strong growth in all our major trading partners, an expansion in worldwide DFI coupled with an improvement in Ireland's cost competitiveness, an improvement that was partly facilitated by a return to corporatist national wage agreements after 1987.

No doubt all nations are entitled to their time in the sun, and Ireland's was during the period 1987–90. However, the optimism has evaporated more recently. As world (and particularly United Kingdom) growth has slowed and the United Kingdom labour market deteriorated, the Irish fiscal correction has stalled, the social partners have begun to revert to their pre-1987 fractious behaviour and unemployment is back at record levels. The extent to which the economic recovery after 1987 depended on favourable external conditions is perhaps becoming more clear.

Conclusion

Grave fears have been expressed concerning the possible effects of a European monetary union on peripheral regions, but the Irish experience would not seem to substantiate these fears. Certainly, for SOEs with inflexible and homogenous labour markets (a stereotype to which Ireland certainly conforms, and towards which the other peripheral economies may be moving), the floating exchange rate does not appear to be a satisfactory option. For Ireland, the major policy choice has effectively been between a link with sterling and the EMS. In 1979, Ireland chose the EMS and, on balance, the subsequent experience has been positive. Inflation has undergone a sustained reduction, trade diversification has been facilitated, and Ireland is now in the front line of prospective members of the monetary union about to take place within the EC.

This does not mean that the periphery has nothing to fear from a full Economic and Monetary Union. Rather, it is the issue of cohesion, or real convergence, which will preoccupy policymakers of the periphery. Ireland has already had the experience of discovering that free trade and increasing returns can produce an economic geography in which peripheral regions lose out (Krugman, 1991). The question of whether the larger EC members are committed enough to give structural aid to the periphery, and whether the aid is sufficiently effective, will prove vital if countries such as Ireland are to be safegarded from another period of industrial decline.

Notes

1 Even pre-revolutionary France found itself in a similar position after a free-trade agreement concluded by Calonne in 1786. However, there was a strongly held expectation that healthy competition would stimulate French producers (Schama, 1989, p. 233).

2 The Census of Industrial Production of 1926 showed less than 8 per cent of the Irish labour force in industry, of which only 4.3 per cent was in manufacturing. With British GNP per capita at 100, in the year 1910 Ireland came in at 62, slightly ahead of Norway and Sweden (60.4 and 60.3 respectively) and well ahead of Italy and Finland (40.5 and 34.6 respectively) (Lee, 1989, p. 513).

3 The Small Open Economy (SOE) theory of imported inflation had by the mid-1970s convincingly won out over the earlier cost–push model, mainly as a result of a series of persuasive econometric studies on UK–Irish price transmission mechanisms (Geary, 1976).

4 In an curious comment on the paper by Dornbusch (1989) on Ireland's attempt at stabilisation in the 1980s, Charles Wyplosz was puzzled 'at the apparent lack of nationalistic feelings in Ireland, where people prefer to leave rather than accept wage reductions'.

5 From being profoundly pessimistic about Ireland's prospects within the EMS, Dornbusch has swung round to optimism and in his Geary lecture in 1990 recounts that 'no sooner had the galleys (of the 1989 article) gone to press, then did the Irish miracle develop: successful incomes policy, less-than-German inflation, major and sustained budget correction, strong growth and a falling debt ratio ... there is a distinct optimism and a can-do atmosphere'.

7

German Monetary Union and Some Lessons for Europe

Willy Friedmann*

Introduction

German monetary, economic and social union came into force on 1 July 1990. Residents of the former GDR gained access to the broad range of Western goods for the first time, and material living conditions in East Germany improved more or less overnight. However, the blessings of free competition have at the same time relentlessly exposed the lack of efficiency in the East German economy. As a result, high public transfer payments from West Germany were necessary to eliminate this discrepancy. In 1991 alone transfers probably amounted to about DM140 billion; that is, almost 5 per cent of West German GNP or roughly two-thirds of East German GNP. This requires really unprecedented efforts on the part of the West German economy, especially as the latter is already working to the limits of its financial capacities. Indeed in 1992 public transfer payments from the West are expected to exceed even this sum.

If we take the monetary field by itself, then the process of integration proceeded comparatively swiftly and smoothly. Fortunately, the loss of D-Mark stability often predicted in the run-up to German unification has not come about. Nevertheless, German monetary union has also had a clear impact on the monetary field. To some extent its secondary effects are still being felt. The current risk of inflation, on the one hand, and the additional burdens arising from high public sector deficits on the other, call for a policy mix that will, for the foreseeable future at any rate, remain fraught with tension; it will only be possible to sustain such a mix by means of a broadly-based social consensus that avoids disadvantages in the field of employment. The potential for conflicts of stability policy can only be eased if all those involved are aware of the limits of the overall leeway for income distribution. This requires both a

* The views expressed are those of the author and do not necessarily reflect those of the Deutsche Bundesbank.

credible consolidation strategy by the government and more regard for the situation on the part of wage policymakers.

Even before the real outcome of this unique economic 'experiment' has emerged, the framework for a new historically unique event is currently being forged, an event which far exceeds the dimensions of German monetary union. The establishment of a European economic and monetary union is now within our reach. At all events, the road to a common Europe has been opened, and the monetary policy roadsigns point in the direction of European monetary union with a single European currency. The advantages which accrue to the European economies are more or less beyond dispute. In the monetary field the main form these will take will be savings in transaction costs, which the well-known EC study put at close to ½ per cent of the Community's GNP.[1] The price paid for these advantages may, of course, prove to be rather high if the new monetary policy order ultimately transpires to weaken the anti-inflationary anchoring of the European currency or if it is possible only to implement the monetary union in Europe at the price of severe real economic friction resulting from the adjustment process.

In the current negotiations by the participating governments the German side is trying to take account of this, *inter alia*, by trying to avoid 'grey monetary policy areas' in designing the institutional framework of the transitional phase to a European monetary union; by committing the later European central bank unequivocally to the goal of price stability and by making sure that it has the requisite formal and material independence; by ensuring, with the application of global convergence criteria, that homogeneity among the participating economies is initially adequate upon their entering into the European monetary union; and, finally, by keeping the danger of tension-fraught conflicts over the aims of the respective national fiscal policies, on the one hand, and the common monetary policy, on the other, within reasonable limits, by avoiding excessive budget deficits.

Only if it rests on these main pillars can European monetary union become a real community of stability and thus a solid foundation for political union in Europe. In other words, the more incomplete the economic convergence, the greater the demands on the ability of the member states to reach a political consensus in order to bridge the resulting economic tension. In a way German monetary union shows how painful the friction generated by the adjustment process can be, given fixed-rate conditions and the high measure of political solidarity necessary to cope with it. In this sense German monetary union can actually be seen as a sort of 'model', although we should not lose sight of the particular features of the German case. At all events, the German example shows the high degree of political consensus and devoted financial effort which is called for and will remain necessary in the near future to bridge the considerable structural differences. In the case of German monetary union it was from the outset clear to all the participants – that is, prior to the subsequent political unification – that this would require the complete renunciation of monetary and fiscal policy sovereignty on the part of the former GDR. In contrast to the European vision of monetary union as the engine driving forward an accelerating process of political integration, German monetary union and its swift implementation are thus a reflection of the unrestricted will for political unification of the two parts of Germany – and did not merely serve as the vehicle on the road to this end. Without the common political accord of all participants, it would not have been possible to deal with the profound adjustment constraints and frictions.

German monetary union: a review of events and implications

Favourable initial conditions
After the political upheavals in the autumn of 1989 on the other side of the iron curtain, upheavals which came as a surprise to everybody, and the virtual collapse of the old system of a centrally-planned economy in the former GDR, there was from the outset no doubt as to the fact that the adequate response to these challenges could only consist of an uncompromising adoption of a free market economy. The question of which promising process of transition would lead to this end was, by contrast, initially the subject of controversy. At first, opinion prevailed that the exchange rate should be retained as an instrument of adjustment; but attention was also drawn to the possible disadvantages of such a model.[2] Yet ultimately most economists advocated a 'soft' transition. This idea was, however, quite quickly frustrated by the understandable impatience of the population and the urgent wish for a political unification of the two parts of Germany. This was increasingly emphasised by a constantly growing influx of immigrants from the former GDR. Under the pressure of these developments, the Federal Government announced as early as the beginning of February 1990, the introduction of the D-Mark into the GDR within the framework of a German monetary, economic and social union – as a first step, so to speak, in the process of German unification. Surprising as these events were to German economic policymakers, the initial conditions in the Federal Republic could hardly have been more favourable. As is clear from table 7.1, the West German economy was in the middle of a sustained and essentially smooth upturn; employment levels on the labour market in the Federal Republic were correspondingly favourable; households' disposable income had just benefited from a major tax reform; public finance had recorded remarkable progress with regard to consolidation

Table 7.1   *Growth and price performance of West Germany*

Year	Real GNP	Unit labour costs	GNP deflator	CPI
Change from previous year in per cent				
1985	1.8	1.9	2.2	2.0
1986	2.2	2.8	3.3	−0.1
1987	1.5	2.4	1.9	0.2
1988	3.7	0.2	1.5	1.3
1989	3.8	0.4	2.6	2.8
1990	4.5	2.5	3.4	2.7
Change from previous period in per cent – seasonally adjusted				
1990				
1st half	3.0(a)	1.1	1.9	1.3
2nd half	2.3(a)	1.0	1.7	1.6
1991				
1st half	2.4(a)	2.2	2.3	1.2
3rd qtr	−0.5(a)	1.3	1.1	1.8

Source: Deutsche Bundesbank, Statistiche Beihefte zu den Monatsberichten den Deutschen Bundesbank Reihe 4.
(a) Also adjusted for working-day variations.

(without the additional burdens resulting from the unification process, the public sector would probably have shown a small surplus in 1990); and aggregate saving in the Federal Republic exceeded investment during the same period by more than 4 per cent of GNP. All in all, this initial position could hardly have been more favourable.

'Money stock upsurge' as a result of the currency conversion
After the principle political decision in favour of the introduction of the D-Mark in the former GDR had been taken, it was important to make adequate arrangements on the monetary side to maintain the stability of the D-Mark in a national and international climate with a heightened awareness of the problem, for the establishment of an efficient East German economy and the requisite transfer of financial and real resources could only succeed on the basis of monetary stability. It was therefore essential that full sovereignty for monetary policy was transferred to the Bundesbank from the outset for the whole extended currency area of the D-Mark.

The question of the terms of the conversion met with particularly lively interest both at home and abroad. From the point of view of monetary policy it was primarily a question of converting all financial assets and liabilities in such a way as to maintain stability. In contrast to a future introduction of a single European currency, there were hardly any reliable yardsticks to go on. In these difficult circumstances it was important to strike the best possible balance between different requirements. On the one hand, inflationary risks resulting from too 'generous' a conversion of the population's financial assets had to be reduced to a minimum, and enterprises' borrowing requirements had to be confined to a reasonable measure. On the other hand, the social and political acceptance for the conversion had to be secured among the population. Finally, the financial burdens on the government resulting from the possibility of an asymmetrical conversion of assets and liabilities were to be kept within limits. The upshot was that the contracting parties agreed on a conversion rate of 2:1, in principle, with the exception of private savings, which were converted at a preferential rate of 1:1 up to certain ceilings. The average conversion rate was 1.8:1.

As a result, the money stocks in the Federal Republic rose by DM180 billion, or nearly 15 per cent, in the middle of 1990. This was more than the Bundesbank considered justifiable over the longer term. In the absence of better information on the demand behaviour for money in the new *Länder*, it had used the estimated economic weighting of Eastern and Western Germany respectively as a guideline at the time and regarded a 'money stock upsurge' of about 10 per cent as a result of the currency conversion as in order. The fact that the actual rise in the money stock was markedly higher was initially no reason for concern as it could be assumed that the 'monetary overhang' resulting from the conversion would largely decline again more or less of its own accord. As there were no investment alternatives available, the total financial assets of the population were held in the form of savings deposits payable on demand, deposits which could also be used for private cashless payments and were therefore to be included in the money stock (M3). Over the longer term, however, it was to be expected that private savers would turn to the new offers of longer-term forms of saving with more attractive interest rates 'outside' the money stock M3 and that the resulting shifts would curb the growth of the money stocks. The East German money stock has indeed been reduced by such portfolio adjustments since the middle of last year. In the summer of 1991, the Bundesbank was prompted by this structural curbing of the monetary expansion to reduce its monetary growth target for this year by 1 percentage point to 3–5 per cent.

In spite of the 'tendencies towards normalisation' of East German cash holdings this reflects, the liquidity supply of the German economy still seems to be quite ample, even though the question of what would constitute an appropriate money supply cannot be answered as accurately as usual as there is no prior experience to fall back on here. The pace of overall monetary expansion in Germany has, moreover, accelerated noticeably since the summer of 1991. In October the money stock M3 exceeded the level of the fourth quarter of 1990 by a seasonally-adjusted annual rate of 4.8 per cent and thus loomed at the upper edge of the new target range (of 3–5 per cent), whereas, at 3.3 per cent, it had dwelt at the lower edge of the target corridor in the middle of the year. Accordingly, German monetary policymakers still think it necessary to keep the latitude for monetary expansion within narrow limits.

Decline in output and employment
The introduction of the D-Mark into the former GDR led to a distinct increase in prosperity for residents there. After decades of supply shortages, pent-up consumer demand erupted in a spending spree which continued until very recently and initially focused almost exclusively on Western products. In the first six months after the introduction of the D-Mark, for example, as many new cars were registered in the new *Länder* as previously over a period of five to six years. A dramatic slump in East German output was the other side of the coin, revealing at one fell swoop the structural competitive weaknesses in the East German economy. In the second half of 1990 industrial production in East Germany was only half as high as a year earlier. At the beginning of 1991 this trend was further intensified by the fact that, with the abolition of the transferable rouble system, enterprises were forthwith only able to make deliveries to their former trading partners in the countries of the former Eastern bloc against convertible currencies. The economic difficulties of these countries aggravated the drop in the export business of East German enterprises. These reasons also played a part in causing the decline in output to persist well into 1991. In that summer, East German industrial production was 40 per cent below its 1990 level. This trend seemed to have come to an end only at the end of 1991. In individual sectors, particularly in the construction industry, the first favourable signs are to be seen. Forecasts by the German Council of Economic Experts and the economic research institutes give grounds for expecting a distinct recovery in production in East Germany for 1992 – albeit a recovery which will start from a very low level.

According to these forecasts no turn for the better is to be expected in the near future as far as employment in Eastern Germany is concerned. In the fourth quarter of 1990 the number of employed persons in the new *Länder* was nearly two million lower than in the first half of 1989, which means that the employment figures fell by about one quarter. This reflects the fact that many members of the workforce have moved to Western Germany or have found a job there, or alternatively have quit the labour force owing to early retirement. At the end of October 1991, the number of unemployed persons in Eastern Germany was more than one million, or 12 per cent of the dependent labour force. In addition, a further 1.2 million persons were on short-time work (table 7.2).

The slump in output and employment is the obvious result of decades of mismanagement which had prevented production patterns adjusting to

Table 7.2   *Population and labour market in Eastern Germany (thousands, average)*

	Population	Employed (a)	Short-time workers (b)	Unemployed (c)
1988	16667(d)			
1989	16609	9858		
1990	16250(e)	8923		
1989I	16665	9930		
1989II	16647	9928		
1989III	16610	9820		
1989IV	16515	9754		
1990I	16366	9582		38
1990II	16268	9158		142
1990III	16201	8759	1295	445
1990IV	16098(f)	8193	1736	642
1991I			1925	808
1991II			1962	843
1991III			1464	1049
September			1333	1029
October			1200	1049
November			1103	1031

Source: Joint Statistical Office (population); Federal Statistical Office (employed); Federal Labour Office (short-time workers, unemployed).
(a) Residents (domicile concept).
(b) Quarterly figures: averages; monthly figures: mid-month levels.
(c) End-of-period levels.
(d) May to December.
(e) January to November.
(f) October to November.

meet the factual conditions of scarcity and the needs of the population. However, the severity of the slump must also be seen in the context of wage policy. Since the former GDR's entry into the monetary, economic and social union the aim has been to adjust the East German pay level to the West German one as quickly as possible. On average, pay was raised by more than 50 per cent against the previous year.

Offsetting this by major financial transfers from the West ...
The difficulties the East German economy has experienced in adjusting to the new situation have tended to be aggravated by the afore-mentioned problems and have made massive fiscal policy support necessary. The volume of assistance, initially conceived as 'start-up finance', was increased several times. In 1991 alone public financial transfers are expected to reach an order of DM140 billion. The funds are used to secure the social welfare of the population, to set up an efficient administration,

Table 7.3   *Public sector deficits(a)*

Year	Receipts		Expenditure	Deficit
	Total	of which taxes		
1970	39.2	22.8	39.8	−0.6
1975	44.7	23.6	51.2	−6.5
1980	46.7	24.7	50.4	−3.6
1981	47.0	24.1	51.6	−4.6
1982	48.0	23.8	52.1	−4.1
1983	47.3	23.7	50.6	−3.4
1984	47.0	23.5	49.8	−2.8
1985	47.3	23.8	49.4	−2.0
1986	46.8	23.4	48.7	−1.9
1987	46.6	23.4	49.0	−2.4
1988	45.9	23.2	48.5	−2.6
1989	46.5	23.9	46.8	−0.4
1990(b)	46.1	22.7	49.2	−3.1
1991(c)	47.0	23.5	51.0	−4.0

Source: As table 7.1.

(a) Central, regional and local authorities and social security funds.

(b) West German public authorities plus section B of the Federal budget and the 'German Unity' Fund; budget figures relative to the West German gross national product.

(c) Germany as a whole, estimated.

to foster investments to improve the infrastructure, and to promote private economic projects. The financing of these enormous burdens on public expenditure was undoubtedly facilitated by the favourable initial position of the public authorities. In view of the unprecedented orders of magnitude involved, tax increases were also necessary. In addition to an increase in excise taxes, a limited-period surcharge on income and corporation taxes was introduced. The public sector deficit in 1991 will probably be of the order of approximately DM120 billion. It will amount to about 4½ per cent of GNP and will thus again come close to the unfavourable situation last seen at the beginning of the 1980s.

... and reversing the German current account

In Western Germany, unification has stimulated economic growth as consumer demand, in particular, rose sharply, and as a growing number of immigrants and commuters increased production capacities. In the second half of 1990 and the first half of 1991 real GNP in Western Germany rose at an annual rate of 4½–5 per cent. Initially, the massive stimuli to demand encountered a remarkably elastic supply of goods in Western Germany. Against the background of favourable external conditions, increasing recourse could, furthermore, be had to foreign capacities through imports of goods from other Western industrial countries, which thereby participated likewise in the growth stimuli emanating from the German unification process. After the West German economy had made available as much as about 5 per cent of its GNP to its foreign trading partners in the form of export surpluses in 1989, the cross-border flow of current transactions soon reversed after German unification. In the first nine months of 1991 the deficit on the German current account rose to more than DM30 billion, compared with a surplus of about DM65 billion in the same period of the preceding year. The considerable decline in West German saving, which reflects the drastic deterioration of the financial situation of the public authorities, has thus, in the final instance, been 'financed' by a rapid swing of the previous surpluses on current account into deficits.

Summary and conclusions

Overall, the German unification process has led to exceptionally heavy burdens being placed on public sector budgets over the past eighteen months, burdens which, in view of the special circumstances, can undoubtedly be absorbed in the interim but which would overtax the capacity of the German economy over the long term.

To this extent, the German experience impressively confirms the simple textbook wisdom that, once one adjustment variable such as the exchange rate has been fixed, the integration of different economic structures results in correspondingly heavier adjustment burdens elsewhere. In the German unification process, fiscal policy was to a certain extent left to bear the full brunt of coping with this task on its own; there was, above all, virtually no support forthcoming in the shape of wage policy. Indeed, surely one of the most bitter experiences of 1990 was that wage policymakers did not shoulder the responsibility they had to bear in this context and instead additionally impaired the East German economy's prospects of catching up with the West by making excessive income claims. This unfavourable policy mix moreover demanded special anti-inflationary steadfastness on the part of monetary policymakers.

The process of monetary policy integration in Western Europe fortunately does not confront the member countries with a similarly difficult task. Nevertheless there are, in principle, considerable structural differences to be bridged. Strict convergence requirements prior to the introduction of a single European currency are the best way to ensure that the willingness for political consensus is not overtaxed.

Notes

1   Commission of the European Communities (1990), 'One market, one money. An evaluation of the potential benefits and costs of forming an economic and monetary union', in *European Economy*, no. 44, October.

2 See, for instance, Economic Advisory Council at the Federal Ministry of Economics: 'Wirtschaftliche Herausforderungen der Bundesrepublik im Verhältnis zur DDR' (Economic challenges for the Federal Republic of Germany in its relations to the GDR), December 1989. Special report of the German Council of Economic Experts, 'Zur Unterstützung der Wirtschaftsreform in der DDR: Voraussetzungen und Möglichkeiten' (Support of economic reforms in the GDP: prerequisites and opportunities), Bonn, January 1990 (specifically paragraph 32 ff.).

8

The Diverse Experience of the Netherlands, Belgium and Denmark in the ERM

Jan Willem in't Veld

The three smaller EMS countries, the Netherlands, Belgium and Denmark, have achieved a marked economic convergence towards German norms in the last decade. All three are small open economies with close economic links to Germany. Table 8.1 shows the structure of exports of the three countries in 1989. It is clear that they have stronger trading links with Germany than the average, yet their experience in the EMS has been quite diverse. Since the inception of the ERM in 1979, the Netherlands has chosen the strong currency option and Dutch monetary policy has closely followed the policy of the Deutsche Bundesbank. On the other hand, in the first stage of the ERM, Belgium and Denmark adopted the soft currency option of a crawling peg *vis-à-vis* the D-Mark and have only at a later stage shifted towards a harder stance.

The economic performance of these three countries has also been quite diverse during the last decade. The Netherlands has indeed been in a quasi monetary union with Germany for some time now. Its experience in the ERM was favourably affected by good starting conditions from the onset, a relatively good inflation record, and close trading links with Germany. Its inflation rate has been lower than Germany's for some time now and over the last decade its interest rate differential *vis-à-vis* Germany has gradually diminished to almost zero. It has, however, followed an independent fiscal policy, which is reflected in high public sector financial deficits and relatively high public debt. Belgium has, after initially shadowing the French franc, gradually adopted a harder stance and introduced corrective measures to reduce wage inflation, improve competitiveness and to reduce fiscal expenditure to stabilise its mounting public indebtedness. During the last years it has achieved a closer convergence to Germany. Denmark entered the EMS with high inflation, high fiscal deficits, and a long history of balance of payments deficits and uninterrupted debt accumulation. A substantial policy shift came with the introduction of a stabilisation package in 1982, suspending automatic wage indexation, reducing public expenditure and adopting

Table 8.1   *Exports to other EC countries (as % of total exports, 1989)*

Exports to:	Exports from:		
	Netherlands	Belgium	Denmark
Belgium	16.0	–	2.1
Denmark	1.7	0.9	–
Germany	28.1	19.8	18.2
Greece	1.0	0.6	0.9
Spain	2.3	2.3	1.7
France	11.4	21.4	6.2
Ireland	0.7	0.4	0.6
Italy	7.0	6.7	4.9
Netherlands	–	14.4	4.4
Portugal	0.8	0.7	0.7
UK	11.7	9.7	12.7
Total EC	80.6	76.8	52.3

Source: *European Economy.*

a fixed exchange rate policy. This hard currency policy has gradually gained credibility and Denmark has, like Belgium, attained considerable economic convergence with Germany over the last few years. However, it has paid a significant price for this in the form of output loss and high unemployment.

The experience of these three countries in the EMS is instructive as it illustrates the process of reputation building. The countries entered the ERM with diverse starting conditions and have acquired their hard currency credibility at different stages. This chapter describes the economic performance of these three countries and the lessons that can be learned from their experience in the EMS. The following section briefly discusses the exchange rate policies pursued in the ERM and the credibility of these policies. All three countries have now achieved a remarkable convergence, but only after a decade of vigorous adjustment policies. The next sections describe the main features of these stabilisation policies and their effects on wage setting. In the final section, the performance of the countries will be assessed with a view to the criteria for transition to the final stage of a monetary union.

Exchange rate policies and reputation in the ERM

The first years of the ERM were characterised by frequent realignments. These were caused by continuing inflation differentials, which were a reflection of divergent economic performances. Table 8.2 shows the changes in central rates of the three currencies *vis-à-vis* the D-Mark that have taken place since the inception of the ERM.

Table 8.2   *Changes in EMS central rates vis-à-vis the D-Mark (per cent change in central rate)*

	Dates of realignments							
	24/9 1979	31/11 1979	5/10 1981	22/2 1982	14/6 1982	21/3 1983	7/4 1986	12/1 1987
Dutch guilder	−2.0	0.0	0.0	0.0	0.0	−2.0	0.0	0.0
Belgian franc	−2.0	0.0	−5.5	−8.5	−4.25	−4.0	−2.0	−1.0
Danish kroner	−4.9	−4.8	−5.5	−3.0	−4.25	−3.0	−2.0	−3.0

The Dutch guilder has devalued against the D-Mark on only two occasions, in September, 1979, when a first adjustment to ERM parities was made, and again in March 1983. During the 1970s, Dutch monetary policy had increasingly focused on maintaining a fixed guilder–D-Mark exchange rate in the snake arrangements. From the onset of the EMS, inflation in the Netherlands had been only slightly above the German rate and for many years in the last decade inflation was actually lower than in Germany (see chart 8.1). Changes in discount rates in Germany are almost always immediately followed by changes in official Dutch rates. In a study of reputation and credibility in the EMS, Weber (1991)

Chart 8.1   *Consumer price inflation: differential vis-à-vis Germany*

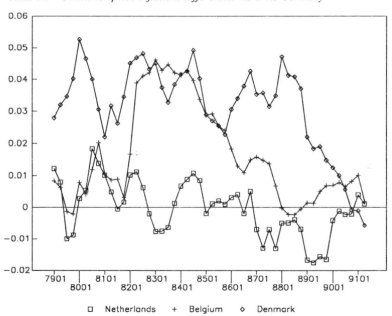

Note: inflation is defined as a proportionate change. Hence 0.06 on the graph represents a 6 per cent differential.

argued that, after Germany, the Netherlands had the highest anti-inflation reputation prior to and during the EMS period. By late 1982, the Dutch commitment to a stable exchange rate policy had gained credibility and the hard currency reputation of the Dutch monetary authorities had become established. Considering this, the fact that in March 1983, the guilder did not appreciate by the same amount as the D-Mark, but devalued by 2 per cent, must have come as a surprise. Despite reassurance from the Finance Ministry that it was a once and for all move, the step was openly criticised by the Dutch central bank, which warned that the gain in competitiveness would only be temporary and that it would lead to higher inflation and higher interest rates. Indeed, financial markets temporarily lost some confidence in the Dutch hard currency policy and the devaluation led to a small increase in the interest rate differential *vis-à-vis* Germany. The official reassurance of their commitment to a stable guilder–D-Mark exchange rate gradually regained credibility and the interest rate differential *vis-à-vis* Germany has remained within 0.5 percentage points for some time (see charts 8.2 and 8.3).

In order to test the credibility of the hard currency policy since the last realignment of the guilder in the ERM in 1983, Koen (1991) constructed rate of return bands on assets of comparable maturity implied by the fluctuation margins in the ERM. He found that on a quarterly basis, that is, based on three months interest rates, the ±2.25 per cent exchange rate band of the guilder was credible and that by 1984 even a narrow band of ±0.5 per cent around the D-Mark was credible. To test whether further devaluations were ruled out in the long term, he also considered long-term interest rates and found that the hard currency policy became credible by early 1986. Based on these tests, Koen concluded that 'it could be said that it took around three years for the exchange rate policy to become fully credible' (Koen, 1991, p. 4).

Belgium entered the ERM with inflation rates only slightly above German rates. In the snake arrangements during the 1970s, exchange rate policy had been directed towards maintaining an exchange rate linkage with Germany and the Netherlands, Belgium's main trading partners. During the first years of the ERM, Belgium maintained a stable exchange rate policy, but in 1981/2 this hard currency stance was abandoned and Belgium switched to the soft currency option. The Belgian franc was devalued by 8.5 per cent as part of a vigorous adjustment policy. Officially it was presented as a new linkage to the set of all the ERM currencies, but Weber (1991) argued that it was a policy shift from a relatively credible exchange rate peg *vis-à-vis* Germany to a soft currency policy of pegging to the French franc. Chart 8.1 shows the inflationary consequences of this move. While inflation fell in Germany and the Netherlands, inflation in Belgium stayed at relatively high levels

Chart 8.2   *Short-term interest rate: differential vis-à-vis Germany*

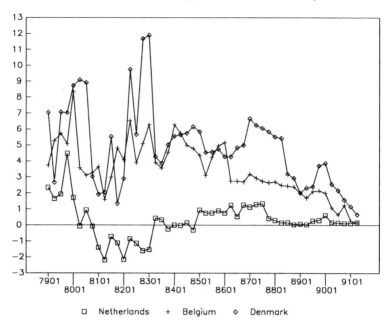

□ Netherlands   + Belgium   ◇ Denmark

and the differential *vis-à-vis* Germany rose to 4 percentage points. Also in the years after 1982 the government directly intervened in the wage formation process. Wages were restrained through these incomes policies and inflation was gradually reduced (see chart 8.1).

Gradually monetary policy became redirected to maintaining a stable currency and this was reflected in the changes in official discount rates, which, like the Dutch rates, followed changes in German rates. By the end of the decade Belgium's commitment to a strong currency had become more credible. In March 1990, the two-tier exchange market was abolished and in June 1990, the government announced that it was linking the Belgian franc more closely to the most stable currency in the ERM. This implied a tightening of the bilateral fluctuation margin *vis-à-vis* the D-Mark to ±0.5 per cent and a commitment to maintaining the central rate *vis-à-vis* the D-Mark in any future realignment. This reduced the risk premium on the Belgian franc and led to a closer convergence of interest rates to German rates (see charts 8.2 and 8.3). Koen (1991) tests the credibility of the hard currency policy and finds that the credibility seems to have markedly improved since 1990 if short-term interest rate differentials are considered. The behaviour of long-term interest rates, however, suggests there is still some long-term credibility gap.[1] Notwithstanding that, Koen concluded that the adoption of a hard

Chart 8.3 *Long-term interest rate: differential vis-à-vis Germany*

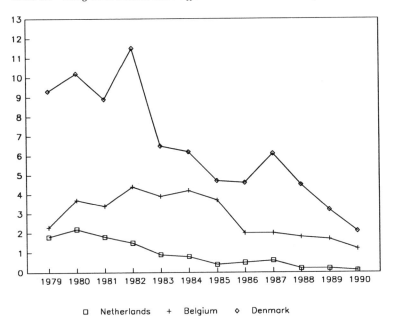

☐ Netherlands   + Belgium   ◇ Denmark

currency policy might have reduced interest rate differentials *vis-à-vis* Germany by as much as 1.1 to 1.5 points.

Denmark joined the EMS with a relatively high inflation rate and a long history of current account deficits. During the first years in the ERM it adopted an active devaluation policy. The Danish krone devalued by 10 per cent against the D-Mark in 1979 and 5.5 per cent in 1981. In 1982, Denmark announced it would seek a stable exchange rate in relation to the EMS basket. This declared fixed exchange rate policy was a significant change compared to the past devaluation policy and it contributed to a dramatic decline in interest rates and wage inflation (Andersen and Risager, 1988, p. 674–8). In consecutive realignments, it followed this linkage to the EMS basket.[2] However, this soft currency policy led to further devaluations against Germany, Denmark's main trading partner. The gradual nominal convergence in the EMS during the second half of the 1980s reduced inflation and interest rate differentials *vis-à-vis* Germany. In late 1989 Denmark joined the Euro-rounds of official discount rate changes, following changes in German official rates. Recently, Denmark has joined the low inflation group of countries as inflation and interest rate differentials in relation to Germany have almost disapppeared. Koen compares the rate of return bands implied by the ERM fluctuation margins with the actual interest rates and argues that, on a quarterly horizon, 'the Danish krone–D-Mark rate was not at all times perceived as free of devaluation risk' (Koen, p. 5). Based on the long-term rates, the credibility gap seems to have been even larger. Although Denmark has attained a remarkable convergence to German standards in the last few years, one cannot yet conclude that it has established a credible hard currency reputation.

Adjustment policies in the 1980s

The nominal convergence attained during the last decade did not come automatically, but has been achieved through the implementation of vigorous adjustment policies and austerity packages. All three countries have in various stages and in different degrees adopted a policy of wage moderation to restore levels of competitiveness lost during earlier years. Labour costs rose sharply in the 1970s and reduced profitability. Chart 8.4 shows the rate of change in normalised unit labour costs. Large increases in the early 1970s were followed by more moderate increases in the Netherlands and Belgium, while the increases in unit labour costs in Denmark remained high. Chart 8.5 illustrates what happened to competitiveness. Relative unit labour costs had risen in each country in the pre-EMS period and international competitiveness had deteriorated. The adjustment policies pursued in the 1980s will be discussed for each country in turn.

The Netherlands

During the 1980s, the Netherlands has registered the lowest price and wage increases among industrial countries. Wage moderation was on the agenda earlier than in other European countries. The 1970s were characterised by high wage increases and Dutch exporters had lost competitiveness, while profit margins had been eroded. In the centralised wage negotiatons, real wage claims had been based on economy-wide productivity growth that included the effects of the rapid increase in exploration of natural gas. High wages had eroded profit margins in the exposed sector and the share of labour in total income had risen from 78 per cent in 1971 to 92 per cent in 1980. Profitability of Dutch manufacturing was estimated to be 40–50 per cent of German profitability and 30–40 per cent of profitability in the United States.[3] The decline in profitability was reflected in a reduced rate of investment. The reduction of the share of labour in total income and the restoration of the profitability of Dutch firms became one of the main objectives of incomes policy.

For some years the government imposed wage restraint on social partners through incomes policy decrees. In 1980/81, cuts were made in the established practices of half-yearly full price indexation. Contractual

Chart 8.4 *Normalised unit labour costs: differential vis-à-vis Germany (percentage change)*

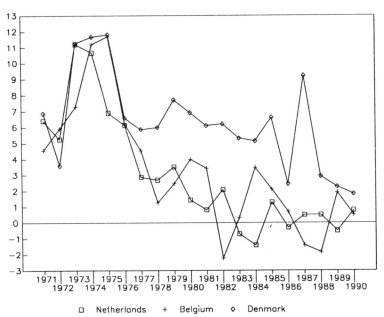

☐ Netherlands   + Belgium   ◇ Denmark

wages fell in both years by 3 per cent. In 1982, price indexation was restored for the average wage earner, but constrained by a flat rate ceiling. In later years, wage formation was left to free negotiations between social partners. In 1983, they agreed to abolish price compensation in exchange for a reduction in working hours. The idea was that this would increase employment, but in reality it helped to improve productivity and led to a rise in the profitability of firms. In the following years, wage settlements turned out to be very moderate, certainly by international comparison. Furthermore, the government reduced the legal minimum wage substantially, which increased employment prospects for the lower paid. These trends have made the development of unit labour costs very favourable for the Netherlands. It has also helped to offset the loss of competitiveness of Dutch industry, caused by the appreciation of the guilder in the ERM. Relative unit labour costs in 1990 were close to their 1981 level and profitability of Dutch firms has improved remarkably since 1980. The share of labour in total income has fallen to 79 per cent and is now close to what it was in the early 1970s.

Labour market performance has not been so favourable in the last decade. Unemployment rose considerably at the beginning of the 1980s and reached its peak in 1983 at 12 per cent, well above the European average.

Chart 8.5   *Relative unit labour costs: differential vis-à-vis Germany,*
1980 = 100

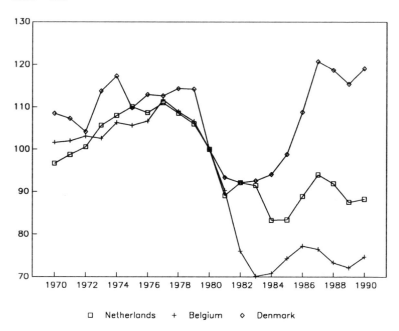

Although unemployment has fallen significantly since 1985, long-term unemployment stayed at a very high level, while the participation rate is one of the lowest in the world. The rising number of beneficiaries under the disability scheme also points to continuing structural problems in the labour market.

Belgium
When the EMS was set up in 1979, the Belgian economy was not in a healthy position. Throughout the 1970s, a number of domestic and external imbalances had accumulated and this was reflected in high and worsening unemployment, a loss of competitiveness, and widening public sector and foreign deficits. In 1981 the current account deficit was 4.5 per cent of GDP, the public sector deficit 13 per cent, and the unemployment rate was 10 per cent and rising. One of the main causes of these imbalances was the dramatic rise in real wages in the early 1970s. Between 1971 and 1975, the real wage rate in manufacturing rose on average by 8 per cent per year. The surge in wage costs was consolidated by a widespread system of wage indexation. Chart 8.4 shows the sharp rise in unit labour costs through the 1970s. It had resulted in a sharp fall in profitability of Belgian firms. The loss in

Chart 8.6   *Current account balances: differential vis-à-vis Germany (% of GDP)*

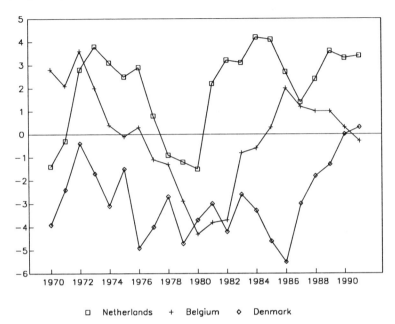

□ Netherlands   + Belgium   ◇ Denmark

competitiveness led to a deterioration of the current account and this put downward pressure on the exchange rate. Another problem was the rapid deterioration of the financial position of the government. Throughout the 1970s government consumption had risen and a generous social welfare system was developed. This had led to widening public sector deficits and a mounting public debt.

After 1982, when a new economic stabilisation programme was introduced, a major reorientation of policy took place. In order to restore international competitiveness, the Belgian franc was devalued by 8.5 per cent in the ERM. The normal mechanism of proportional indexation was suspended and consumer prices were temporarily frozen to prevent a new price–wage spiral. In addition, substantial cuts in public spending were announced. Although the suspension of wage indexation was later lifted, it was replaced by a flat rate system and real wages remained frozen till 1986, while a 'competitiveness norm' was set. This meant that the government could intervene in the wage formation process when the wage rise would exceed average wage growth, in common currency terms, recorded in the seven main trading partners. The slowdown in wage growth that was achieved was more marked than in many other countries and the profitability of enterprises improved. The combination of the 1982 devaluation of the franc and wage restraint led to an improvement of competitiveness. Relative unit labour costs decreased by 27 per cent between 1980 and 1983. The current account position improved significantly and since 1984 Belgium has recorded surpluses. Interest rate differentials with Germany were reduced and the monetary authorities gradually replenished foreign exchange reserves. Labour market conditions also improved, although unemployment remained high.

The government has introduced various measures since 1982 to improve labour market flexibility as part of a very active labour market policy. More stringent qualification conditions were introduced for the generous unemployment benefit and welfare system. As Layard, Nickell and Jackman (1991) stressed, if these changes were effective, they should have changed labour market behaviour. In addition, greater flexibility was introduced in the labour force's conditions of employment (in particular working hours).[4] However, long-term unemployment remains a serious problem. Special levies on labour income in the form of 'index skips' were introduced to finance labour market programmes and assist public finances. These stabilisation policies have led to some improvement in the public financial position. The general government's borrowing requirement fell from 13 per cent in 1981 to 6 per cent in 1990. Government deficits recorded in the 1980s, however, have been much higher than those recorded in other European countries. The net public debt–GDP ratio has risen to 120 per cent and a substantial part of this is held abroad. Primary fiscal surpluses have been recorded since 1985 but these have not been sufficient to stabilise the debt–GDP ratio. The corrective policies of wage restraint, fiscal consolidation and the move towards a hard currency policy in the EMS seem to have had a favourable impact on the Belgian economy, which has now achieved much closer convergence with Germany than in the early 1980s.

Denmark

The Danish economy has changed dramatically over the last decade. Severe imbalances that had built up through the 1970s have been markedly reduced. By 1982, the economic situation had become increasingly difficult. Denmark had had a long history of uninterrupted current account deficits. The string of deficits over more than two decades had led to an accumulation of foreign debt of 36 per cent of GDP in 1983. Wage costs had accelerated and the competitiveness of Danish firms had deteriorated. The public sector deficit had risen to 9 per cent of GDP. With widespread uncertainties in the financial markets, interest rates had reached record high levels, which led to rising interest payments. In 1982 a new coalition government took office and introduced a comprehensive stabilisation programme. The medium-term objective was to stimulate a strong expansion of production and employment in

Table 8.3   *Unemployment rates*

	Netherlands	Belgium	Denmark
1978	3.43	7.24	7.29
1979	3.49	7.50	6.19
1980	4.13	7.89	7.00
1981	6.26	10.16	9.16
1982	8.82	11.89	9.79
1983	11.16	13.17	10.44
1984	11.18	13.21	10.06
1985	10.05	12.31	9.05
1986	9.18	11.63	7.82
1887	8.66	11.32	7.83
1988	8.28	10.28	8.59
1989	7.37	9.29	9.32
1990	6.47	8.79	9.58
1991	6.46	8.84	9.79

the private sector, in particular the export sector, and to reduce the size of the public sector. The programme consisted of the following elements: a policy to maintain a stable exchange rate in the ERM (a reversal of earlier devaluation policies); the implementation of an incomes policy to improve competitiveness and lower inflation; and a sharp tightening of fiscal policy to reduce the budget deficits. It was hoped that this would lower inflation and interest rates and gradually also improve Denmark's external position. The incomes policy package included a suspension of the automatic wage indexation scheme and ceilings on wage increases. These policies were maintained for the following years and significant and rapid progress was made in bringing the public sector balance into surplus.

The fiscal contraction was accompanied by an unusually strong expansion in the subsequent four years. It is suggested that the factors that contributed to the surge in private consumption were the financial wealth effects due to the fall in interest rates and the associated rise in house prices. Giavazzi and Pagano (1990) argue that these direct effects cannot fully explain the expansion and that the part left unexplained can be attributed to changes in expectations about future fiscal policy. The experience of Denmark would show that fiscal contractionary measures can be expansionary if they are believed to be 'part of a credible medium-run program of consolidation designed to permanently reduce the share of government in GDP ... (and thus) taxation in the future' (Hellwig and Neumann, 1987, p. 137–8). However, a process of financial liberalisation (similar to that in the United Kingdom) may have also contributed to the expansion of demand.

Table 8.4   *GDP growth*

	Netherlands	Belgium	Denmark
1979	2.4	2.1	3.5
1980	0.9	4.3	−0.4
1981	−0.6	−1.0	−0.9
1982	−1.4	1.5	3.0
1983	1.4	0.4	2.5
1984	3.1	2.1	4.4
1985	2.6	0.9	4.3
1986	2.0	1.6	3.1
1887	1.1	1.9	−0.7
1988	2.7	4.3	−0.4
1989	4.0	4.0	1.3
1990	3.4	3.5	0.9
1991	2.0	2.2	0.9

Source: *European Economy.*

However, competitiveness deteriorated further as unit labour cost continued to rise by more than in Denmark's main trading partners, due to weak productivity performance and an effective appreciation of the krone. This caused a further weakening of exports, while imports were boosted by the strong growth of private consumption. In 1986 there were signs that the economy was overheating with increasing wage pressure and rapid consumption growth, caused by wealth effects due to the rise in real estate prices and the dramatic fall in interest rates. The government responded with a deflationary policy package to tighten fiscal policy and dampen credit-financed consumption by new legislation and tax reforms (the 'potato diet').[5] This deflationary policy and the subsequent fall in real estate prices led to a fall in private consumption and resulted in two years of negative GDP growth in 1987 and 1988. This was in sharp contrast to the emerging boom in the rest of Europe. A positive effect of this recession was the reduction in inflation that was achieved and the improvement in the external position. The current account moved into surplus in 1990 for the first time for 27 years. A heavy price was paid in terms of unemployment though, which rose to almost 10 per cent.

ERM effects and the cost of disinflation

The corrective policies pursued in the three countries have some striking similarities. The main feature of the adjustment programmes has been to restrain wages in order to improve international competitiveness. Whilst this was achieved in the Netherlands largely by free wage negotiations between the social partners after 1982, in Belgium and Denmark wage rounds were settled by government or parliamentary intervention for many more years. Such strict incomes policies are controversial though and, judged by final outcomes, the effect of past incomes policies seems to have been small.[6] More recently, the emphasis has shifted to the improvement of general labour market conditions and wage incentives from labour market institutions.

There is some evidence that the disinflationary policies have led to changes in the wage determination process. Membership of the ERM has meant increasing anti-inflation reputation, which may have changed the price expectations formation process, and/or changed the underlying structures of the wage determination process. Expectations may be based on past and current experiences and it may take some time before an announced anti-inflationary policy becomes credible. Such a policy shift will affect the wage formation process. Anderton, Barrell and McHugh (1991) found that in the majority of ERM countries a downward shift in the wage determination process has occurred. They report several structural stability tests to which estimated wage equations are subjected. In general, they found that for the majority of ERM countries, wage equations estimated over previous years tended to overpredict wage growth in the 1980s. The downward shift in wage formation was particularly clear in Belgium in the period till 1984, while there seemed to be a stabilisation in the second half of the decade. The results for the Netherlands also support the view of a downward shift in the early 1980s. The results for Denmark are less clear, although there is arguably some evidence of a downward shift from 1988. These shifts in wage determination have clearly been associated with the harsh policy measures that have been introduced in these countries and which seem to have succesfully signalled the anti-inflationary resolve.

One of the factors that determines wages is unemployment. High and rising unemployment will put downward pressure on wage setting. When the long-run effect of unemployment on wages is small, then the implication is that for a given disinflation a high sacrifice must be paid in terms of unemployment. Dornbusch (1989) argues that ERM membership can give rise to high 'sacrifice ratios'.[7] All three countries have had relatively modest growth in comparison with other EC countries. Although Denmark experienced relatively buoyant growth in the early 1980s, this was followed by a slump in the second half of the decade. Large and persistent labour market imbalances are also features that all three countries have in common. Even when total unemployment has fallen, long-term unemployment remains high.[8]

The relatively poor economic performance of these countries seems to give support to the view of high sacrifice ratios. The anti-inflationary reputation has been acquired at the expense of output loss and higher unemployment. The structural change in wage determination that Anderton, Barrell and McHugh (1991) found appears at least in some countries to be related to a parametric shift of the unemployment coefficient in wage equations. This implies that there has been a fall in the sacrifice ratios related to disinflationary policies, as the increase in unemployment required for a given reduction in inflation has fallen. During the 1970s unemployment had a small or even insignificant effect on wage setting, but this effect has risen in the 1980s. A larger influence of unemployment on wages is desirable, in particular for countries with a history of high inflation, as it reduces the costs of disinflation.

Table 8.5 gives an indication of the changes in wage flexibility that have occurred in the 1980s. It shows the significant structural changes in the long-term effect of unemployment on wages for each of the three countries. The wage equations are similar to those reported in Anderton *et al.* (1991), but a parameter shift in 1982 is included. For the Netherlands no significant change in the unemployment parameter can be found. However, for Belgium there is evidence of a structural change. The effect of unemployment on wage setting was insignificant before 1982, but is significant in the years after 1982. After the shift we can say that in the long run a 1 percentage point rise in unemployment would lead to a 0.5 per cent fall in wages. Wages appear to have become more flexible in the second half of the decade, or at least more responsive to unemployment. A similar parameter shift appears to have occurred in Denmark. The long-run effect of unemployment on wages is larger after 1982 and the change is significant. Before 1982, a 1 percentage point rise in unemployment was associated with a 0.5 per cent fall in wages, while after 1982 the results suggest that the long-run effect can be as high as 3.2 per cent.[9]

The evidence in table 8.5 is based only on a simple test for structural breaks,[10] but the results are informative. Previous sections have described the changes in unemployment benefit systems, such as more stringent

Table 8.5   *Structural changes in wage determination*

| | Long-run unemployment effect | |
	Before 1982	After 1982
Netherlands	−0.0106	−0.0106
Belgium	..	−0.0058
Denmark	−0.0055	−0.0323

Note: The long-run relationship is $W/P = a + bU + cT$, where W/P *is the real wage,* U unemployment and T the tax wedge.

qualification conditions, and the measures that have been implemented to improve the flexibility of the labour market. Layard, Nickell and Jackman (1991) stress that such measures may lead to a higher influence of unemployment on wage determination and increased wage flexibility. There appears to be evidence of this in Belgium and Denmark. This implies that the sacrifice ratios have fallen, and that the cost of disinflationary policies have been reduced.

Convergence and preconditions for monetary union

The Maastricht Treaty for Economic and Monetary Union states specific convergence criteria for transition to the final stage of monetary union. These are: an inflation record of less than 1.5 percentage points above the, at most, three best performing countries; no excessive fiscal deficits, by which is meant a budget deficit exceeding 3 per cent and a stock of gross public debt exceeding 60 per cent of GDP; having respected the narrow fluctuation margins in the ERM without realignments for at least two years; and long-term interest rates not exceeding that of the, at most, three best performing countries by more than 2 percentage points. Not all these criteria are binding. In particular, the second criterion on budgetary positions is formally only a guide for judgement. Although it can be derived from the 'Golden Rule' formula, it seems somewhat arbitrary as simple EMS averages. In its simplest form, the equation that gives the required primary balance for the debt–GDP ratio to stabilise at its present level, is $p = (i–g).d$, where p is the primary balance, i the nominal interest rate, g the nominal growth rate and d the desired or present debt–GDP ratio.[11] This simply states that the non-interest surplus must be large enough to offset the snowball effect, that is, the increase in the debt–GDP ratio due to interest payments.

Inflation and interest rate differentials have converged sufficiently to German rates, as is clear from charts 8.1 and 8.3, and no realignment has taken place since 1987. At present, Denmark would satisfy all four criteria, although its record on inflation and interest rate convergence is too short to meet the specified two years examination period. Belgium and the Netherlands do not meet the budgetary conditions.

Belgium's position is most precarious. Since the early 1980s, when it was recognised that the public sector had to be reduced in size, fiscal policy efforts were concentrated on reducing public sector dissaving. Fiscal deficits gradually fell to nearly 6 per cent of GDP in 1990, from a peak of 13 per cent in 1981 (see table 8.6). Primary surpluses, that is, excluding interest payments, have been recorded since 1984, but gross general government debt has continued to grow during the 1980s to about 133 per cent of GDP. To overcome the so-called snowball

Table 8.6   *Public sector finances (% GDP)*

	Netherlands		Belgium		Denmark	
	Fiscal deficit	Public debt	Fiscal deficit	Public debt	Fiscal deficit	Public debt
1979	3.7	43.0	7.3	74.0	1.7	27.0
1980	4.0	45.9	9.2	79.9	3.3	33.5
1981	5.5	50.3	12.8	93.4	6.9	43.6
1982	7.1	55.5	11.0	102.3	9.1	53.0
1983	6.4	61.9	11.3	113.4	7.2	61.6
1984	6.3	66.1	9.0	118.6	4.1	65.9
1985	4.8	69.6	8.5	122.7	2.0	64.1
1986	6.0	71.3	9.1	127.2	−3.4	58.3
1987	6.6	75.2	7.1	131.7	−2.5	56.3
1988	5.2	77.5	6.6	133.7	−0.2	57.9
1989	5.2	79.7	6.6	130.7	0.7	58.0
1990	5.4	81.7	5.8	130.1	1.4	59.2
1991	4.7	83.4	6.1	131.6	1.6	60.0

Source: OECD, *Economic Outlook*, and *European Economy*.

effect, through which the government is forced to borrow to service its debt, larger primary surpluses must be achieved than have been so far. More than half of today's debt is due to interest payments made over the past decade.[12] Although the snowball effect seems to have come to a halt now and the net debt ratio appears to have stabilised in recent years, this is mainly due to higher GDP growth. The budgetary situation is highly vulnerable to variations in the rate of economic growth. Furthermore, much of the public debt is of a short-term nature (one quarter of total debt has a maturity of less than one year) while foreign currency debt amounts to nearly 20 per cent of GDP. This also makes future budgetary positions very vulnerable to changes in exchange rates and interest rates. The official announcement in 1990 of linking the franc more closely to the strongest currency in the ERM should help to bring interest rates down and facilitate fiscal consolidation. However, a drastic reduction of public debt is desirable in order to offset the effects of an anticipated increase in pension payments in the next decade due to the ageing of the population. More severe reductions in public expenditure are needed and it seems inevitable that the burden will have to fall on social expenditure and public employment, as government investment has already been drastically reduced, from 3.6 per cent of GDP in 1980 to 1.4 per cent in 1990. The extremely high public sector indebtedness, the highest in the OECD after Ireland, remains Belgium's most severe handicap.

Although the Netherlands would, at present, like Belgium, not meet the budgetary condition for EMU, its financial position is less precarious.

Public deficits have been large throughout the last two decades, but smaller than in Belgium. Despite the efforts of various coalition governments to reduce budget deficits, primary deficits have still been recorded in the last few years and the gross debt–GDP ratio has risen to over 80 per cent of GDP. Further cuts in public spending are urgently needed to achieve the primary surpluses required for stabilisation of the debt–GDP ratio. Most of the fiscal cuts so far have been made in government investment, which has fallen from 3.3 per cent of GDP in 1980 to 2.3 per cent in 1990, low by international standards. The meagreness of present levels may risk the quality of the infrastructure and seem to rule out any further cuts. The burden will have to fall on social spending and further cuts in the Dutch welfare system are expected in the near future. The government's objective to stabilise the debt–GDP ratio by 1994 is expected to be met one year earlier. Compared with Belgium, the Dutch fiscal position is less worrying. The Dutch authorities have always pursued fairly conservative methods of debt-financing. No debt has been issued in foreign currency and the Dutch position has always been that the public sector deficit must be financed domestically from private sector savings, which have by international standards been relatively high. Large current account surpluses have also facilitated the financing of the deficits. Also in contrast to, for example, Belgium, the prospect of an ageing population is less alarming, as the government pension fund has assets of almost 40 per cent of GDP to match its future liabilities of the same amount.[13] Its future financial position is therefore less vulnerable to anticipated demographic developments than in many other countries. Despite this, Blanchard *et al.* (1990) argued that there is a substantial long-term sustainability gap when pensions and the effects of ageing on public health care spending are taken into account.

The financial position of Denmark's public sector has changed dramatically in the early 1980s, and Denmark is one of the few countries that has registered budget surpluses for much of the second half of the decade. The turnround in public finances was the result of substantial spending cuts and tax increases. Denmark has presently some of the highest tax rates in the EC. Fiscal consolidation was also facilitated by relatively low initial debt.[14] Although recently higher public deficits have been recorded, these have not been excessive and may well disappear in the near future. Denmark's major handicap in the last decade has been its low domestic private savings, reflected in the string of current account deficits. These culminated in a high foreign debt, which peaked at 40 per cent of GDP in the mid-1980s, and large interest payments abroad. One of the causes of the turnround in the external position in 1990, when for the first time since 1963 a current account surplus was recorded, was the delayed effect of the recession. Foreign debt has fallen to around 35 per cent of GDP, but although private savings have risen in recent years, it remains to be seen whether a structural improvement in Denmark's external position has been achieved.[15]

Conclusions

The 1980s were characterised by a remarkable nominal convergence in the three smaller member countries of the ERM. Inflation and interest-rate differentials with Germany have almost completely disappeared now. The Netherlands has been in a de facto monetary union with Germany for some time, while Belgium joined this pseudo union in 1990. Denmark's experience in the ERM has been more diverse, but it has recently achieved a noticeable convergence. The convergence has not come about automatically, but vigorous adjustment policies have been implemented in each country over the last decade. There is evidence that some of these harsh measures have been effective and have reduced labour market rigidities. It appears that the effect of unemployment on wage setting has risen over the last decade. This may have facilitated convergence and reduced the cost of disinflation. Progress on fiscal consolidation has been less impressive. Belgium's public debt is one of the highest of the industrial countries and the rise in the Dutch public debt has not come to a halt. Efforts to reduce budget deficits and to stabilise public indebtedness have not been very succesful in either country so far. More measures are urgently required.

Notes

1 Factors that could explain the long-term interest rate differential are the relative thinness of Belgian capital markets, which may cause an upward bias in interest rate differentials, and increasing concerns about Belgium's fiscal stance (see Koen, 1991, p. 6–7).

2 In March 1983, the Danish krone actually revalued against most other ERM currencies. Only by heavy intervention and a large increase in interest rates could the considerable speculative pressure be resisted.

3 OECD Economic Survey, Netherlands, 1984, p. 16.

4 OECD, Economic Survey, 1987/88.

5 The key measure was the cut in the tax value of the mortgage relief deduction and the deduction for other interest.

6 Incomes policy measures can only influence negotiated wages, but almost half of the wage increases consists of wage drift (see, for example, OECD Economic Survey, Denmark, 1989/90).

7 Robertson and Symons (1991) claim that membership of the ERM has increased the cost of deflation for low-inflation countries, but lowered the cost for high inflation countries. Anderton, Barrell and McHugh (1991) do not draw the same conclusion, however.

8 A higher ratio of long-term unemployed may reduce the effect of unemployment on wage setting. For the Netherlands, Graafland and Huizinga (1988) find that the downward pressure from the long-term unemployed on wage

setting has become smaller, which indicates the relevance of insider–outsider considerations.

9 These figures indicate the scale of the effect of unemployment on wage bargaining, but the effects on wage and price inflation depend upon the dynamics of the whole wage and price system.

10 More tests are reported in Anderton *et al.* (1991).

11 This suggests that the relevant concept is the *net* debt–GDP ratio. For practical purposes, though, the Maastricht Treaty refers to gross debt–GDP ratio.

12 OECD Economic Survey, Belgium, 1990/91, p. 86.

13 Keuzenkamp and van der Ploeg (1991), p. 232.

14 Public sector assets exceeded its liabilities before 1978.

15 Nielsen and Sondergaard (1991) examine equilibrium and disequilibrium causes of the external indebtedness.

9

Real and Nominal Convergence in the EMS: the Case of Spain, Portugal and Greece

Bénédicte Larre and Raymond Torres*

Introduction

Over the last five years the functioning of the EMS and its macroeconomic impact have stimulated economic research. Not surprisingly, there is little consensus on the extent to which the EMS system has produced positive effects in countries with high inflation rates. Some economists are of the view that EMS participation can bring inflation down only at the price of a deep recession. Others minimise the adjustment costs, and stress that joining the EMS strengthens credibility of the anti-inflation resolve of governments. However, what is usually not questioned is, first, that in the short to medium run, joining the EMS with high rates of inflation does imply some cost in terms of output and employment and second, that rates of inflation will eventually converge (in the longer run) across countries.

The main aim of this chapter is to show that these two conclusions may be wrong, especially in the case of South European economies, with living standards below the average of other EMS countries. Greece joined the European Community in 1981, Spain and Portugal in 1986. Among these three countries only Spain participates in the exchange rate mechanism of the EMS (since June 1989). Before explaining the basic framework, it may be useful to describe underlying trends in these countries. Chart 9.1 plots their inflation rates over the last twenty years. Inflation performance was very similar in the 1970s, but the 1980s saw some notable divergences. Greek inflation has remained in the range 15–25 per cent during the last ten years, whilst inflation has been reduced somewhat in Portugal. The Spaniards have had a great deal more success in bringing their inflation into line with the rest of Europe. However, even Spain continues to record relatively high inflation: 1.5 percentage points

* The views expressed are those of the authors and do not necessarily reflect those of the OECD.

Chart 9.1 *Inflation: Greece, Spain and Portugal*

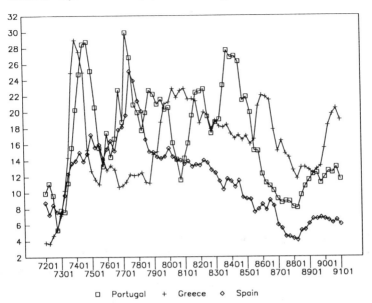

Source: OECD.

above the OECD average, and 2.5 points above the core EMS countries average. The cumulative inflation differential since 1985, when Spain joined the EC, is 15 per cent and the peseta has appreciated in nominal terms *vis-à-vis* other EMS currencies, bringing the real appreciation to nearly 20 per cent over the last six years. Even so, Spanish exports have significantly outpaced export market growth and the basic balance of payments remains in comfortable surplus. A similar conclusion stands for the Portuguese escudo, although it does not (yet) belong to the ERM of the EMS. By contrast, the Greek economy combines a fragile balance of payments position and a continuous nominal drachma depreciation.

Can South European countries sustain a positive inflation differential?

In theory, a positive inflation differential can be explained by two sets of factors. First, to the extent that an economy is catching up, prices have to grow faster than in more developed countries, leading to an 'equilibrium' differential. Secondly, structural rigidities may lead to 'disequilibrium' inflation, while at the same time inhibiting the catch-up process.

The catch-up process and equilibrium inflation

Analysis of the process whereby the less advanced economies catch up with the more advanced ones does not come explicitly within the province of the neo-classical theory on which modern economics is founded. However, starting from the equilibrium conditions of the neo-classical growth model, it is possible to highlight the various aspects of the catch-up process and the implications for output and price convergence.

In the neo-classical growth model, average labour productivity is a function of the efficiency of the economic system (also known as the rate of technical progress) and the average quantity of capital goods per worker (or capital intensity). In other words, the more efficiently the means of production are used and the greater the amount of productive equipment, the higher the average income. Neo-classical theory thus explains the international disparities in labour productivity described earlier, primarily by technological backwardness and a shortage of capital.

In neo-classical growth theory, the efficiency of factors of production is determined by technology, or more broadly by the 'stock of useful knowledge', to use Kuznets' expression. To the extent that there is no impediment to the dissemination of technological knowledge, the efficiency of the way factors of production are used is thus related intrinsically to the ability to assimilate this knowledge.

Olson (1982) and Abramowitz (1986) have made major contributions to the analysis of technological progress and diffusion. According to them, living standards do indeed converge over the long term, but the speed of catch-up and the economic rise and decline of nations are determined to a large extent by the existence of a 'favourable environment' comprising both economic factors (particularly the degree of development of market mechanisms), social factors (level of education), sociopolitical factors (pressures from lobbies, social structures, property law), cultural and other factors. The existence of a favourable environment determines an economy's long-term level of efficiency and the speed at which it moves towards this level, thus influencing both the level and rate of growth of productivity.

In a recent article, Lucas (1990) expanded the neo-classical model by adjusting the rate of technical progress (which is considered to be exogenous and identical in all economies) for the effect of the accumulation of human capital on productive performance. The recent literature on endogenous growth cited in this chapter has both widened and deepened our understanding of the growth process. In particular it helps us understand developments in these three countries.

In steady-state equilibrium the marginal rate of return on capital is determined by the rate of technical progress and labour productivity. These two variables operate in opposite directions. The more efficiently factors of production are used, the higher the rate of return on capital.

On the other hand, the higher labour productivity is, the lower the rate of return on capital. This is so because, in the neo-classical model, the returns on factors are considered to be diminishing. Capital accumulation raises labour productivity but lowers the marginal return on capital.

The inverse relationship between labour productivity and the return on capital shows that, when differences in income levels do not reflect technological backwardness, autonomous forces exert powerful pressures towards catch-up. In this view, therefore, catch-up is a spontaneous process. These spontaneous forces result in investment flows to low-income countries – attracted by the high returns to be found there – or in labour migration. The more developed countries have imposed a wide range of immigration controls, which proves that part of the workforce from the poorest countries is sufficiently skilled; hence, the backwardness of the poorest countries cannot be explained solely by technological factors.

As there are fewer impediments to capital movements than to migratory flows, investment, along with technology, is one of the main means of catching up. Investment and technology are basically complementary to one another. The diffusion of technical progress may indeed be autonomous, but it can also be embodied in the capital goods acquired from the most advanced countries, primarily via two channels: resident economic agents import technology, or foreign firms set up in the country, in turn importing or producing investment goods. However, these two forms of catch-up have different macroeconomic effects; when the catch-up is of a technological nature, it enhances total factor productivity, whereas when it is via capital accumulation it results rather (to the extent that technical progress is partially autonomous) in a narrowing of the gap between labour productivity levels.

Imperfections in factor and goods markets may make investment in low-income countries more uncertain, thereby reducing the expected rate of return on capital. Overall, the determinants of domestic and foreign investment, which are notoriously difficult to quantify, may be divided into three categories. First, the effective marginal productivity of capital, which in an open economy is essentially a function of the cost of inputs and their productivity: second, the degree of uncertainty attaching to the profitability of an investment: and third, institutional factors, and particularly impediments to the free domestic and foreign circulation of goods and factors of production.

Accession to a customs union like the European Community boosts both the actual and expected rate of return on capital. To the extent that imports are used as inputs in domestic production, the removal of customs barriers results in a reduction of average and marginal production costs. The greater the share of imported inputs in total inputs, the greater the resulting improvement in the rate of return on capital. This supply-side effect is accompanied by a demand stimulus, since the removal of import barriers and the resulting relative fall in import prices causes domestic real disposable income to rise.

From the macroeconomic standpoint, the dismantling of market barriers means that tradeable goods and services will have the same prices in different countries. In contrast, the price levels of non-tradeables will be lower in the less developed countries; this is why there is an inverse relationship, identified by Balassa (1964), between per capita income and purchasing power parity. Relative wage levels also diverge in the long run across countries in line with the differences in marginal productivity between them. As Southern European countries catch up with EC average productivity, real wages could rise at a higher rate than elsewhere. Consumer prices as a whole will rise more rapidly since price levels in the non-tradeables sector will move closer to those in the tradeables sector. During the catch-up phase, inflation rates in the less-advanced countries will thus diverge somewhat from those in the rest of the Community. The differential will be smaller if the nominal exchange rate in the less-advanced countries is allowed to appreciate.

Hence, a positive inflation differential does not necessarily point to a loss in external competitiveness to the extent that this is accompanied by a rise in living standards and an upgrading of the production structure of the economy. The structural changes associated with the catch-up process will cause price aggregates to rise more rapidly in poor relative to rich countries. A poor region, which offers a higher profit rate than average, attracts 'foreign' investments, thus exerting pressure on existing resources (demand effect) while at the same time upgrading output.

In sum, neo-classical theory shows that countries can catch up through two main channels: technological progress and capital accumulation. But the existence of a favourable environment and sufficiently developed market mechanisms is also essential, though these are difficult to single out from other factors and to quantify. During the catch-up process (that is, to the extent that productivity grows more rapidly than in more developed countries), an upwards adjustment in the price level takes place, leading to a positive inflation differential that is sustainable for some period in time. It is of course difficult to quantify the scale of equilibrium inflation differential for the countries we are discussing, but it has been suggested that it could be between 1–2 per cent. If this is the case then countries that are catching up can be expected to experience a real exchange rate appreciation of this magnitude. The latter are equilibrium properties, in the sense that they reflect a favourable investment environment.

Disequilibrium inflation

Experiences of European economies, even with comparable living standards, suggest that rates of inflation may fail to converge across countries in the face of shocks. Monetary authorities may prefer to accommodate a certain rate of inflation, as it would imply a sizeable adjustment cost in terms of output and job creation, that is, a significant degree of slack would be required in order to bring inflation down to its target.

The size of the slack that is 'necessary' to bring inflation down by a certain proportion depends upon two main sets of factors. First, according to the credibility theory, it all depends whether agents believe in the anti-inflation resolve of the central bank. The degree of independence of the central bank, the public-debt burden, the size of the public deficit and in certain countries the actual level of foreign exchange reserves (as a guarantee for the value of the currency) may be important determinants of credibility.

Structural factors, notably regarding the wage formation system, market imperfections and rigidities, may also increase the cost of disinflation. To the extent that a temporary rise in prices is quickly embedded into the wage–price setting, expectations for high inflation are boosted, thus raising the real costs for reducing inflation. The degree of indexation of an economy crucially depends upon the kind of institutional wage–price formation system. It has been argued that centralised and very decentralised wage bargaining systems traditionally favour relatively low inflation rates, whereas in countries with systems in between, inflation is relatively high. The exchange rate regime may be another important element. A flexible exchange rate system may reduce the credibility of monetary policy, so stimulating inflation expectations in the face of inflationary shocks.

Structural impediments to lower inflation

This section reviews the main structural weaknesses of the three Southern European countries, some of which may explain the high inflation proneness in the three economies. The rapid growth of the 1960s and early 1970s masked the structural problems of the Southern European countries. These became more visible in the wake of the first oil shock. EC membership and the opening up of markets that it brought with it forced the pace of structural adjustment.

Despite Spain's 1970 trade agreements with the EC, and Greece becoming a Community member in 1981, these two economies were still relatively sheltered from foreign competition in the mid-1980s. In Spain, a traditionally protectionist country, asymmetrical conditions prevailed after the 1970s: tariff barriers were maintained even though the other European countries had dismantled their quantitative restrictions on a wide range of exports from Spain. Greece was in the same situation. It obtained access to the Common Market in the early 1960s for many classes of exports, while maintaining its tariff barriers and levying special import taxes. These barriers probably explain in some measure why Greece's production structures and trade specialisation have remained virtually unchanged since the end of the 1960s.

By contrast, in terms of the weight of foreign trade in GDP, the openness of the Portuguese economy in 1980 was already comparable to that of the major European countries. The explanation lies in its membership of EFTA and its long tradition of trading with the colonies and Brazil. At the time of joining the European Community, its tariff barriers were 5 per cent, equivalent to EC rates, against 17 per cent in Spain. However, import licences and quotas were still in force.

By comparison with the rest of the Community, agriculture still accounted in all three countries for a large share of value-added and employment. The level of agricultural productivity was half the EC average (a quarter in the case of Portugal). Geographical factors apart, there are many reasons for the poor performance of the agricultural sector: heavily-subsidised prices, a rural population with too low a level of education to make proper use of modern production techniques, inadequate infrastructures (roads, electricity, irrigation, and so on) and inefficient distribution channels.

In Greece, the land reform of the 1950s resulted in a proliferation of smallholdings. In Portugal, misgivings dating from the 1974 expropriations deterred investors for many years; in 1985, investment accounted for only 3 per cent of agricultural value-added, against an EC average of 20 per cent. However, the agricultural labour force constitutes a resource that can contribute to the catch-up, provided the skill level is improved.

As in other OECD countries, the weight of the public sector together with wide-ranging price controls has hampered the free play of market forces. Public enterprises, used to differing degrees for short-term regulatory purposes (to boost activity), and often not managed in accordance with economic criteria, have accumulated substantial losses constituting a heavy drain on savings. Central government subsidies and capital transfers have helped to keep loss-making enterprises afloat and have been detrimental to efficient resource allocation.

In the mid-1980s, financial markets were still in their infancy, with some distinctive features: little or no competition between banks and financial institutions, a large proportion of public corporations serving non-financial objectives set by government; narrow capital markets; a limited range of savings instruments and a preponderance of public debt securities; credit controls (Greece and Portugal) and administratively fixed interest rates; compulsory portfolio requirements for banks; and a high proportion of subsidised credit. The variety of regulations made for poor resource allocation and transaction costs were generally higher than elsewhere.

The three countries still had both social (education and health) and economic infrastructures (communications) that lagged far behind those of the other European countries, all of this creating an environment that made it difficult for these countries to catch up. Thus, in Spain, at the end of the 1970s, over two-thirds of the male population in the middle-age group (25–44 years) had completed no more than the compulsory period of primary schooling (over 80 per cent in the case of Portugal), whereas in most of the other European countries the proportion was under 50 per cent. Technical and vocational training was also inadequate, especially in Portugal where only 5 per cent of young people were receiving any such instruction in the mid-1980s. In 1985, while infant mortality in Spain was close to the European average, in Portugal and Greece it was considerably higher. In addition, poor roads, transport systems and telecommunications in the three countries undoubtedly hampered development and were a cost to the productive system.

The trade liberalisation that the Southern European countries' membership of the European Community brought with it has been gradual. Well before the formal date of membership, trade agreements had been signed with member states and a transitional period was subsequently provided for, varying in duration according to the country and products concerned. At the same time, over the past ten years or so, as in several other OECD countries, microeconomic reforms have been implemented on several fronts to promote structural adjustment. The process varied in scale and timing across the three countries. In the early 1980s, even before joining the EC, Spain had begun to reorganise its hardest hit industries, while labour market reforms brought some wage restraint. A little later, in 1984, Portugal embarked on a gradual process of market reform, beginning with the financial markets, a process that gathered momentum with the coming into office of a new government in 1985. Greece, though it joined the EC before Spain and Portugal, did not fully dismantle its tariff barriers any earlier. Tariffs were brought into line with EC rates only in 1986 and the import tax was not abolished until 1989.

The catch-up

It is difficult to establish direct links between structural reforms and the catch-up process. Reforms operate on a number of fronts, they are spread over time and interact in a number of ways. In addition, it takes some time for economic agents to react to new conditions, and the general thrust of macroeconomic policy also plays a part. However, diverging trends in the three Southern European economies can shed some light on these links.

During the 1960s and early 1970s, the boom in investment and the adjustment in productive structures greatly stimulated income growth in the three countries. Investment ratios were high – more than 20 per cent of GDP on average over the period. Value-added in industry grew by more than 10 per cent per year. The level of industrialisation, which was still relatively low in all three countries at the start of the period, meant that there was considerable potential for rapid growth. Real GDP grew at an annual rate of some 7 per cent between 1960 and 1973, compared with an average of 5 per cent for Europe as a whole leading to a narrowing of income differentials.

In the aftermath of the first oil shock, relative levels of per capita income fell in all three countries. The steep increase in investment gave way to a pronounced decline caused partly by the fall in exports; furthermore, the political uncertainties of 1974–5 in the three countries meant that the climate was not conducive to either domestic or foreign investment. Lastly, the worsening public finance situation may also have had a crowding-out effect. Since 1985, the catch-up has been fairly brisk in Spain and Portugal, where relative incomes are virtually back to the levels of the early 1970s, but not in Greece where the income differential widened compared with the other OECD countries.

The growth of relative per capita income, adjusted on the basis of purchasing power parities, may usefully be broken down into three components: first, the growth of total factor productivity (TFP), which measures the gains in the productive sector's efficiency; second, the change in the ratio of inputs (employment and capital stock) to the number of inhabitants. This ratio reflects various factors, including demographic variables, the participation rate of the population of working age and unemployment; and third, the change in the terms of trade, which depends on (exogenous) fluctuations in raw material prices and (partly endogenous) changes in production and foreign trade patterns. Such a breakdown of relative per capita incomes shows that the increase in the employment–population ratio has been the main factor behind income growth in Spain; since the mid-1980s, labour productivity has not increased much faster than in the other OECD countries. By contrast, in Portugal TFP gains have been the main engine of income growth. In Greece, all the factors referred to have contributed to a relative decline in per capita income.

The intensity of investment in Spain and Portugal has had a positive impact on productivity and the employment–population ratio, two components of relative incomes. In Spain, productivity in those sectors which have been the targets of foreign investment has risen twice as fast as the national average. In aggregate terms, growth of labour productivity undoubtedly slackened in the second half of the 1980s, but this was due to the slowdown in the process of capital–labour substitution caused by wage restraint. Total factor productivity, which is adjusted for the substitution effect, has in fact accelerated since 1983–4. There is a link between productivity and investment. All in all, investment in Spain and Portugal has resulted in both substantial job creation and more efficient economic systems. In Greece, on the other hand, the persisting sluggishness of investment has caused both productivity and the volume of employment to level off.

That living standards have evolved differently in the three countries is due partly to the fact that Spain and Portugal were quick to lift import barriers and export subsidies. In Greece, on the contrary, the impediments to free trade were removed slowly. The result was that Spain and Portugal enjoyed a sharp improvement in their terms of trade immediately after joining the EC, the positive impact being all the greater in that tariff barriers and import quotas had been high prior to membership. The 'trade creation' effects easily outweighed the 'diversion' effects. The only exception was in agricultural products, on which Community tariffs were on average higher than those applied by the countries of Southern Europe prior to their joining. In Greece the improvement in the terms of trade in 1981–2 was small. Supply-side restructuring increased the terms-of-trade gains in Spain and Portugal, the concentration of production in the most efficient sectors generating economies of scale.

However, progress was uneven in reducing market rigidities. Far-reaching labour market reforms are still needed in the three Southern European countries, both to ease the legislation in force and to improve the quality of labour supply. In Spain, the flexibility of the labour market was enhanced by the introduction of fixed-term employment contracts, which also opened the way for part-time work and employment-training programmes. As a result of these measures, the new jobs could be adapted to changes in supply and demand conditions. But flexibility was in fact confined to new jobs, and regulations with respect to permanent employment remained virtually unchanged. In Portugal too, fixed-term contracts were used to enhance the responsiveness of the labour market. Real wages were also remarkably flexible. The labour legislation reforms of February 1989 eased the restrictions on individual or collective layoffs and improved unemployment insurance; some provisions were also introduced to regulate the application of fixed-term contracts. In Greece, on the other hand, the regulations on part-time work, overtime and fixed-term contracts have not been eased and the system of wage formation is fairly rigid.

There have been further differences in the evolution of the economies of these countries. The size of the public sector has been reduced in Portugal and Spain by way of privatisations and efforts have been undertaken to reduce public deficits. By contrast, the Greek public sector is oversized and the PSBR exceeds 20 per cent of GDP. (Further details on macroeconomic developments in these countries can be found in Chapter 1.)

The effects of the contrasting developments are most strongly brought out by comparing developments in Greece and Spain. Structural reforms

Chart 9.2   *Developments in the Spanish economy*

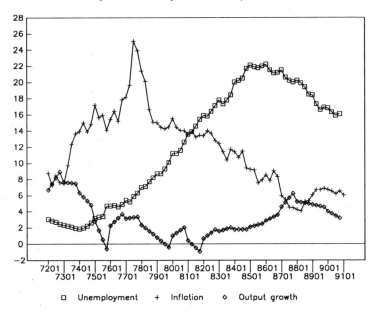

Source: OECD.

in combination with restrictive aggregate demand policies have been major factors behind the reduction of inflation in Spain. Chart 9.2 plots output growth, unemployment and inflation in Spain. Unemployment rose steadily from 1974, and between 1978 and 1982 output growth was also slow. As a result some spare capacity developed in the economy and inflation fell slowly. The contrast with Greece is clear. Chart 9.3 plots the same variables for Greece. Inflation has remained high, and although unemployment rose in the early 1980s, it remained low by European standards.

The inflation performance in Spain

Among the three countries, only Spain fully participates in the EMS. In that country, wage moderation and, since 1985, favourable import price developments appear to have been the main factors behind the fall in inflation since the end-1970s. But excess demand has stimulated profits, so preventing inflation from easing further in recent years. Service prices are particularly buoyant; by contrast industrial prices have moved broadly in line with foreign prices, thus implying a squeeze in industrial profit margins. The latter were high by all standards in the mid-1980s, explaining the subsequent rather limited costs of inflation. However, it

Chart 9.3   *Developments in the Greek economy*

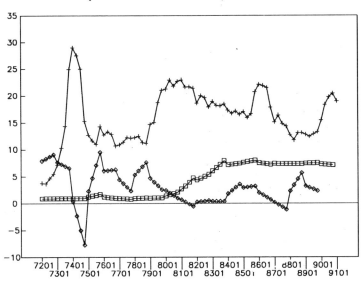

Source: OECD.

appears that inflation has not been just a result of an equilibrium catch-up of relative prices, and it is clear that there are disequilibrium structural factors behind it. This may cast doubts on the sustainability of the present expansionary phase in a context of quasi-fixed exchange rates.

Evidence of disequilibrium inflation

There are indeed signs of a relatively strong inflation proneness in the Spanish economy. During the second half of the 1980s, inflation in the services sector (excluding rent) exceeded inflation in the manufacturing sector by two percentage points, the strongest differential among OECD countries after Australia. In fact, even during the early 1980s, at a time when the economy was very weak, service prices again outpaced industrial prices. By contrast, in many other countries during that period, service prices were growing broadly in line with industrial prices. This suggests that in Spain services prices quickly react to expansionary shocks, while the response to recessionary shocks is much slower. The analysis of sacrifice ratios provides additional evidence of the relatively high inflation proneness exhibited by the Spanish economy. Evidence produced by the OECD indicates that the rise in unemployment or the loss in output necessary to bring inflation down by one percentage point is twice as large in Spain as in other EMS countries.

With fixed exchange rates in the next phases of monetary union, credibility of monetary union may be even further reinforced. Nevertheless, structural factors leading to some degree of inflation proneness may still persist, so rendering the adjustment to inflationary shocks more costly. The lack of competition in the services sector, labour market rigidities and inadequate public services tend to increase the inflation stickiness of the Spanish economy.

Wage formation and the labour market
Econometric results show that in Spain the response of wages to unemployment is very weak. Disinflation forces could have been much stronger had wages and labour markets been more flexible. The duality of the labour market, which comprises permanent workers enjoying a high degree of protection by international standards, and temporary workers with relatively precarious job contracts, is a key factor. The very rigid rules that protect permanent workers make them excessively immune to overall economic trends. In case of 'economic' dismissals, a prior administrative authorisation is required in Spain, and dismissal costs (two years of salaries in some cases) are high by international standards.

As a result, temporary contracts, which can be renewed for six-month periods up to a maximum of three years, have become widespread, explaining all of the net job creation (two million jobs) since 1985. However, many employers (in particular in small enterprises) are reluctant to transform temporary contracts into permanent ones, suggesting that the cost involved is too high compared with the benefits of having a stable well-trained workforce. This has produced detrimental effects on overall productivity, as skills acquired by temporary workers are partly lost if they have to find another job. It has also increased frictional unemployment.

The very limited professional and regional mobility of labour is another important hindrance to the functioning of the labour market. In a third of enterprises, the old labour legislation, the so-called 'ordenanzas laborales', are still in force. Hence, the various tasks in the enterprise are irrevocably attributed to specific workers, eventually leading to productivity losses. At the regional level, the high cost of housing strongly deters mobility of employment. Moreover, the scheme which provides an income support to agricultural workers ('empleo comunitario') could be abolished so as to enhance regional mobility and prevent abuses.

The inefficiency of the public employment offices (INEM) is notorious, probably increasing the natural unemployment rate by exerting insufficient controls. A related problem is that employers cannot rely on INEM to fill job vacancies, so that 95 per cent of hirings are effected directly by the firms. Private employment offices are not allowed in Spain, which is at odds with the successful experience of such labour intermediaries in some other OECD countries, such as France. These problems have been compounded by the extension of unemployment benefits to temporary workers, further increasing the opportunity cost of work (and the natural unemployment rate).

The strong deterioration of external competitiveness, combined with the greater openness of Spain, has produced a shift out of sectors necessitating low skilled workers. This has strengthened the need to intensify training. The government, with the help of the EC social fund, has elaborated well-designed training programmes, but these are administered by INEM, which may not be very efficient.

Many aspects of the 1940 system of wage negotiations, which involved a very rigid nationwide industrial branch-based framework, still operate in Spain. The specific situation of individual enterprises and regions appears to play a limited role in the wage formation process. In most cases (that is, for 75 per cent of Spanish workers) the level of wage earnings as well as general work conditions are decided at the national, or industrial branch level. This system may deter investments and the creation of new enterprises in underdeveloped areas. As a result, the very high level of unemployment prevailing in poor regions such as Extremadura has had little impact on wages. On the contrary, even though wage levels were already close to the national average in 1988, they have rapidly increased ever since. This may have contributed, together with the lack of infrastructure, to the limited amount of foreign direct investment that flows to this part of the country.

Lack of competition in the services sector and inadequacy of
public services
Prices for most services have risen rapidly, and their rate of increase has been significantly above average. The most inflationary items in the services price index are transport, private health and medical services, private education, restaurants and domestic services. In the last two cases, there are some catch-up effects, the price levels of those services being rather low by international standards. However, in the case of transportation, private health and education, high inflation is more due to the lack of competition and inefficiencies in the provision of public services. Collusive behaviour stems from the intervention and various regulations introduced by liberal professional syndicates (the so-called 'colegios profesionales') which set minimum prices and impose barriers to entry. Moreover, the private transport sector is highly regulated, with the state fixing tariffs which usually increase rapidly during expansionary periods and moderately during recessions.

Despite the expansion of public spending (notably investment) the infrastructure equipment of the country seems to remain insufficient and inadequate. There is widespread dissatisfaction with the public health system, which explains the shift to private doctors and hospitals. The public education system raises similar problems. As for the transport system, the limited (if any) improvements in the railway network and delays in the improvements of roads are notorious. Moreover, there seems to have been some overlap of projects, notably as regards the connection between Madrid and Seville, capital of Andalucia, one of the poorest regions in the country. It has been decided that the two cities should be connected by high-speed train (the first in Spain) and a high-speed motorway, the international airport terminal of Seville has been greatly enlarged and modernised, and the main road access to the city improved (including the construction of a ring-road). Although this upgrading of connections and communications with less developed regions may be justified on equity and efficiency grounds, the superimposition of so many costly projects is more difficult to understand.

Costs of inflation and policy constraints
The fact that the disinflation process appears to have slowed down raises the question of the cost of inflation. Inflation has been accompanied by a widening of profit margins in the service sector and a profit squeeze in industry. Sectors exposed to international competition have only slightly increased prices, so that the real exchange rate measured by industrial-price inflation has only marginally deteriorated since EC entry. By contrast, unit labour costs have progressed significantly faster than both domestic industrial prices and foreign unit labour costs. As a result, industrial profit margins have fallen both in absolute terms and *vis-à-vis* Spanish competitors.

The persistence of a positive inflation differential owes more to disequilibrium processes associated with structural rigidities and excess demand than to the equilibrating process of relative price adjustment associated with catch-up itself. However, it is clear that so far the costs for the economy have been rather limited. First, Spanish exports have largely outpaced world markets. Hence the sharp deterioration in relative unit labour costs does not appear to have affected competitiveness conditions of the export sector. Second, foreign direct investment in industry has continued to increase from the already very high levels reached in 1987, suggesting that Spanish industry continues to enjoy favourable conditions by international standards.

Nevertheless, as the recent weakening of both exports and foreign investment suggests, action is needed to avoid a premature break in the expansionary phase. Both developments may however be the result of the slowdown in activity in Europe as a whole, and there does not appear to be an emerging balance of payments problem, as deficits are supported by structural capital inflows. These direct investment inflows are a major factor in the catch-up process.

Conclusions

The example of Spain shows that the combination of EMS membership and structural deficiencies poses a serious problem for the flexible operation of monetary policy. In 1989–90, in order to reconcile EMS constraints and internal objectives (that is, reduce money supply and inflation), controls on domestic credit expansion and on foreign capital inflows were imposed. In early 1991, most of these restrictions were removed. Capital controls allow the authorities to keep interest rates higher than they would otherwise be, and this tighter monetary stance has helped to offset the effects of fiscal policy. Once capital controls are removed the need to make clear policy choices becomes more pressing. To the extent that the peseta cannot appreciate further within the EMS, monetary authorities are short of instruments to combat inflation, stressing the need for tackling the main underlying sources of inflation.

More generally, the analysis of the experience of the economies of Southern Europe suggests the following. First, the good economic performance of Spain and Portugal is attributable largely to foreign investment and the existence in the early 1980s of substantial unexploited resources, mainly an abundant supply of cheap labour. Second, structural reforms have given a considerable boost to investment, the most effective measures in this regard being the deregulation of the labour market, and in particular the introduction of more flexible methods of recruitment and the lifting of restrictions on imported goods following EC membership. Third, the example of Greece shows that the increased welfare to be gained from the opening-up of markets is all the more limited when supply conditions are not improved. By helping to make economies more flexible and adjusting production structures, structural reforms permit rapid growth while at the same time avoiding unsustainable disequilibria. Finally, catch-up is not therefore a spontaneous process, but depends very much on the degree of development of market mechanisms and the quality of social and economic infrastructures.

Criteria for macroeconomic convergence between these economies and the rest of Europe are not easy to establish. Moreover, as shown in this chapter, it is not clear that macroeconomic convergence is desirable. Indeed, persistence of inflation differentials may be a property of a sustainable macroeconomic equilibrium even in a fixed exchange rate system. In the case of Spain, there is evidence that the inflation differential has been mainly due to catch-up effects, as it goes hand-in-hand with structural change. Thus, the strength of foreign capital inflows and sizeable export market gains suggest that the positive inflation differential has not fundamentally affected the external competitiveness of the Spanish economy. More recently, however, remaining structural rigidities have played an increasing role, leading to some kind of disequilibrium inflation. In the context of a booming economy, the persistence of labour market imbalances, insufficient infrastructures and public service systems and the lack of competitive forces in certain service markets have led to an increase in aggregate inflation, so eroding profitability of the exposed sectors. The question of how long the Spanish economy can sustain this unbalanced growth process is difficult to answer. In any case, we would argue that successful participation in the EMS requires action on the structural front.

10

An Ecu Zone for Central and Eastern Europe: A Supportive Framework for Convergence

Stefan Collignon

The widening of the European Community in the wake of European Monetary Union sets an even more ambitious challenge of economic performance convergence for potential applicant countries than for the twelve existing members of the Community. For the twelve EC countries can count on a wide range of coordination and support mechanisms, such as the European Monetary System with the Exchange Rate Mechanism, the Common Agricultural Policy or structural funds, while outside applicants have to make all the efforts alone in order to converge to the established norms of the Community.

However, the difficulties are not the same for all potential candidates. In the countries which were part of EFTA, and now form the European Economic Space, market economics has been well established for many years, while countries in Central and Eastern Europe are only beginning to restructure and learn the rules of the new market mechanism. For these latter countries, economic convergence means simultaneously the institutional establishment of economic norms compatible with the European Community and adjustment to these norms. The speed of this adjustment will determine if and when the fast-reforming countries of Central and Eastern Europe will be able to join the Community.

This chapter will concentrate on the challenges of economic convergence in the fast-reforming countries in Central and Eastern Europe, as this is the most difficult problem to solve. That former EFTA countries have an easier task to converge becomes apparent when one takes the rate of inflation as the predominant norm indicator; Austria, Norway and Switzerland have been close to the EC standard and to either the D-Mark or the Ecu for some considerable time. Sweden is less in line with these performances but recent policy changes express a strong commitment to reduce inflation and maintain a fixed Ecu-peg (see charts 10.1 and 10.2). It is therefore not unreasonable that those countries will be able to achieve the necessary convergence on their own account. It is, however, much less likely that the fast-reforming countries in Central and Eastern Europe will be able to restructure their economies, stabilise macroeconomic

Chart 10.1   *Inflation differentials for Finland, Norway and Sweden vs Germany*

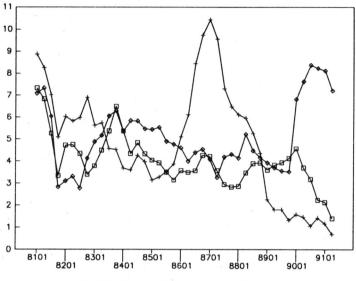

Source: Datastream.

Chart 10.2   *Inflation differentials for Austria and Switzerland vs Germany*

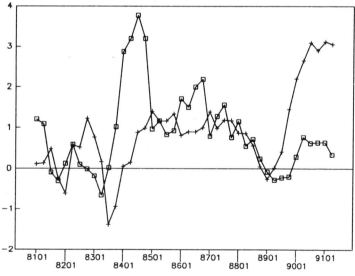

Source: Datastream.

Chart 10.3   *Monthly inflation over a year previously for Hungary and Czechoslovakia*

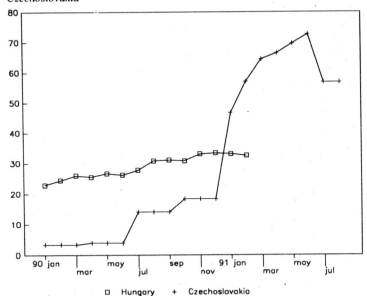

Source: Datastream.

Chart 10.4   *Monthly inflation over a year previously for Poland (000s)*

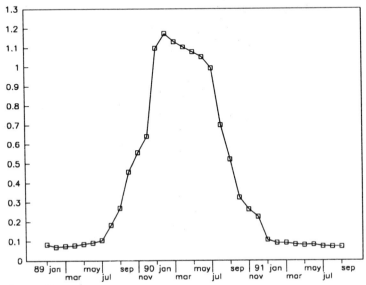

Source: Datastream.

performance and converge to the EC norms without outside support. Charts 10.3 and 10.4 give information on recent inflation performance. We will therefore look, first, at the specific difficulties arising out of the systematic transformation process, and subsequently consider the proposal of the creation of an Ecu zone as an institutional framework for monetary cooperation between East and West.

Economic stability and currency convertibility as fundamental norms of a monetary economy

In a centrally-planned economy, money has only a very limited role as a 'lubricant' for consumer transactions while resources are allocated by the plan. Accounting units are 'material quantity coefficients'. Real resources, rather than money, are used as 'stores of value'. Hence the use of money is not fully developed.

If money is used as a unit of account, and simultaneously as a store of value, it fulfils a function as a means of deferred payment. This effectively means that the promise to pay later establishes credit contracts between economic agents, in exchange for which a title of ownership is issued. Thus, with the phenomenon of credit, there is a counterpart created which is capital, that is, the right of ownership over resources. Some of the essential functions of money were therefore missing in the former centrally-planned economies.

The consequences of this amputation of money functions have been important, because money as a means of exchange was always readily available and never scarce. However, resources were scarce in the planned economy and hence served as a store of value. This in turn contributed to the shortage of goods in these economies (Riese, 1991).

From these considerations it follows that if money is to be the store of value, it is going to become scarce. The three prime tasks of systematic transformation are, therefore, the creation of so-called legal property rights, which lie at the root of ownership titles and are necessary to provide collateral for credit; adequate control of money in order to make it valued so that agents will always agree to exchange their goods against it; and that once money has become scarce it becomes convertible into commodities, but the true litmus-test of money's scarcity is its external convertibility. These tasks establish three policy axes.

First, *privatisation* represents the systematic change in property rights and economic decision making. It necessitates a reliable legal framework and, ultimately, its purpose is to make the supply side of the economy more elastic and efficient so that it may respond flexibly to the price signals of the markets.

Second, *price liberalisation* is to give companies the autonomy to manage resources and production in accordance with monetary market signals, subject to a hard budget constraint. Third, *currency convertibility* in internal and external markets requires a coherent and stable macroeconomic environment, so that microeconomic price signals can operate as a rational incentive structure. Without trade liberalisation and external currency convertibility, integration into world markets is incomplete and resources are not used in the most efficient way. The success of privatisation is therefore partly dependent on this macroeconomic framework.

Early convertibility can speed up the transition to a market economy by providing the discipline of foreign competition; by 'importing' foreign price ratios and allowing trade liberalisation to suit the conditions of world markets (thereby opening up the domestic market and providing economies of scale); by speeding up the process of creating property rights (Bofinger, 1991); by providing an exchange-rate peg as a nominal anchor for macroeconomic stabilisation policies; and by preventing the disintegration of traditional trade links with former CMEA partners.

Several countries in Central and Eastern Europe and, in particular, Poland, Czechoslovakia and Hungary, are now firmly committed to programmes designed to achieve both privatisation and full convertibility. However, most of them have so far stopped short of removing all exchange restrictions on current account transactions (Greene and Isard, 1991), not to mention the capital account.

Other countries more to the east, and in particular the republics of the former Soviet Union, are still at the beginning of the systemic transformation. The uncontrollability of budget deficits and money creation in the Soviet Union which is due to a number of political, social and economic contradictions, pushes in the direction of each republic trying to take control individually, issuing its own currency and attempting separate stabilisation. The success of these stabilisation attempts will always have to be measured against the norm of currency convertibility.

The benefits of currency convertibility

According to the OECD definition, full convertibility allows residents and non-residents to exchange national currency against foreign currency or against other foreign commercial or financial assets (Aglietta, 1990). Therefore, in order to achieve currency convertibility, certain basic requirements have to be fulfilled. Price reform must have created an environment in which economic agents are free to respond to the signals of economic scarcity. Sound macroeconomic policies must establish that money is scarce. An adequate level of international liquidity has to be available. Finally, an appropriate exchange rate has to be set and a mechanism to maintain it has to be found.

Currency convertibility is ensured if outflows of payments for goods, services and capital do not exceed the inflows except for short periods.

However, the monetary flows related to commercial and financial assets (capital movements) are far more volatile than those related to transactions in goods and services (the current account balance without debt service). The former depend on a general evaluation of asset security and interest rates, the latter on the competitiveness of exchange rates. It may therefore be necessary to restrict capital flows for some limited time by means of capital controls. The controls can be progressively lifted, provided that the elasticity of the supply side has improved, so that adjustment to exchange-rate changes takes place at lower social costs, and after a reasonable degree of confidence in the stability of the new regime has been established. Ultimately capital account convertibility responds to the norms of a market economy. Before Eastern European countries are able to join the EC which, by that time, would use the Ecu as a single currency, they need to have achieved full convertibility, including capital accounts. But the way to get there may be a gradual one.

It is commonly accepted that current account convertibility for residents and non-residents is essential for the integration of domestic price structures with the world economy and should therefore be established most rapidly,[1] as this has beneficial effects for reforms in the real sector (Bofinger, 1991). On the other hand, capital account convertibility can help to attract resources from abroad (Greene and Isard, 1991). The willingness of foreign investors and companies to move capital into a country crucially depends, firstly, on investment security, that is, whether or not the interest, after-tax profits and initial capital outlays can be fully repatriated. Secondly, it depends on expected yields of the investment projects and these are a function of competitiveness at a set exchange-rate level.

An undervalued currency renders export production profitable, and imports expensive. It is therefore likely to attract productive investment for exports. Inversely, an overvalued currency supports imports and discourages investment in export industries. The resulting current account surplus encourages borrowing abroad and therefore increases the use of finance capital at the expense of local savings. Therefore, an undervalued currency can help to establish credibility of the reforms, for the improvement of export performance is consistent with the convertibility commitment and long-term growth. On the other hand, an overvalued currency would encourage heavy borrowing in foreign currency, but the resulting current account deficits will undermine confidence in the sustainability of the policies pursued. The threat to credibility increases with the degree of overvaluation with respect to the long-term equilibrium exchange rate (Edwards and Edwards, 1987).

The effectiveness of convertibility in attracting private capital inflows is a consequence of a successful combination of a stable legal (political) and economic environment with a competitive exchange-rate policy.

Exports will then improve, long-term foreign capital will start flowing in and foreign currency reserves increase. The creditworthiness and reputation of the currency is strengthened. Yet this too may turn out to be dangerous. For if the greater credibility is to attract capital inflows, particularly of short-term 'hot money', to a degree that significantly appreciates the exchange rate, the long-term benefits of an undervalued currency are lost and the credibility of reforms will collapse. It is therefore paramount to stabilise exchange-rate fluctuations in order to maintain the long-run viability of the reform process.

The stability of the exchange rates poses the problem of choosing a currency to peg against. If the purpose is to stimulate growth, rather than stabilise debt repayments, then the currency, or a currency basket, of the main trading partner should be selected and the debt portfolio adjusted in order to eliminate detrimental effects of a possible currency mismatch (Collignon, 1990). For Central and Eastern Europe, but also for the Western republics of the former Soviet Union, this choice should clearly be the Ecu.

Whatever nominal anchor is chosen, it is of paramount importance to generate confidence that exchange-rate expectations will be stabilised. Convertibility could prove to be counter-productive, if governments lose the popular support for their policies and have to abandon their commitment to sound macro policies and convertibility. It may therefore be desirable to strengthen the confidence and the credibility of reform policies by providing some outside support. The creation of an Ecu zone intends to address this problem.

How to achieve currency convertibility

The most direct route to convertibility is to restrict domestic expenditure, stimulate exports and encourage net capital inflows. Poland, Czechoslovakia and, to a lesser degree, Hungary, have tried to achieve this by dramatically reducing budget deficits (sometimes even achieving a surplus) and implementing large devaluations. Experience after one and a half years shows that it is possible to realise a certain degree of convertibility (primarily for current account transactions by companies and non-residents) within a short time, but this success is subject to an extremely harsh stabilisation programme causing not only a short-term fall in production and subsequent increase in unemployment, but also jeopardising future growth as the reduction in government expenditure prevents urgently needed investment in infrastructure. Furthermore, the initial maxi-devaluations were followed by a refuelling of inflation which requires a further tightening of fiscal and monetary policies. Consequently, social or political tensions have arisen that may ultimately lead to relaxation of the tight adjustment policies. Under these circumstances, the credibility of reform policies and thus of the convertibility commitment is easily lost. Clearly there exists a danger that Eastern Europe could fall into a vicious cycle of repeated unsuccessful stabilisation attempts of a Latin American type (Dornbusch, 1987, and Edwards and Edwards, 1987). One way out of this dilemma may be to 'borrow credibility from abroad'. Integrating a programme for currency convertibility in Eastern Europe into a long-term programme of economic convergence to possible membership of the European Community including monetary union and greater access to the Single Market could also help to secure popular support for reform policies when structural adjustment and external conditions start to hurt.

Outside support for currency convertibility
It would be naive, and even wrong, to believe that the outside support of Central and Eastern Europe could or should take the form of net resource transfers, similar to what happened in East Germany. Such transfers are not feasible in view of their scale and the burden they would impose on public budgets or private capital markets in the West; neither would they inhibit the development of an export-led growth strategy by keeping exchange rates overvalued and preventing excess demand for domestic products which would trigger the investment income mechanism.[2] The experience of devoloping countries has proved again and again trade is better than aid.

In view of these difficulties, some authors (Steinherr, 1990; Brabant, 1991; Aglietta and de Boissieu, 1991) have suggested a more gradual route to currency convertibility, following the example of the European Payments Union of the early 1950s. Others have suggested (Bofinger, 1991) a more stringent approach of incorporating Eastern Europe's currencies into the European Monetary System or even a monetary union. The proposal to create an Ecu zone, as outlined in the second part of this chapter, aims at a more intermediary and flexible transitory solution of providing outside support to monetary credibility (but not a net transfer of funds, except in the very short term).

The central idea behind the scheme of an Eastern European Payment Union is that the countries formerly united in Comecon have very deeply separated markets that cannot be bridged in the short run. Over time, their machine park will be replaced and competitiveness improved, enabling them eventually to change over to fully-convertible currency trade relations. According to this view, competitiveness is exogenous to the exchange-rate regime. The plan hinges on the assumption that the structures of production and trade in the former Comecon are of only very limited elasticity and substitutability (Aglietta and de Boissieu, 1991). This may be true in the short run, but does not fully take into account the effects of the very far-reaching systemic changes taking place in Eastern Europe. According to a study by the World Bank, experience in

Poland, Hungary and Yugoslavia in 1990 shows that exports can increase significantly in response to appropriate exchange-rate policies.[3] There is therefore evidence of a greater trade response to the exchange rate than generally assumed by the defenders of the Payments Union.

Furthermore, former Comecon trade relations were overshadowed by the weight of the Soviet Union. The fast-reforming countries of Central Europe found it unacceptable to be tied down by old trade patterns and a dominating partner, and this is why they have so far vehemently refused the idea of an Eastern European Payments Union. Nevertheless, although the breakdown of traditional markets has certainly made the burden of adjustments harsher in those countries than anticipated, it is clear today that there is no alternative to a rapid transition to currency convertibility in the fast-reforming countries. But for more slowly reforming countries, where the preconditions for convertibility, such as balanced budgets, trade liberalisation, and so on, have not yet been met, or where the structure of traditional trade patterns cannot be integrated into the world market before a fundamental reallocation of investment and capital has taken place, as in some of the previous Soviet republics, a Payments Union may prevent the complete collapse of trade and production (Dornbusch, 1991). Such a Payments Union could also use the Ecu as a reference unit and therefore complement the Ecu zone as an 'outer circle'.

The monetary approach to the problem of economic transformation which is also favoured by the IMF sees currency convertibility and competitiveness not as an exogenous phenomenon but rather as being dependent to a large degree on monetary (and fiscal) policies (Bofinger, 1991), therefore the exchange-rate regime is crucial. But the different economies of Eastern Europe each follow their own programme of reform, with different depths and speeds. This makes it impossible for them to be immediately integrated into the European Monetary System. What is therefore needed is a more flexible route to currency convertibility which will allow gradual convergence to the standards of the European Community. We propose to achieve this through the creation of an Ecu zone in Central and Eastern Europe.

The creation of an Ecu zone

The creation of an Ecu zone seeks to establish a 'community of solidarity' (*Solidargemeinschaft*) between the countries of Eastern and Western Europe. Both sides make sacrifices and both sides obtain benefits. It is suggested that 'after millennia of quarrels and wars Europe will finally become a space of friendly cooperation for all its inhabitants' (Havel, 1991). In this spirit, the creation of an Ecu zone in Central and Eastern Europe is to be seen as an antechamber to the European Community, preparing the future accession of those rapidly-transforming countries to the EC by opening the Single Market and providing a framework for compatibility and convergence with the standards of the Community.

In order to achieve this, a cooperation mechanism has to be set up. At its core stands the idea that the success of European integration has always been based on 'working together' rather than *'chacun pour soi'*. Furthermore, cooperation is not only needed between East and West, but also within the East.

It is therefore suggested that the countries in Eastern Europe who wish to be part of such a zone pool part of their foreign exchange reserves for use as collateral in a specially set up Eastern European Stabilisation Fund, to which a convertibility standby facility is granted by the European Community. The pooled funds will also be used for interventions in exchange-rate stabilisation. As we will see, despite its cooperative and multilateral nature, the mechanism is to function in a highly flexible and individualistic way, allowing each country to proceed with transformations at its own pace. Our proposal combines different features from the Payments Union approach, the Franc zone in Africa (Vizy, 1989 and Guillaumont, 1984) and the European Monetary System in a new and original way.

The instruments of monetary cooperation in the Ecu zone would be the Ecu Zone Surveillance Board, the reserve pool with the system of convertibility standby facilities (Eastern European Stabilisation Fund) and the Ecu zone exchange-rate mechanism.

The Ecu Zone Surveillance Board

The Ecu Zone Surveillance Board (EZSB) is the governing mechanism of the arrangement. Its functions are to ensure the management and proper functioning of the reserve pool and the system of convertibility standby facilities (that is, it will administer the Eastern European Stabilisation Fund, see below), to coordinate the Ecu zone exchange-rate mechanism and to monitor the compatibility of macroeconomic policies with the convertibility commitment and to ensure that sound policies are pursued.

The Board would consist of a small management team responsible for the day-to-day running of the reserve pool administration and its cooperation procedures. It would also have an Advisory Council of representatives from the Eastern European authorities and from the newly-created European Monetary Institute and also from the IMF. It may also prove useful to have the EBRD and the BIS represented in this Council.

The Council will conduct the surveillance on a permanent basis, aimed at detecting the emergence of external disequilibria and at fostering appropriate corrective action as early as possible. It will insist on necessary adjustments through the conditional clauses attached to the convertibility standby facilities (see below). Voting rights in the

Council would have to be subject to negotiation, but it is important that the Council cannot set conditions in contradiction with those of the IMF. The EZSB's specificity in comparison to the IMF lies in the very short-term convertibility standby facility aimed at providing added credibility to the local Eastern European countries and in the political fact that an institutional cooperation mechanism with the EC allows a gradual opening of the single market for Eastern European products in parallel with the progressive removal of current and capital account restrictions.

The Ecu Zone Surveillance Board would act as a forum for trade reforms to work in concert with monetary policies. This is important for two reasons. First, while the lifting of restrictions on capital account transactions may well generate a real appreciation, successful trade liberalisation would probably require a real devaluation of the domestic currency in order to help the export sector expand as the new structure of relative prices replaces the old protective structure (Edwards and Edwards, 1987).

Second, if the Single European Market is not opened to goods and services from Eastern Europe, growth in the transforming economies will stagnate, given the necessity of restrictive stabilisation policies. Hence, direct capital investment and foreign lending will cease after the initial competitive rush to occupy market positions, and debt service will become increasingly more difficult. It is therefore desirable, in the interests of all parties concerned, to have an institution which helps to manage and smooth these contradictions.

The Ecu zone also adds credibility to the political aim of becoming full members of the Community at a future date, thereby stabilising democracy in the transformation process. The Surveillance Board has an extremely important role to play in bringing economic and monetary policies in the participating countries into line with the standards of the European Community. It will serve to adjust economic policies in Eastern Europe to the long-term target of membership of the Community. In this respect it serves as a link between membership candidates and the Community. At a time when many new systems, regulations and procedures related to a market economy are installed, it is preferable to take into account and possibly to import EC legal and regulatory frameworks, rather than having to change them again after a few years. Within the European Community this learning and convergence process has been supported by the existence of the European Monetary System. For a variety of reasons, Central and Eastern European countries would not be able to join this system which, in any case, will disappear with the realisation of a single currency in the Community. The Ecu zone would provide an appropriate fallback position.

The creation of an Ecu zone as proposed here has the advantage of giving economic and political credibility to the transition period in

Eastern Europe. Sacrifices in terms of economic adjustment today may be more acceptable if it is clear that at the end of the road full membership in the prosperity club of the European Community is assured. The same applies to the 'luxury' (Portes, 1991) of national sovereignty; if the aim is ultimately EC member status which by definition implies loss of some sovereignty, why wait for what may never be reached rather than giving up some today and reaching the goal? The proposed scheme of an Ecu zone is therefore only applicable to countries that are truly willing and committed to becoming members of the Community.

The reserve pool with the system of convertibility standby facilities

In order to create an Ecu zone for Eastern Europe, an Eastern European Stabilisation Fund (EESF) will be set up *ad hoc*. The EESF will be administered by the Ecu Zone Surveillance Board.

The central banks of the participating Eastern European countries will open accounts with the Eastern European Stabilisation Fund to which they transfer a significant amount of their total foreign currency reserves, including reserves in the local currency of Ecu zone trading partners (that is, Zloty, Forint, and so on). A benchmark from the zone Franc is 65 per cent, but in the Eastern European market less may be required. The EESF accounts are denominated in Ecu. The central banks of the participating Eastern European countries are entitled to keep the non-deposited part of their foreign exchange liquidity in other currency outside the Ecu zone for current transactions. Foreign exchange reserves of private banks and companies can be independently held with outside institutions and would not normally fall under the reserve pooling requirement.[4] The amounts due to be deposited are reassessed on a quarterly basis in consultation with the Ecu Zone Surveillance Board.

The transmitted reserves are pooled by the Eastern European Stabilisation Fund and managed by the Ecu Zone Surveillance Board as a convertibility back-up and as an intervention fund for the Eastern European currencies. In exchange, the European Community through the European Monetary Institute (later the European Central Bank) sets up a system of convertibility standby facilities for all currencies participating in the Ecu zone.

The common reserve pool is used to provide cover for the Ecu zone countries' day-to-day foreign exchange requirements. In addition to the EESF account, each central bank operates a working account with the Bank for International Settlements (BIS) for its normal daily foreign exchange transactions. This working account is balanced on a daily basis by debiting the EESF reserve pool account if its balance is negative, or by crediting it if it is positive.

If all the countries' working accounts with the BIS lead to an overall deficit of the EESF account, the debit is covered by drawing on the European Community's convertibility standby facilities. The purpose of the BIS working account is therefore to express the individual foreign currency reserves of the participating Eastern European countries, while the EESF's account (reserve pool) is to indicate the aggregate reserve position of the region. The EC convertibility standby facility serves to upgrade credit balances in local currency into hard currency balances. Thereby, regional cooperation in the East and between East and West will be encouraged.

If a country carries positive balances on the BIS current account, these are remunerated at an interest rate which reflects the opportunity cost of alternative reserve holdings. Negative balances are debited according to a sliding scale of interest rates depending on the size of the deficit, with the intention of discouraging large imbalances.

The European Community's convertibility standby facility system consists of three facilities: the Very Short-Term Financing Facility (VSTF) of unlimited amount for 45 days, renewable once; the Short-Term Monetary Support (STMS), unlimited for six months, renewable once, subject to conditionality from the Ecu Zone Surveillance Board (EZSB); and the Medium-Term Financial Assistance, subject to conditionality from the EZSB. These funds may complement normal IMF lending and should be used rather sparingly.

This system of standby facilities is designed to provide primarily short and very short-term financing for balance of payments needs due to transitional difficulties and thereby assure the credibility of the convertibility commitment. Member countries are not to make use of the EC facility to meet sustained outflows of capital and therefore the Ecu Zone Surveillance Board must insist that appropriate adjustments in policies are made. In case of justified structural adjustment finance requirements, the IMF is to provide loans subject to the usual conditionality. The cooperation between the IMF and the Ecu Zone Surveillance Board (of which the IMF is a member) will ensure that sound macroeconomic policies prevail in the Ecu zone and this is the precondition (and guarantee) that those countries will make the necessary progress towards future EC membership. But the implied political commitment is likely to add to and to strengthen normal stabilisation programmes by the IMF.

The commitment by the EC countries to provide the necessary short-term standby funds establishes the credibility of the currency convertibility promise in the Ecu zone. However, this commitment does not imply unlimited and unrestrained access to foreign exchange by Eastern European countries (see p. 206). Being standby credits with limited duration they have to be repaid in hard currency at the agreed settlement date. If local currencies have been devalued in the meantime, their monetary authorities carry the risks and the costs.

The modalities of these standby facilities follow the model set by the European Monetary System credit mechanism: for other balance of payments financing the IMF would act as a lender. This establishes an operational hierarchy between the International Monetary Fund, the Ecu Zone Surveillance Board and the Eastern European countries. The reason for having a level between the IMF and the countries concerned is that the implicit political commitment would strengthen the credibility and social acceptability of adjustment policies and accelerate the East's access to the Community's single market.

The Ecu Zone Exchange Rate Mechanism (EZERM)
The exchange rates of Eastern European currencies are pegged to the Ecu. The level of this peg is to be chosen in such a way that exports at the prevailing rates are highly competitive. In the medium term, they will produce export surpluses. In this way the evolution of the foreign reserves in the reserve pool will prevent excessive drawing on the EC convertibility standby facility. The accumulation of foreign exchange will also improve the credibility and reputation of Eastern monetary policies, thereby facilitating the removal of barriers to the flows of capital and goods and services between East and West.

However, as we have seen, the opening of the capital account can result in the short run in large destabilising capital flows: excessive inflows lead to unsustainable currency overvaluations which ultimately need to be corrected by harsh devaluations. This volatility of exchange rates would prevent a consistent long-term strategy based on export promotion.

In order to stabilise the peg, exchange-rate interventions will be necessary. These interventions will be undertaken by the Eastern European central banks, who would buy their own currencies if they fell beyond the acceptable level against the Ecu. They would use the funds available through the EESF in order to purchase their own currency. Repurchasing of their own currency by central banks reduces their money supply and therefore contributes to monetary discipline and economic stability.

For their intervention the Eastern European central banks will, first of all, use the currencies deposited in the reserve pool of the EESF. This will have no impact on the money supply in the Community and therefore contains no risk of inflationary effects. If these funds are insufficient, Eastern European central banks can draw on the convertibility standby facilities. These facilities give access either to the EC Central Bank's own foreign exchange reserves (for example, US dollars) or to private Ecu created by the EESF. The lending of existing foreign exchange reserves leaves domestic money supply in the Community unchanged and therefore bears no risk. The creation of private Ecu by the EESF could cause an increase in domestic EC money supply if it were financed by drawing on central banks. This risk can largely be eliminated if the convertibility standby facility is financed by the treasuries rather than the central banks. The costs of contributing to the EESF would be shared by the twelve EC countries in proportion to their relative Ecu weights. In this way the solidarity of cooperation is assured.

The purpose of the Ecu Zone Exchange Rate Mechanism is also to provide a credible anchor for the domestic stabilisation efforts of the participating economies, and a synchronisation of their monetary, trade and economic policies with those of the European Community, leading the way to future entry of those countries into the EC.[5] However, this does not necessarily imply that fixed exchange rates would be desirable in order to stabilise the economy. In fact, if real wage reductions are resisted by some kind of indexation, or if substantial budget deficits are maintained, the resulting inflation would cause a currency overvaluation under a regime of fixed exchange rates.[6] This could interrupt the economic reform process, leading to widespread popular disenchantment which would further undermine the credibility of reforms. A slight currency overvaluation might be useful to bring single digit inflation rates to German levels, by increasing unemployment and thereby putting pressure on wages. But this strategy is inconceivable for bringing down double digit inflations, which are predominant after the internal price reforms in Central and Eastern Europe. Therefore, in view of the different strategies of economic development chosen by the countries involved, flexibility of exchange regimes in time and space is required.

The nature of the exchange-rate regime is to be decided by the Ecu Zone Surveillance Board in accordance with the specific requirements of each country. Several possibilities are conceivable.[7] First a fixed but adjustable peg with an Ecu central rate and relatively large fluctuation margins, similar to the exchange-rate mechanism of the EMS but with larger bands which may be gradually reduced. This means that the intervention fund requirements and therefore the costs to the EC would be less than they would be with narrower bands. Occasional readjustments of the central rates or reductions in fluctuation margins are allowed after agreement with the Ecu Zone Surveillance Board. Second, a crawling peg with preannounced nominal devaluations of the Ecu central rate is required in order to allow for the structural resistance factors in the early transition period to a market economy. It might be desirable to indicate that over a certain period the preannounced devaluations will be gradually reduced to zero, so that after the initial period the economy converges to a fixed but adjustable peg. Third, there should be a crawling peg with stable real exchange rates to compensate for inflation rate differentials with the EC. Here the purpose is to maintain competitiveness and possibly an undervalued currency. This may be useful in order to crowd in export production and thereby give an impulse to growth, but it is unlikely to increase trust and confidence in the currency, and is therefore unlikely to attract large volumes of foreign capital. It should therefore only be considered for a short period of time while price reform leads to unpredictable changes in the general price level.

In contrast to the European Monetary System, the participating countries in the Ecu zone would not necessarily all be subjected to the same regime. Each country could follow its own speed of development and economic reform, without being influenced or hindered by the performance of its partner countries. In view of the great variety of economic conditions and problems in Eastern Europe, a flexible approach to convertibility is required. Some countries may wish to change from one regime to another after internal economic conditions have changed. It is important that decisions are taken in conjunction with the Ecu Zone Surveillance Board, reflecting the need for economic cooperation, the general policy aims of convergence to EC standards and the convertibility standby facilities of the EC. It is likely that over time the Ecu Zone Exchange Rate Mechanism will resemble the present EMS. It is however necessary to present an adjustment mechanism if actual development deviates from the target, and to assess the potential costs and benefits of such a mechanism.

The adjustment process and costs and benefits of the Ecu zone

What happens if one or several countries encounter short-term foreign exchange difficulties?

The EC standby facility comes into play when the EESF account turns into a deficit, that is when the participating Eastern European countries collectively become a debtor to the rest of the world. In order to prevent such an event for more than very short periods the Ecu Zone Surveillance Board monitors the development of each participating country and indicates the appropriate action. Non-compliance will meet with the withdrawal of the standby facility. The resulting loss in credibility and access to finance is a powerful 'stick' to prevent misbehaviour.

The adjustment mechanism is triggered by the following arrangements. If a country's balance in the BIS current account remains continuously below 20 per cent of its reserve deposit at the EESF reserve account for more than 45 days, the EZSB can request the country's monetary authorities to raise interest rates, tighten fiscal and monetary policy or to take any other necessary measure in order to increase the country's foreign exchange reserves.

If the current account debit in the BIS approaches an amount equivalent to the foreign exchange deposit at the EESF, or even exceeds it, additional adjustment measures are required. The Ecu Zone Surveillance Board can request that the national central bank increases its reserve deposit with the EESF by drawing on the other 35 per cent of its reserves or ask the central bank to draw on foreign exchange held by commercial banks and financial institutions in the public and private sector outside the central bank. If these measures are insufficient, the central bank can be obliged to increase its reserve pool deposits by drawing on its IMF facilities, and thereby to submit to IMF conditions of sound macroeconomic policies. If the reserve loss is due to fundamental imbalances, the central rate against the Ecu is readjusted. Simultaneously, the Eastern European economic and monetary authorities have to comply with the Ecu Zone Surveillance Board's recommendations for internal adjustment. Parity adjustments are to be undertaken only after 'multilateral approval' by the EZSB and must be part of a more far-reaching adjustment package. If a country refuses to implement the necessary adjustment measures, the convertibility standby facility system is withdrawn. Given the reserve deposit, this should cost the other countries of the Ecu zone little, but would have serious consequences for the credit rating of the country concerned, most probably leading to an immediate suspension of currency convertibility. In view of the significant drawbacks it is unlikely that a responsible government would refuse to cooperate. The mechanisms for adjustment may appear harsh and may imply a certain loss of national sovereignty, but they are a guarantee that sound macroeconomic policies will prevail and this is a precondition for currency convertibility and open markets.

The convertibility standby facility system is essential in strengthening confidence in local currencies and convertibility in hard currencies. It increases the creditworthiness of all participating countries. Therefore the accumulation of credit balances between two different Eastern European countries will attain the same status as hard currency balances with the West. This would contribute to the stabilisation and further development of regional trade. Furthermore, increased credibility and creditworthiness is a way of encouraging private capital inflows. Under those circumstances it is likely that foreign exchange reserves in Eastern Europe would increase rather than diminish. It is therefore possible that the convertibility standby facility may not even have to be used. The simple fact that it exists may be enough to improve internal stability. The risk of drawing on the standby facility would only occur when the aggregate balance of reserve pool deposits became negative. Given the control mechanism through the Ecu Zone Surveillance Board, this is not very likely for any considerable period of time.

As mentioned above, the creation of an Ecu zone would require sacrifices and provide benefits for both Eastern and Western Europe.

The potential costs of the Ecu zone
For the European Community the greatest risk lies in excessive drawing from the unlimited convertibility standby facility for current account

Table 10.1   *Foreign exchange reserves and current account in Poland, Czechoslovakia and Hungary*

	GDP 1990 (bn Ecu)	GDP relative weight compared to EC %	Convertible currency current account as % of GDP(1990)	Foreign exchange reserves IV/90 (m.Ecus)	Foreign exchange reserves as % of current account deficit
Poland	50.6	1.03	−2.4	3651.6	301
CSFR	37.8	0.80	−1.1	895.9	215
Hungary	26.1	0.50	−0.3	869.1	1110
EC12	4895.5	100.0	0.003	0	0

Source: World Bank (1991) and IMF.
Note: 1 Ecu = $1.23.

operations. However, the risk is contained by its very short-term nature. The danger of pumping money into a bottomless hole is to be avoided by the Surveillance Board and the reserve pool.

Two parameters may help to evaluate the potential risk: the current account deficit and the amount of foreign exchange reserves. Assuming that the scheme is at first restricted to Poland, Czechoslovakia and Hungary, the relative weight of these economies compared to the EC in terms of GDP is low. The 1990 deficit of these three countries was 1.7 billion Ecu or 1.5 per cent of their collective GNP. Foreign exchange reserves are also high: estimates for the end of 1991 are all in excess of 2.5 and 3.5 billion Ecu, a considerable improvement on the previous year. One should therefore not overestimate the potential costs of such a convertibility standby system.

The opening up of the Single European Market to products from Eastern Europe may also be considered by some partial interests in the West to represent a cost, but overall increased supply of competitive goods is a benefit, particularly if the opening of the markets can be managed in a coordinated and gradual way.

The Eastern European countries participating in the Ecu zone are required to surrender part of their economic sovereignty if the foreign reserve condition requires an adjustment process. But in the long run, the same is true of the need to cooperate within the framework of the European Community. This is, of course, a political choice. One cannot participate in economic cooperation, let alone in a Community, and maintain unlimited sovereignty. But if these countries wish to join the European Community at some future date, as they proclaim, then it may be better to make the decision now, when new systems are created, rather than later, when the systems have to be changed again.

However, the decision to join the Ecu zone does not prevent a flexible and individual response to the specific national conditions of development in each country. Many issues will be settled 'bilaterally' between the national authorities concerned and the Ecu Zone Surveillance Board as the executing organ of the Cooperation Agreement.

The potential benefits of the Ecu zone
The benefits of the suggested scheme for Eastern Europe are considerable. They obtain immediate convertibility of their currencies for current account transactions and possibly quite soon for a notable proportion of capital account transactions. The convertibility guarantee upgrades financial balances arising from transactions with other Eastern European Ecu zone members because it improves the acceptability and credibility of local currencies. This removes the incentive to divert established trade flows in order to earn hard currency which is so detrimental at present. Instead, regional trade is integrated into the world market, and the creation of the Ecu zone would support the continuation of established trade and production patterns where desirable. Intra-regional trade could thereby become an additional engine of growth. The alternative would be a more 'centre'-oriented trade. Experience from other parts of the world shows that integration based on such centre-oriented structures is always fragile when confronted with shocks (Collignon, 1990a).

Economic cooperation in the Economic Surveillance Board will help to find solutions to the specific problems of participating countries. High inflation countries will have added credibility in their policy commitment to reduce increases in price levels; heavily-indebted countries will have a powerful partner with an institutional interest in maintaining solvency and reducing debt service and promoting local exports; and all Ecu zone members will benefit from easier access to the single market of Western Europe, as the Community will want to avoid financing large deficits with those countries. Participating countries obtain a political commitment to future full EC membership backed up by concrete deeds and procedures and a strategy which allows convergence to the Monetary Union of the Community. Without this institutional framework, EC membership may have to be delayed further than necessary.

The benefits for the European Community are also significant. With regard to security, the creation of an Ecu zone for Eastern Europe would reduce the dangers of external shocks that could destabilise the integration process of the European Community and, in particular, the convergence process in the transition to EMU and the single European currency. This is because the simple existence of the Ecu zone arrangements is likely to strengthen the credibility of reform policies and because the Surveillance Board will have a direct involvement in maintaining sound economic policies. Economic stability in Eastern Europe will contribute to social and political stabilisation of the continent as a whole.

The creation of the Ecu zone will improve and strengthen the credibility of the transition of formerly-state-planned economies to a fully-developed market economy. The international standby guarantee and the increasing adoption of EC norms and regulations will make the regime change irreversible and economic behaviour will change accordingly. Western Europe's neighbours will thereby join the mainstream of European civilisation.

The convertibility of local currencies and the increasing stability of their exchange rates against the Ecu will create vast new opportunities for European businesses. New markets will open up and large investments will contribute to a new growth dynamic. The extension of the Eastern frontier will thereby benefit all members of the European Community without exception.

A macroeconomic framework permitting rational decision making will be provided. Only if macroeconomic stability is achieved will it be possible to make rational micro-decisions. This applies to trade and investment as well as to the external financing of joint ventures or infrastructure development projects. The creation of the Ecu zone would ensure that the amounts invested are properly and efficiently used.

One microeconomic consequence of the Ecu zone would be greater international use of the Ecu for the financing of loans and trade credits (Jozzo, 1991). It should also assist the project establishing a private Ecu-denominated settlement system between East European countries which is at present being pursued by the Ecu Banking Association.

Time scale and participation

Assistance for Eastern Europe is urgent. Important decisions are being taken now. The creation of the Ecu zone should therefore not wait until the European Community has finalised its monetary integration, which at the earliest will be in 1997 and at the latest 1999. A clear and credible announcement now can act as an important signal for changing expectations in East and West, even if it takes some time to set up the institutional framework. Creation of the Ecu zone should be linked to the new European Monetary Institution to be created at the beginning of 1994. The time between now and 1994 should then be used by the candidate countries to fulfil the preconditions of economic reform, which are necessary for the proper functioning of the zone.

It is obvious that the cooperation mechanism suggested could work only for countries that are firmly committed to the development of a market economy. They must also have the wish and the profile to be likely candidates for future membership of the European Community. At present, this applies primarily to Hungary, Czechoslovakia and Poland but the group of possible participants might change in the future. Once an Ecu zone has been created and its success has become apparent, other candidates committed to a market economy, possibly some republics from the former Soviet Union, may be considered.

Notes

1 Current account convertibility is defined by IMF Article VII: '... no member shall, without the approval of the fund, impose restrictions on the making of payments and transfers for current international transactions'.
2 For further details on the critique of net resource transfers see Herr, Tober and Westphal (1991).
3 World Bank (1991), p. 21. However, it can be argued that this increase was a one-off affair due to domestic lack of purchasing power after the stabilisation shock. But evidence from Hungary suggests that 'enterprises responded to market signals ... and that the shift was motivated by economic considerations' (OECD, 1991, p. 94). Evidence from Chile (see Edwards and Edwards, 1987) also shows that a competitive exchange-rate level fosters the creation of new export industries.
4 The rules and regulations of centralising and controlling foreign exchange by the central bank are therefore left to each country.
5 A similar approach is also favoured by J. Attali (1991).
6 See Dornbusch (1987), chapter 4 for an analysis of Latin-American experiences.
7 See Bofinger (1991) for details. For monetary policy implications see Dornbusch (1988).

11

External Implications of EMU

John Williamson

The Maastricht Summit has paved the way for a move to full monetary union (EMU) in Europe. However, there are unlikely to be very dramatic consequences for international monetary arrangements. The G7 will still be able to operate a system of target zones among the three major currencies, although it will doubtless still be rather coy about admitting it. It will still talk about the need to coordinate fiscal policy, but fail to endorse any principles that would make a reality of this aspiration. All three blocs will still refuse to treat any of the others as a nominal anchor, while not getting around to constructing a system where the nominal anchor is provided collectively according to agreed principles. The multiple currency system will remain, though presumably with the Ecu diminishing the role of the dollar (and perhaps the yen) somewhat, but since capital mobility will remain high, the consequences for the distribution of seigniorage will be minimal.

Perhaps the principal external impact of EMU will be a decreased European willingness to manage the dollar if another occasion arises when it becomes seriously misaligned and the United States is in the hands-off phase of the policy cycle (see Bergsten, 1986, for a description of the tendency of United States external economic policy to go through a cycle). The stakes involved are nonetheless modest compared with those at the intra-European level.

Target zones

The G7 has operated a system of 'reference ranges' since the Louvre Accord in February 1987. The original reference ranges have been 'rebased', that is, realigned, several times, notably in late 1987 after Black Monday, and at times the dollar was allowed to appreciate more than the reference ranges would have suggested. Nonetheless, exchange rates have been vastly more stable in the (almost) five years since the Louvre Accord than they were in the equivalent preceding period, and misalignments have been negligible by comparison. While some academics doubtless still maintain that this had nothing to do with the new-found willingness of the G7 to manage exchange rates, that is certainly not the view of the markets.

Would EMU lead to a change in the present regime of target zones? It would obviously change it in one way: the Ecu would replace the D-Mark as the second currency (along with the yen) for which the G7 would set a reference range against the dollar. (The G7 does not set reference ranges for the pound, French franc or Italian lira; hence the absorption of these currencies in the Ecu would not reduce the number of reference rates that would have to be set.)   However, there seems to be no reason why replacement of the D-Mark by the Ecu should either encourage or impede any other change in the target-zone regime. There is no reason why it should cause a change in the width of the zones (which is now a sensible 10 per cent or so, as opposed to the impracticably narrow 5 per cent when the G7 launched its reference ranges after the Louvre Accord). It will be no less irrational to keep the zones secret than it is now.[1] Substitution of the Ecu for the D-Mark will not in itself lead to any increased automaticity, or even presumption, in the policy response when a rate hits the edge of the zone; presumably the only required reaction will still be to consult. Reference ranges will still not crawl to offset differential inflation, unless and until the G7 decides to make that policy change, which it could do just as well whether or not EMU occurs.

Admittedly target zones could be scuppered if the architects of EMU took at face value one piece of bad academic advice that is currently on offer:

> To the extent that the European Central Bank's charter specifies, as we believe it should, the pursuit of price stability to be its primary objective, it should not be expected to stabilize the value of the Ecu in terms of the dollar within an imposed band. For a conflict may otherwise arise between the European Central Bank's price stability objective and its exchange-rate stabilization obligations. (Genberg and Swoboda, 1991)[2]

This argument is presumably based on the assumption that an 'imposed band' has to be a constant nominal band. If it turned out that United States inflation were faster than was consistent with European price stability at a fixed nominal exchange rate and Europe had accepted the obligation to defend such a fixed rate against the dollar, then it would of course have to expand the money supply and inflate. But the argument is unambiguously erroneous if applied to target zones as advocated in Williamson (1985), because of three key design characteristics: the target zones are wide (plus or minus 10 per cent), they crawl to offset differential inflation, and they have soft margins. Imagine a worst-case scenario in which the Federal Reserve decided to stoke up a monetary expansion and allowed it to generate a United States inflation. In the first instance this would cause the Ecu to appreciate towards the top of the zone, which would insulate the European money supply from any immediate impact. As United States inflation got under way, the Ecu target zone would appreciate against the dollar and thus continue to repel inflation. Only in an extreme situation where the Ecu hit the edge of the band could any inflationary impact potentially arise, and that would be a crystal-clear case for exploiting the soft margins and allowing the Ecu to move outside the target zone. There is no need to throw away the advantages of managing the exchange rate because of an improbable contingency that could be met quite easily within the rules of the system should it ever materialise.

Would reference ranges, which are half-baked target zones that still lack some key features as noted above, be more vulnerable to the Genberg–Swoboda critique? They are now wide enough to cope with any reasonable disturbances. They are, if anything, still too soft rather than too hard. Thus the only relevant design feature that is still missing is the automatic crawl to offset differential inflation. In practice it seems rather unlikely that the European Community would acquiesce in unchanging zones in the presence of a significant inflation differential. But the moral is not that target zones need to be abandoned so as to permit the European Central Bank to be sure that it can insulate European inflation from that in the United States, but that reference ranges should crawl to offset differential inflation.

Policy coordination

This is another field where the G7 has come a long way from the policy *laissez-faire* of the early 1980s, but has nevertheless not embraced a convincing intellectual position. The existing system of policy coordination is based on a set of indicators, as agreed in principle at the Tokyo Summit in 1986. It appears that each of the participants is expected to project each of the principal macroeconomic variables (growth, inflation, current account, money supply, and fiscal deficit in particular) over a medium-run time horizon. The IMF staff then assess whether these projections are individually plausible and collectively consistent. If not, the G7 presumably discusses what policy modifications might be called for in order to achieve a set of desirable outcomes.

Such a procedure could be maintained if EMU occurs. The only question would concern participation. Would four members of the European Community continue to participate individually, or would a representative of the EC take their place? The latter not only seems unlikely, but also inappropriate unless and until fiscal policy is largely centralised. It would, however, be easier to accept the proposal of Dobson (1991) that the central bankers should start to participate regularly in all stages of the G7 coordination process, since this would involve adding only four extra participants instead of seven.

The existing process suffers from three weaknesses. One is its lack of institutionalisation, which means that its continuation is at the mercy of the particular personalities involved. The danger is that the process could vanish without trace if and when it once again becomes really needed in order to restrain dogmatic ideologues with a psychological need to defy conventional wisdom. A second weakness is that there are no presumptions as to how policy should react to deviations of outcomes from objectives. The third weakness is that the process of policy coordination is not integrated with that of exchange-rate stabilisation (the reference ranges).

The 'blueprint' offered by Williamson and Miller (1987) contained proposals for remedying those three weaknesses. The first and second weaknesses would have been addressed by endorsement of the blueprint as a set of presumptions about the formulation of intermediate targets and the use of policy instruments to pursue those targets. They are to be thought of as presumptions rather than rules, because economic reality is too complex to give assurance that every contingency can be covered by a set of rules. Obviously, however, one would want to see explicit justification for any decision to override the presumptions. The third weakness of the G7 indicators is also addressed by the blueprint, since the target exchange rates would be chosen with a view to achieving target current account positions in the medium term assuming that activity is at 'internal balance'. Fiscal policy would need to be consistent with the target current balance positions (at internal balance) in the medium term.[3] If the current fiscal stance differs from that consistent level, its base path should envisage gradual convergence towards the target; but deviations from that base path would be allowed in the interest of cyclical stabilisation, as measured by an endogenously-determined target for the growth rate of nominal domestic demand.

The G7 shows no interest in developing its indicators along these lines (or according to any competing set of principles). Despite my attachment to the blueprint, I have become doubtful whether it will be adopted, for I fear it is a victim of what one may term the 'reformer's dilemma': in the absence of a crisis, there is no pressure to reform; but when a crisis comes, there is no time to design an adequate reform. 'One market, one money' (Commission of the European Communities, 1990, p. 195) argues that 'a distinctive effect of EMU would be to give a decisive boost to the search for a genuine multi-polar regime'. It would be nice to believe it, but the supporting arguments seem pretty weak.[4]

The numeraire

Current arrangements for reference ranges and policy coordination do not provide for a numeraire. All of the participants are expected to pursue price stability, but there are no mechanisms that tend to pull a country that succeeds or fails better than some other back into line. (That assertion depends on the validity of the claim advanced earlier to the effect that the reference ranges would be readily modified if they appeared to have become anachronistic because of differential inflation.)

It is true that the G7 has added a commodity price indicator to its list. However, its purpose is to provide an early warning signal of inflation, not a numeraire that would dictate a deflationary policy to reverse price rises that have already occurred if the value of money in terms of the commodity basket were to decline.

Replacement of the D-Mark by the Ecu would be unlikely to change the lack of a numeraire. It would still be inconceivable that Europe would agree to accept the dollar (let alone the yen) as numeraire, that is to maintain a fixed nominal exchange rate whatever consequences that might have for inflation. And it would still be inconceivable that Japan (let alone the United States) would accept the Ecu as the numeraire.

Indeed, one of the great political certainties that must be taken as a datum in suggesting international monetary reforms is that none of the three major poles will be willing to accept any of the others as providing the numeraire. It is only slightly less unlikely that some commodity standard will make a comeback, because economic policymakers are too realistic to embrace the new-classical faith that reversing price rises can be done without a cost in terms of lost output provided credibility can be established.

Hence it would appear that the only conceivable approximation to a numeraire would be the sort of arrangement suggested in the blueprint. This specifies what are supposed to be state-of-the-art principles for calculating target growth rates of domestic demand, and then calls for these to be compared with actual expected growth rates. Both targets and actual rates would be summed across countries. If the aggregate actual exceeds (falls short of) the aggregate target, then the average level of interest rates of the participants should be raised (lowered). In particular, that would mean that, if two currencies were close to the edge of their target zone, the weak (strong) currency country should be the one that would change its interest rate in order to defend the zone.

This would provide a symmetrical rule for determining world monetary policy, with a strong (but not exclusive) focus on achieving and maintaining price stability, by virtue of the specification of the targets for demand growth. The G7 could adopt such a rule with or without the replacement of the D-Mark by the Ecu as the world's third key currency: hence EMU seems, once again, essentially irrelevant to the design of the future international monetary system.

The multiple currency system

Little by little, the world has moved from a situation during the years of Bretton Woods where the dollar was the dominant international money, to one today where the dollar is first among equals. The foreign exchange market is still conducted overwhelmingly in dollars, with very few transactions that go directly between non-dollar currencies, and foreign exchange intervention is also predominantly in dollars. But all other roles of international money are now shared. Apart from raw materials, trade transactions are invoiced predominantly in the currency of the exporter. Of those currencies that retain a peg, only some 40 per cent peg to the dollar, with mutual pegging in the EMS and basket pegging both having eroded the dollar's role. Private loans are denominated in a range of industrial country currencies, with the share of the dollar falling in recent years. Similarly, reserves are held in a mix of hard currencies, with the dollar's share having fallen to under 60 per cent.

It is surely inevitable that the international role of the Ecu will exceed the sum of those played by the currencies that it replaces. Non-member countries in Europe, as well as many countries in Africa and the Middle East and perhaps South Asia, are likely to find the Ecu the most natural peg. The large capital market will enhance the use of the Ecu to denominate loans. The use of the Ecu as a vehicle currency, to denominate trade transactions, will increase. (European Commission, 1990, makes a brave attempt to quantify some of these effects.) And all those factors are likely to increase the proportion of reserves held in Ecus above what would otherwise be held in the component currencies.

While I do not doubt this conclusion, I challenge whether it is nearly as important as often seems to be claimed. Since the developing countries that peg their currencies do not invoice in their own currencies, there is no particular gain to an industrial country in having its currency used as a peg. Loans do not necessarily generate fee income to the country in whose currency the loan is denominated in these days of offshore banking. Use of one's currency as a vehicle currency brings only modest gains, estimated by 'One market, one money' at under 0.05 per cent of Community GDP. Even having one's currency used as a reserve currency generates almost no seigniorage in these days when international capital mobility means that funds placed in one currency are promptly intermediated back to another if that is where borrowers prefer to borrow, rather than leading to lower interest rates. Once again, therefore, EMU will not make much difference.

If that conclusion is correct, it also casts doubt on the size of the problem posed by the need to run down reserve holdings that will be excessive after the Ecu has replaced the national currencies. 'One market, one money' (European Commission, 1990, p. 183) estimated the superfluous reserves that would be created by monetary union as over $200 billion. It is argued that an attempt to dispose of these holdings will put downward pressure on the dollar in the foreign exchange markets. This sum is, however, small compared with the size of total United States overseas assets and liabilities. If capital mobility is indeed high, however, a small dollar depreciation should be expected to cause borrowers to shift their borrowing from dollars to Ecus and lenders to shift their lending from Ecus to dollars, thus limiting the real impact of the rundown of dollar reserves. Admittedly it is not clear that the markets always work as rationally as this, but, provided they believe the authorities are managing exchange rates to prevent bandwagon movements pushing rates outside target zones, such a scenario seems plausible.

Concluding remarks

A tripolar monetary system incorporating the Ecu as a third currency alongside the dollar and yen will not have very important effects on the way the international monetary system operates. The Ecu will replace the D-Mark in the G7 arrangements for reference ranges and policy coordination, but it will neither render those arrangements impractical nor necessitate their further development. The Ecu will not become the numeraire for the global economy, and its enhanced international role will not matter much, except to those whose patriotic heartbeat is quickened by the thought that their currencies are used by foreigners.

The most significant impact of EMU would arise if the present arrangements for international coordination and exchange-rate management break down, which is certainly conceivable given their lack of institutionalisation and the history of a United States policy cycle. As argued by Henning (1991, forthcoming), it would in that event seem altogether less likely that Europe would react as passively as it did in the early 1980s when the dollar went through the ceiling and intensified the difficulty of bringing inflation down in Europe (although the problem of designing a suitable response would still remain). It would seem even less likely that Europe would be prepared to support the dollar under circumstances where it was perceived that the United States was not doing its share too. Of course, a American understanding that Europe would react that way will tend to diminish the danger of current cooperative arrangements breaking down. Perhaps that is indeed the major external impact to be expected of EMU. (Questions of the consolidation of European representation in the international financial institutions will arise only if and when monetary union is followed by a more real political union than will conceivably win British acquiescence, even after Maastricht.)

While it is argued that the external implications of EMU are of somewhat limited significance, this does not imply that European monetary union is an unimportant subject. It does, however, suggest that the critical questions are those on which the European debate has indeed focused, notably whether EMU will increase the probability of avoiding future monetary debauchery and whether adequate alternative adjustment mechanisms exist to compensate for loss of the exchange-rate instrument.

Notes

1 G7 officials defend their practice of keeping the zones secret with the argument that their credibility would be undermined if they found themselves unable to defend a zone that had been publicly announced. Some of us would consider that an advantage: officials who pick indefensible zones deserve to lose their credibility. But what officials who make this argument never seem to have understood is that there is a fundamental difference between having to defend a disequilibrium rate that has been inherited from the past, as the Bretton Woods system obliged countries to do when differential inflation (for example) had disturbed equilibrium, and defending a rate that is the best estimate of an equilibrium rate, which is what they rightly do under the present regime.

2 Centre for Economic Policy Research (1991) makes a somewhat similar argument, though focusing on the danger of undermining the independence of the European Central Bank if the finance ministers are given the authority to determine the Ecu's exchange-rate policy.

3 See Williamson in Blommestein (forthcoming) for this amplification of the original blueprint proposal.

4 The three effects expected to yield this result are:

(i) As the spill-over effects of Community policies on the rest of the world would be larger than those of individual member states, the need for, and the benefits of policy coordination would increase.

(ii) As the number of actors would be reduced, some of the usual obstacles to coordination would be alleviated.

(iii) A greater bargaining power for the EC, which would have a single voice, might also affect the distribution of gains between the Community and the rest of the world.

See European Commission (1990, p. 191).

12

Cohesion as a Precondition for Monetary Union in Europe

Iain Begg and David Mayes

Introduction

Regional disparities are a characteristic of all economies. In the European Community the gap between the most and least prosperous regions is greater than in most nation states and the tensions this engenders are bound to be a major issue for the EC as economic integration goes further in the 1990s. The implications of monetary union have been extensively analysed in terms of what the costs and benefits are for the countries which agree to forgo the use of an independent monetary policy (for a good summary, see Goodhart, 1989). It is generally accepted that once a country joins a monetary union, an external deficit that might have been accommodated by depreciation of the currency will, inside a monetary union, tend to lead to higher unemployment.

Most of the discussion of EMU centres on economic hurdles and assessments, such as the technicalities of the transition from EMS to EMU, the need for nominal convergence and the costs and benefits for different participants. Implicit in this is the presumption that if the 'technical questions' can be satisfactorily resolved, EMU can proceed. Despite the concern expressed in the Delors report about the dangers of regional imbalance (Committee for the Study of Economic and Monetary Union, 1989, p. 18), little attention is given to the effects of monetary union on regional disparities.

This disregard of the regional dimension of economic integration betrays a wider neglect of the political economy of monetary union. It must however, be recognised that political acceptability is, ultimately, the real test of the viability of a union. Cohesion is a major part of this, and consequently has to be addressed, since it will inevitably be one of the key conditions for the achievement of monetary union. Although the Single Act and the Maastricht Treaty contain references to social and economic cohesion, it is not easy to identify either what is meant by the term or what priority it merits in the debate on monetary union. The agreement at Maastricht to create a cohesion fund and the intention to consider the whole issue of budgetary contributions in the negotiations over the next-five year budget perspective early next year indicate clearly that the priority is considerable.

The Delors report notes that in an integrated market, the balance of payments would cease to be a highly visible and sensitive indicator of external imbalance. 'None the less, such imbalances, if left uncorrected, would manifest themselves as regional disequilibria.' Consequently, according to the report, once exchange rates have been irrevocably fixed in a monetary union, 'imbalances among member countries would have to be corrected by policies affecting the structure of their economies and costs of production if major regional disparities in output and employment were to be avoided.'

The aim of this chapter is to elucidate these matters by examining the disparities in social and economic wellbeing in the EC and considering their significance in the process of economic and monetary union. We begin by defining cohesion and its role in the process of achieving EMU. The third section considers how the move to EMU affects cohesion, while the fourth section examines the adequacy of existing policy to meet the resulting difficulties. We then consider what further action is called for before drawing our conclusions.

Much of the concern about the preconditions for EMU has focused on the need to attain nominal convergence. Little attention has been paid either to 'real' convergence – the degree to which living standards differ in different parts of the Community – or to divergences in economic structures which are likely to affect regional competitiveness in the more exposed conditions of an EMU. We have argued elsewhere (NIESR, 1991) that *structural convergence* (adaptation which produces more closely related structures of economies in different parts of the EC economy) and *behavioural convergence* (increasing similarity in various behavioral phenomena such as labour markets, savings ratios, formal or informal systems of welfare support or the character of industrial relations) require attention if an EMU is to be sustainable.

The new Treaty agreed at Maastricht gives a vague indication of the meaning of cohesion (Article 130A). Cohesion is prone to being interpreted in differing and sometimes inconsistent ways. For some, it is considered to be synonymous with convergence of real incomes; others adopt a much more political definition, seeing cohesion in terms of what is needed to sustain a willingness to remain part of the Community. Confusion can also arise where there are multiple objectives, some of which can conflict with others. Advancing social cohesion, for example, may call for spending programmes to assist marginalised groups in society or to counter long-term unemployment. But if this implies expenditure in more favoured regions, it would exacerbate, rather than diminish, regional income inequality and accentuate problems of economic cohesion.

Ultimately, the test of cohesion in the European Community will be whether or not different constituencies accept that it makes sense to remain in the Community, implying that political rather than economic criteria will be paramount. Nevertheless, cohesion is inevitably bound up with divergence in economic and social welfare. A simple definition is that it is the degree of disparity between different regions or groups within the European Community which is politically and socially tolerable. It may, however, be important in the context of a major change such as the creation of an EMU to look at the direction of changes as well as levels of target variables. Thus, if one of the effects of EMU is to enable less-favoured areas to grow more rapidly than they would otherwise have done, the change might be considered cohesive. At the same time, if more prosperous areas endure higher unemployment because of EMU, political antagonism may be aroused, even if the region remains relatively prosperous.

A basic question for the EC as it contemplates the creation of an EMU is whether it needs to adopt explicit measures to advance economic and social cohesion prior to EMU, or whether such policies can be relegated to secondary importance. From a technical perspective, both a single market and an EMU can function in a perfectly satisfactory manner without any policies to promote cohesion. It follows that it is political imperatives which are central to a search for cohesion, rather than economic necessity. Indeed, without cohesion, the polity may not be able to agree to proceed down the road to monetary union.

A successful policy for cohesion must ensure an adequate diffusion of economic advantages from the growth centres to other regions, without stifling the creation of those advantages. Regions which have their competitiveness damaged by the integration process have to be persuaded that this is ultimately in their own best interests, while regions that gain have to recognise that their gains stem in part from others' losses. Acute regional imbalances can be damaging to an economy if they lead to a conjunction of overheating in more favoured regions and under-employment of resources in others. While it can be argued that market mechanisms ought to be able to resolve this by stimulating the movement of factors of production, it has to be recognised that the implied mechanism may require greater factor mobility than has been attained in Europe. We have taken the view that in spite of the rhetoric about 'the market', the European economy of the 1990s neither conforms to the assumptions of the neo-classical model, nor is it likely to be attractive or desirable to seek to make it do so.

The European tier of government has very limited room for manoeuvre to redistribute resources. The Community budget amounts to just 1.2 per cent of EC GDP and more than half of it is hypothecated to support for agriculture. While some of the CAP spending does help to raise incomes in disadvantaged parts of the Community, notably Ireland and Greece, the resources specifically available to assist cohesion amount to just 0.3 per cent of GDP. This, as the MacDougall report (1977) showed, is a tiny sum compared with the redistributive effects of taxation and public expenditure within nation states. According to the MacDougall estimates, potential regional disparities are diminished by 40 per cent on average as a result of these flows. In order to achieve this scale of redistribution from the six richer to the three poorer member states for the Community of Nine in 1975, the Community budget would have had to have been increased by 6–7 per cent of GDP. Since then, the accession of Greece, Spain and Portugal has hugely increased the number of less-favoured regions. It is implausible to expect the Community budget to grow sufficiently to reach an adequate magnitude for a similar redistribution in the 1990s. Yet, as we have shown elsewhere, much could be done with the existing Community budget if assistance was focused on areas most in need (NIESR, 1991).

The magnitude of existing disparities

The economic and social disparities within the Community are much wider than those within most unitary states or federal systems. Political and administrative structures also vary considerably and there are major gaps in infrastructure in many of the less-favoured regions. Geography also plays a part in shaping regional competitiveness, since there are systematic advantages for core areas of the Community in being able to access final and input markets. It is no coincidence that the areas designated for assistance by the European Commission are predominantly on the periphery of the Community.

Conventionally, it is disparities in economic indicators – usually some measure of income per head or of unemployment – which are used to compare the welfare of different regions. Tables 12.1 and 12.2 present the most recent data on GDP per head (measured in purchasing power standards which adjust for differences in price levels between member states but do not adjust for regional differences) and unemployment rates for each of the member states of the Community. For the multi-regional countries, the tables also show the regions with the highest and lowest values on the respective indicators.

The data on GDP per capita reveal a range from under 40 per cent to over 170 per cent of the Community average using the 'Level II' disaggregation of regions.[1] Even at the Level I disaggregation, the most prosperous region has a per capita GDP three and half times that of the least prosperous. By comparison, in the United States, the state with the highest GDP per head (Connecticut) is just double that of the poorest (Mississippi).

Table 12.1   *Disparities in GDP in the European Community*
(Index, EC12 = 100)

Country	GDP index 1980	1989	Highest region	GDP index 1980	1989	Lowest region	GDP index 1980	1989
Belgium	104	101	Antwerpen	127	122	Hainaut	82	75
Denmark	108	107						
Germany/W	114	112	Hamburg	179	173	Lüneburg	81	78
Greece	58	54	Sterea Ellada	80	69	Ipeiros	42	39
Spain	74	77	Baleares	90	104	Extremadura	47	49
France	112	109	Ile de France	158	162	Corse	na	79
Ireland	64	67						
Italy	102	104	Lombardia	135	139	Calabria	58	57
Luxembourg	118	129						
Nether-lands	111	102	Noord-Holland	125	119	Flevoland	na	66
Portugal	55	55	Lisboa/V Tejo	71	70	Centro	44	45
UK	101	107	South East	119	131	N Ireland	77	79

Source: Eurostat Rapid Report 1991, no. 2.
Notes: No data are available for the new länder in East Germany, the French overseas departements or the Portuguese Islands. In these countries, the missing regions would have lower GDPs than the regions shown. In the United Kingdom, the regional disaggregation is less than in other countries. In the Netherlands, the artificially high figure for Groningen has been disregarded.

Table 12.2   *Disparities in unemployment in the European Community*

Country	Rate (%) April 1991	Highest rate (%) region	April 1991	Lowest rate (%) region	April 1991
Belgium	7.6	Hainaut	13.1	W Vlaanderen	4.0
Denmark	8.8				
W Germany	4.5	Bremen	8.4	Stuttgart	2.7
Greece	8.1	D Makedonia	10.0(a)	Kriti	2.5(a)
Spain	15.8	Andalucia	24.2	Baleares	8.4
France	9.3	Languedoc-R	13.6	Alsace	4.9
Ireland	16.9				
Italy	9.9	Sicilia	21.2	Trentino A A	3.3
Luxembourg	1.7				
Netherlands	8.0(a)	Groningen	13.6(a)	Zeeland	5.6(a)
Portugal	4.2	Alentejo	10.3	Centro	2.1
UK	9.0	N Ireland	16.8	Grampian	5.0

Source: Eurostat Rapid Report 1991, no. 3.
(a) 1990 data.

Over a long period, the trend of disparities appears to have fluctuated in response to overall growth in the Community. Broadly speaking, when the EC has grown rapidly (as in the late 1980s or prior to the mid-1970s), regional disparities have tended to narrow, whereas in periods of slower overall growth, they have been more inclined to widen. At first sight, the observed association between rapid growth in the Community and a narrowing of disparities seems auspicious for cohesion. However, as the analysis in the next section shows, the changes in prospect for the less-favoured regions as a result of integration are not encouraging.

Changes in GDP in the 1980s also give cause for concern. Greece has been particularly disappointing, slipping from 58 per cent of the Community average to 54 per cent and being overtaken by Portugal. Two of the other least-favoured member states (Ireland and Spain) have done rather better, both increasing their relative prosperity, while Portugal has marked time.

A more worrying feature of change in the 1980s is that several of the least-favoured regions failed to keep pace with their respective member states during the decade. Thus, in Spain, poorer regions such as Galicia and Asturias fell further behind between 1980 and 1989, whereas the more prosperous regions such as Catalonia or Madrid enjoyed relative improvements. Similar differentials are evident in Northern England relative to the South (see Begg and Guy, 1992), in the Mezzogiorno and in Wallonia. The inference to be drawn from these figures is that an intensification of competition has made it more difficult for less competitive regions to keep pace.

Labour market indicators also show substantial divergences, often exacerbated by differences in natural rates of population growth. Thus, the unemployment rate in 1990 ranged from 24 per cent in the south of Spain, around 20 per cent in the worst affected regions of the Mezzogiorno and 17 per cent in Ireland to 2.7 per cent in Baden-Württemberg and 1.5 per cent in Luxembourg (Commission of the European Communities, 1991b). By contrast, in the United States in 1988, the spread was from 2.4 per cent in New Hampshire to 10.9 per cent in Louisiana. Because of social and institutional differences between regions, however, comparisons of unemployment rates, even using supposedly harmonised data, are neither wholly reliable, nor a convincing proxy for regional prosperity. Greece and Portugal, for example, do not register high rates of unemployment, even though they manifestly lag behind the rest of the Community in terms of prosperity.

The effect of EMU on disparities

Most of the argument in this chapter focuses on the characteristics of the path to EMU, thereby putting a relatively heavy weight on what may turn out to be purely transitional effects occasioned primarily by the need to achieve convergence in appropriate nominal indicators and the increasing impact of the unification of the market. However, other effects are deeper seated and longer lasting, continuing to apply during the EMU itself. In what follows we distinguish these two categories of impact and effect and further distinguish between their macroeconomic and microeconomic components.

Macroeconomic impacts
Many of the issues involved in the macroeconomic analysis of EMU are discussed in Chapter 1. There is no obvious set of criteria for analysing their impact on regional disparities. There has been considerable debate whether economic and monetary union is in general likely to lead to a narrowing or widening of disparities. The general implication of 'One market, one money' is that disparities will tend to narrow. Other studies tend to be more agnostic (Padoa-Schioppa, 1987, for example), expecting some regions to gain and others to lose at all levels of current advantage relative to the average. However, no one suggests that there will be major reductions in disparities as a result of EMU alone even in the long run and in the short run there is considerable evidence that many of the most disadvantaged regions will tend to lose out (Nam *et al.*, 1991, O'Donnell, 1991).

The most disadvantaged regions in the Community (objective 1 regions in the parlance of the Community's structural funds)[2] are concentrated in Greece, Portugal, Ireland, Spain and Southern Italy. Only Ireland and Spain have made significant progress in reducing inflation, and Greece also faces the problem of a large government deficit. The transition to monetary union would require further deflationary policies, and this will widen disparities in the Community, and make it less cohesive. An excessive and extended worsening in disparities will lead the voters in the worst affected areas to press for offsetting measures, the most obvious of which, in the face of such difficulties, would have previously been a downward realignment of the exchange rate. However, the EC has decided not only to move ever closer to a common inflation rate but feels that as far as possible the union and the single currency should be formed round existing exchange rates with parities being allowed to vary within increasingly narrow bands. The Maastricht summit seems to have recognised that this may cause problems and has set up a 'Cohesion Fund' of some 1bn Ecu to address the problems of transport and infrastructure in member states with GDP per head less than 90 per cent of the EC average (that is, Greece, Portugal, Ireland and Spain).

This process of narrowing in on existing nominal exchange rates implies that real exchange rates are close to the rates required to achieve a sustainable EMU. It is not, however, necessarily the case that existing rates are near their long-run stable values. Insofar as real exchange rates are above their long-run values, the adjustment will have to be undertaken in other markets, particularly the labour market, which is notoriously slow in many member states. The inevitable consequence is higher unemployment. These high levels of unemployment may continue to persist even after inflation has been brought down, and the transition period may be lengthy, and certainly too long for governments to survive within the electoral cycle.

A second feature of the transition is that interest rates will fall in the more inflation prone countries. This does not entail that real rates of interest will also fall. High price inflation has often been associated with low and indeed negative real interest rates. Tight monetary policy in the run-up to monetary union is unlikely to let Community-wide real rates fall and indeed they may increase, especially in the previously high inflation economies. The real gain in the high inflation regions is likely to be in nominal rates, in part because it improves the cashflow position of firms and this in itself acts to improve firms' ability to invest.

The move to monetary union should reduce the risk premia on loans to high inflation countries, and this should produce a relative fall in their real interest rates. It is suggested in 'One money, one market' that a ½ per cent fall in real interest rates could lead to a 5–10 per cent increase in GDP in the long run, although the time profile for any such falls is difficult to sort out. Both the stimulus and the response are likely to be spread over a number of years. However, dynamic gains will always tend to dominate static benefits as they are compounded as time passes. If of course the initial changes in real interest rates are negative then the cumulative causation would be negative, especially if added to a short-run period of deflation to achieve convergence. Kaldor (1971) was particularly concerned about such a negative spiral on the United Kingdom's original entry to the EC. Similar arguments can readily be applied to the move towards EMU, especially from countries starting with an overvalued exchange rate. Those member states that have already achieved very low rates of inflation have little or no scope for further improvement in nominal or real interest rates. For them the benefits of EMU have to come through other, largely microeconomic mechanisms.

The completion of the internal market and the implementation of the social programme are the other major developments affecting the cohesion of the Community. Their implications are discussed at length in NIESR (1991), and that study concludes that their impact may not necessarily be positive. The removal of internal barriers may lead to relatively higher growth in the less-favoured regions, but it can be argued that the gains from the removal of barriers may be mainly located in the advanced regions. These areas already benefit from economies of scale associated with large agglomerations of activities, and these may be enhanced by an increase in the size of the available market.

The problems of regional disparities might be ameliorated by significant levels of labour migration. However, the evidence of the last thirty years suggests that interregional labour mobility in Europe is low, and that it may even be declining. Social obstacles to migration may make the progress to monetary union more problematic than it otherwise needs to be. The social dimension of the internal market programme may even exacerbate the problem (Ermisch, 1991). The spread of advantaged region non-wage benefits to less-advantaged regions raises labour costs without necessarily raising productivity, and hence makes the less-advantaged regions less attractive as locations for productive activity.

Microeconomic effects

Two aspects of the nature of the individual regions affect the overall impact of monetary union. The first is the structure of the region and the second the nature of the response. The greater the involvement of the region in exports to other member states, then the greater will tend to be the favourable impact. However, it is not just current exporters who gain but those who have been held back from exporting by currency risk as well. The form of the gain to exporters occurs in two parts. The first is simply the cost of foreign exchange transactions, which will be eliminated. The second is the costs of risk. These costs can be borne in a number of ways, by taking out appropriate cover, by taking the risk and getting caught out from time to time and by avoiding the risk altogether by not undertaking the foreign transactions. All of these will have an adverse effect on traders and their removal should reduce costs and hence enhance competitiveness.

Transactions costs related to exchange rates are relatively small, variously estimated as anything between 0.15 to 1 per cent of GDP in 'One market, one money', depending on the proportion of output which goes to other member states. In general the smaller the state the greater the benefit because more of their output tends to be traded, but when it comes to the individual regions the same does not apply, as poorer regions tend to concentrate their trade with their own member state and have lower trade proportions. They also tend to have a higher proportion of small firms, which gain less from the move to EMU. While the simple transaction cost gains may be largely static in character, those from the reduction in risk may be dynamic in the same way as outlined for interest rates in the macroeconomic case.

The more multinational the firm, the more it tends to be able to gain in terms of internal costs from EMU. It no longer has to price in different currencies for intrafirm transfers, its treasury operations are simplified, as are its accounting procedures. The beneficiaries are not only internal to EC countries, since competitors from outside the member states and regions will also be experiencing lower costs which will enhance their ability to compete.

Many of the microeconomic costs and benefits of an EMU occur at the last stage, what we have labelled 'E-day' elsewhere (Mayes and Burridge, 1991), when the single currency is actually implemented in the member states. Although risks may be reduced as currencies move closer and closer to fixity and it may also be possible to reduce transactions costs at the same time, it is not until the currencies show no fluctuation that the treasury and foreign exchange operations can be fully simplified. There is thus unlikely to be much in the way of microeconomic benefits to offset the macroeconomic costs of EMU for disadvantaged regions in the main part of the transitional phase. The gains will become apparent once convergence has been achieved.

Multinational firms may in fact be able to anticipate some of the gains, for once it becomes clear that the Ecu is to be established as the single currency, they can simplify some of their systems at an earlier date. It is not clear yet, however, from the Maastricht agreement, how much uncertainty has been reduced. Stage 3 is possible for 1997 and some action intended for 1999 in any event, but with an unspecified number of members. A specific asymmetric uncertainty is added for the United Kingdom with the possible exercise of the 'opt out' clause even if the conditions for participation have been met. Firms tend to put off taking action in the face of uncertainty, particularly since it is clear (Mayes and Burridge, 1991) from previous currency changes that the necessary lead-in time can be quite short, certainly less than four years. It must be emphasised that in the final change to the single currency, all firms will incur a cost. They will have to convert their prices and accounting and payments systems if nothing else. These issues are addressed further in the conclusion to this volume.

In the changeover to a single currency, it is necessary to assess whether the costs will be evenly spread over the regions. The more firms are solely involved in domestic transactions then the more the changeover is likely to be a cost rather than a benefit. There is thus an important distinction between peripheral regions, which have no borders with other member states and border regions, which although disadvantaged and some distance from the core of the Community, nevertheless have both existing cross-border transactions and the potential for a considerable expansion in their size. There is also a fixed cost element in the change (the new system has to be purchased and understood), even though much of the cost will be proportionate to the scale and complexity of operations. Hence, costs will tend to fall more heavily on small firms, exacerbating the lower incidence of benefits that we have already noted. Given the greater share of small firms in the activity of the less advantaged regions, this pattern will tend to be anti-cohesive.

Taken together there is strong macroeconomic and microeconomic evidence that the transition period to EMU will be anticohesive for the least advantaged regions. Although there will be longer-run gains, the transition has to be negotiated successfully first. It is highly unlikely that the possibility of longer-run gains for some will prove an adequate compensation for general short-run losses, both in achieving the transition to convergence and in implementing E-day. These findings will be emphasised by additional external losses in those regions which are likely to be adversely affected in relative terms by the completion of the internal market, as suggested by Nam *et al.* (1991), for example. Action to improve cohesion in the short run is therefore required and the proposed Cohesion Fund in the Maastricht agreement reflects this.

The adequacy of the current policy package in furthering cohesion

The approach to policy

The EC uses two main mechanisms to try to achieve cohesion. The first is furthering integration of the Community, particularly through the completion of the internal market and the move towards a single currency, although the 'social dimension' is also seen as a means of extending the benefits to all of its citizens. By opening up the market it is intended to increase the competitiveness of European producers towards the best possible in the world, particularly by having a large home market, which permits economies of scale and the removal of unnecessary transactions costs. This freeing up of the market should, on the one hand, maximise the opportunities for growth in the Community as a whole and, on the other, provide the maximum opportunity for the market to reallocate resources efficiently across industries and locations.

As we have suggested in the previous section, although this policy may be increasing the rate of growth and level of GDP per head for the Community as a whole, some of which trickles down to all regions of the EC, it is likely to widen some disparities, particularly those with the regions which are currently most disadvantaged as a result of peripherality. The Community therefore seeks to offset this through a second major plank of policy – structural intervention. This is administered through three funds, jointly referred to as the structural funds: the European Regional Development Fund (ERDF), which is the largest and was formed in 1975, the Guidance section of the agricultural funds (EAGGF) and the European Social Fund (ESF). The use of the funds, which was previously on a somewhat *ad hoc*, project-by-project basis, was reformed in 1988, leading to a doubling of size in real terms over the period up to 1993, a coordination of the three funds and a focus on five objectives. The objectives and the allocation of funds are set out in table 12.3. Their principal characteristic is that regions that are most disadvantaged, as measured by GDP per head, receive the lion's share of the funds. These regions are denoted by objective 1. Two other sets of regions are also defined as needing assistance, traditional industrial areas in decline, designated largely on an unemployment criterion (objective 2) and rural areas with adjustment problems (objective 5b). Objectives 3, 4 and 5a are not defined by region and can be applied anywhere in the Community where the need arises, although in practice much of this tends to be within the objective 1 regions. As noted above, the objective 1 regions are concentrated in Portugal, Spain, Greece and Ireland.

The form of the policy is governed by Article 130A of the new treaty, with its focus and importance defined by Article 130B. The general rationale is to try to create some 'equality of opportunity' for the regions of the Community to compete within the Single Market by investing in a wide range of 'infrastructure'. Thus infrastructure includes not just roads, bridges, dams and other forms of structures for utilities and transportation, but investment in communications, facilities for industry (industrial parks, networks of business services) and in the human capital stock through vocational training. By creating this framework, disadvantaged regions can develop their own sources of indigenous growth, specialising in their own sources of strength rather than merely hoping to attract some of the diminishing supply of footloose direct investment, which is based largely on the existence of low costs. In recent years this more traditional approach to regional policy has been discarded in favour of a focus on indigenous development (see O'Donnell, 1991, and the chapter by Kowalski in Albrechts *et al.*, 1989, for example).

It is, however, true that where new and more permanent investment can be attracted, particularly in manufacturing, this will act as a focus for further investment from component suppliers, business services and

Table 12.3   *Structural funds – instruments and allocation 1989–93*

% of total funds		Objective	Instrument	Ecu bn
63	1	Lagging regions	All funds	38.3
12	2	Declining regions	ERDF, ESF	7.2
12	3	Long-term unemployment	ESF	7.5
	4	Youth unemployment	ESF	
6	5a	Agricultural adjustment	EAGGF	3.4
5	5b	Rural development	All funds	2.8
2		Other		1.1
Total				60.3

Source: European Commission.

the whole network of consumer services to meet the demands of the expanding workforce and rising levels of income per head. The policy, therefore, is also aimed at providing the conditions where such investment could take place if that was the sensible market conclusion, but without the panoply of state aids that previously led to a distorted pattern. (State aids are restricted under the the EC's competition rules, their resurrection under the guise of regional policy poses problems where the richer regions are able to offer greater 'sweeteners' than the less-favoured ones.)

The evidence for the success of this policy is still to come, in part, purely because the doubling of the structural funds is still only in progress. However, there are some indications that where an effective partnership can be developed between the various levels of government, industry, financial institutions and local educational and research institutions it is possible to develop indigenous sources of growth (Camagni, 1991, and Hingel, 1991).

The structural funds form only a small part of what the member states spend on their own regional problems, although in countries like Portugal, Greece and Ireland, which are entirely objective 1 regions, these funds amount to 3–5 per cent of total investment (see table 12.4) and up to 20 per cent of the relevant infrastructure investment. The way the funds are spent is itself intended to be part of the cohesive process as it involves a partnership between the Commission, the member state and lower tiers of government in forming the Community Support Framework, which establishes how the money is to be spent, with the responsibility being devolved to the member state according to the principle of 'subsidiarity' (responsibility for action should lie with the lower tier of government

Table 12.4   *ERDF and structural fund commitments as a*
percentage of investment and GDP in Objective 1 regions, 1993

| Country | ERDF only | | All funds |
	Investment	GDP	GDP
Greece	7.8	1.7	2.9
Ireland	6.3	1.3	2.7
Portugal	6.0	2.1	3.7
Spain(a)	3.0	0.8	1.2
France(a)	10.0	2.2	4.6
Italy(a)	2.8	0.6	0.9
UK(a)	2.1	0.4	0.9
Total Obj. 1	4.1	0.9	1.6
Total all EC	0.6	0.1	0.3

Source: Fourth Periodic Report, Commission estimates.
(a) Objective 1 regions only: in France this is limited to Corsica and the overseas 'départements', and in the United Kingdom it is only Northern Ireland.

where possible, subject to its being efficient and not involving any substantial spillover effects into other member states).

The Community is concerned that its funds should add to the spending which would in any case have taken place in the member states and, in the doubling of the funds, insisted that the new funds should represent an increase of at least the same amount on the spending in those regions. To help ensure this, all projects have to be cofinanced by funds from within the member state, normally on a 50–50 basis. Only the United Kingdom seems to experience any difficulty in establishing that the additionality principle is being followed and this appears to be because of the way public finance is administered, not because the actual practices are particularly different (see House of Lords, 1991).

Structural assistance is not only provided in the form of grants but also in loans through the European Investment Bank (EIB). These loans enable borrowers to obtain funds at the best rates available, as the EIB is triple A rated and passes on these terms with a commercial margin, thus enabling those in the more inflation prone member states to lower the costs of borrowing considerably. All the loans are, however, in hard currency terms so it is not possible for borrowers also to gain from exchange-rate depreciation. A second advantage of the involvement of the EIB is that it lends for projects which are much closer to industry and hence enables firms themselves to restructure.

Taking these structural instruments together, Franzmeyer *et al.* (1991) have shown that the pattern of spending clearly favours the less-favoured regions. However, focusing on expenditure tells us only part of the story as the funds also have to be raised from the regions. The net impact on the regions is the difference between what is currently achieved and what would have been achieved without the Community's intervention.

The Community budget

The Community does not try to redistribute funds as such across the member states and regions. It has expenditure programmes, on the one hand, and four instruments for raising revenue, called 'own resources', on the other. These do not inherently balance up into a pattern of net contributions which relate closely to either the ability to pay or to need on the basis of relative disadvantage. This has to be assessed at the level of the member states as it is they, not the regions, which provide the funds direct to the Community, although of course they in turn will have raised their resources across the country. Ireland and Greece, which are both covered by objective 1, are the clearest net beneficiaries, but Portugal, which is also entirely objective 1, receives relatively less in proportionate terms, while Spain, which has a large number of objective 1 regions and a GDP per head substantially below the Community average, is close to becoming a net contributor. On the other side of the coin, the Netherlands and Denmark are net beneficiaries despite being among the most favoured of the member states.

This pattern does not help cohesion, to say the least, and it was the subject of successful protest by the United Kingdom, which was becoming a substantial net contributor despite being around average GDP, that resulted in the Fontainbleau agreement. A new budgetary perspective for the five years 1993–8 now has to be agreed and this provides an opportunity to try to reorganise the budget on a more equitable basis. The Spanish are already pressing for transfers to assist them, supported by the other member states with substantial objective 1 regions.

The source of the inequity is straightforward and we have argued elsewhere (Begg and Mayes, 1991) that the more appropriate solution is to tackle that source directly rather than try to correct it subsequently by transfers. Spending on agricultural price support dominates the current EC budget (table 12.5). As Franzmeyer *et al.* (1991) show this does little to assist the least-favoured regions relative to the rest of the Community. This is principally because it was devised for the Community of Six and focuses on 'northern' products. As a result the budget as a whole only gives a relatively limited transfer of resources towards the less-favoured regions in *gross* terms. On the revenue side, the first two resources relate to agricultural levies and to customs duties, which are not strongly related to GDP, although the third resource based on VAT does follow it much more closely. The fourth resource is related to GDP but it is not normally called upon at present. Hence rebalancing the budget to provide a more equitable and cohesive pattern could be achieved by altering the emphasis on agriculture, ceasing to support prices generally and focusing the support on farmers and indeed on other parts of the rural economy in need.

Many of the Community's programmes are aimed at specific aspects of improving competitiveness, such as those relating to R&D. This results in distributions of expenditure towards those regions which have the greatest resources for undertaking R&D, rather than trying to provide facilities for the less-favoured regions. There is thus no reason for expecting that all programmes should reflect a pattern which favours

Table 12.5   *Preliminary draft community budget for 1992*

	Ecu mn	Per cent
EAGGF guarantee section	34660	53.2
Structural operations	17965	27.6
Other policies	7748	11.7
Repayments and administration	3833	5.9

the less-favoured regions. A choice, therefore, has to be made, over the degree to which positive programmes for improving the ability of the less-favoured regions to compete can be expanded or made more effective and the degree to which there needs to be transfers to those regions because the positive measures are insufficient. Beyond a certain point the rate of return on 'infrastructure' investment becomes too small to make it worthwhile. However, by the same token, there are disadvantages at the margin to transfers, as they can act as a disincentive both to those who are providing the transfers through greater taxation and to those who are receiving them, who may become dependent in a way that seems prevalent, for example, in Southern Italy. NIESR (1991) makes a balanced set of recommendations for the way forward to improve cohesion over the rest of the decade.

There is debate over whether the resulting multi-speed approach to closer integration is economically beneficial. It is clearly not conducive to cohesion as it creates a group of member states that cannot enjoy the full benefits of integration. Nor does it remove the need to assist those regions. Even though the full short-run costs of adjustment may have been avoided, adjustment is still required at some stage. In the meantime the rest of the member states reap the cost advantages of monetary union and hence make the problems of convergence worse rather than better. This implies that, despite the costs to the Community of improving cohesion, such spending is necessary if the Community is to be able to continue its path to closer integration.

Requirements to enable monetary union to proceed

Given that a political judgement is needed to determine what constitutes cohesion, it is unlikely that a precise set of targets to be met can easily be identified. Moreover, the requirements for cohesion can be expected to vary through time: major disparities which, though unwelcome, are acceptable today, may cease to be so once monetary union has been in place for some time. Maintenance or achievement of cohesion implies not only a strategy to diminish existing disparities, but also the establishment of mechanisms to deal with regional shocks that may arise as a consequence of monetary union.

As noted above, there is no purely technical reason for cohesion to be considered a precondition for monetary union. Nevertheless, the question of whether it is possible to move towards monetary union in the absence of a policy to assure cohesion has to be considered. This question was posed in relation to the single market and the answer was a commitment to double the Structural Funds and to concentrate their resources in the least-advantaged regions. Already, at the Maastricht summit, a new

'Cohesion' fund has been agreed, albeit with comparatively modest initial resources. The fact that the new fund will be written into the Treaty suggests that it could become a more potent instrument, especially in conjunction with the proposed changes to Structural Funds rules aimed at easing co-financing stipulations.

Although it is clear that the EC recognises that it has a responsibility to support its least-favoured regions, what is at issue is how big a commitment it needs to make. The risk is that if sufficient priority is not assigned to cohesion, the pace of economic integration may have to be slowed, either because too few regions are persuaded that the benefits are sufficient to outweigh the costs or because Member States where regional problems are concentrated can exercise their political power when unanimous decision-making is required. At the same time, if policies to assure cohesion impose excessive demands on the regions and member states which have to provide the resources, they may judge that the entire process does not warrant the effort.

In the transition to monetary union, the immediate threat to cohesion comes from the obligation on some of the weaker member states to attain nominal convergence. Substantial short- to medium-term credits and, possibly, derogations for single market rules may be required, especially for a country like Greece which faces intense fiscal pressures. The longer-term demands on policy will, however, be largely concerned with improving the underlying competitiveness of less-favoured regions so as to give them equality of opportunity in the integrated European economy. This will call for both improved use of existing Community policy instruments and a search for new ones that respond to emerging needs.

Even within its own terms there is substantial scope for the Community to improve its use of the structural funds. The attempt to improve cohesion can be improved, first by ensuring that funds are focused on the projects that will achieve the greatest payoff, simplifying the administrative barriers, ensuring that high standards of evaluation and monitoring are followed. Secondly, a rather wider view of what constitutes investment in the social and economic infrastructure could enable a more cohesive approach to the development of the less-favoured regions, improving education, health and social provision as well as providing more direct support for industry. Thirdly, the effective use of the new infrastructure to achieve improved growth in the less-advantaged regions comes from the actions of the private sector. If those efforts are to be better integrated it would be an advantage to involve industry and the social partners in the decision making at an early stage. The Community stresses the advantages of partnership between the Commission, member state and regional administrations in deciding upon the priorities for the use of the structural funds and in their administration, extending that argument to the private sector would complete the logic.

In NIESR (1991) we suggested that both routes towards closer cohesion, encouraging indigenous growth and assisting those currently disadvantaged need to be considered, putting forward a form of social security transfers as a means of assisting lower income households. One of the problems with existing Community expenditures in the less-favoured regions is that there is no particular guarantee of where in the income distribution the payments go. It would be possible for the transfers to be going from the less well off in advantaged regions to the better off in the less-advantaged regions. This would be particularly likely when payments go towards equipment rather than local labour.

An inevitable question in relation to cohesion will be how much should be spent. The fact that disparities in the Community have not narrowed appreciably in the last decade suggests that the immediate answer is that what has been done thus far is 'not enough'. Improvement in the formulation and delivery of policy can go some way towards narrowing the gap, but there are natural limits to what limited spending can achieve. In the light of this, the Community, if it is serious about cohesion, will almost certainly have to look at some form of inter-regional equalisation system. This, as the calculations in the MacDougall report show, would require funding of a different order of magnitude from that currently available to the Community. Given that there are deep-seated objections to increases in a central budget that would confer more power on a Brussels bureaucracy, it is important to distinguish the form of delivery from the purpose of income transfers. Nevertheless, as the EC becomes more integrated politically and economically (whether or not a federal structure evolves) there is a compelling logic pointing in the direction of explicit inter-territorial transfers.

With a starting-point of a budget of just 0.3 per cent of Community GDP devoted to structural policies, it is obvious that the scope for action on cohesion faces severe resource constraints. Even with sufficient political will to stimulate change, it is difficult to see major increases in the budget being politically acceptable or even quickly agreed. The agreement at Maastricht for a fresh look at the Community budget in order to relate it more to ability to pay is a positive step, but realism suggests that it will take some time to be enacted.

It can be argued that cohesion demands that the Community should set itself objectives for the improvement of the real economy in less-favoured regions, and should not be content with attaining target levels of financial commitments. The simplest form of target would be to reduce disparities for various groups, for example, that by 1998 no region should have a GDP less than 60 per cent of the EC average or that no region should have unemployment exceeding 200 per cent more than the EC average. Alternatively one could have targets which relate to disparities for the Community as a whole. Thus one could argue for a reduction of 10 per cent in the variance of regional GDP in the Community (as measured by the weighted coefficient of variation). However, this measure is also affected by the spread of the upper tail of the distribution, which is outside the scope of the policy.

Conclusions

Although cohesion exists as an issue that has to be dealt with in the Community even without economic and monetary union, the requirements for convergence before such a union can start, in particular, exacerbate the problems of cohesion. Removing the non-tariff barriers to trade, fixing exchange rates and constraining macroeconomic policy and the use of state aids all reduce the mechanisms that the least-favoured regions and the member states in which they are concentrated can use to improve their relative position. Furthermore, the combination of the natural immobility of labour in the EC and the requirements of the social dimension of the process of closer integration put even more pressure on labour markets, which are typically slow to adjust. As a result the burden for achieving cohesion falls firmly on the rest of the Community.

At its extreme, the failure to achieve adequate cohesion could lead to the disintegration of the Community or the creation of a division between those which can adjust to the preconditions of monetary union and those which cannot, within the initial time frame. It is not surprising that those who find that the current system is not offering all the benefits it might demanded concessions in the intergovernmental conferences and are taking the argument on to the negotiations over the next five-year budget perspective.

Thus, although convergence of real variables like GDP per head and unemployment may not be requirements for EMU in the technical sense, a measure of closer cohesion is in practice. Since this is primarily a matter of political judgement it is difficult to say how far such changes will have to go. There is a lot of pressure, for example, for the redoubling of the structural funds over the years 1993–8 which, given the problems of absorption, would probably go as far as is reasonable in pursuing the idea of trying to establish equality of opportunity to compete in the single market through investment in the infrastructure of the least-favoured regions. Combined with tighter administration and the provision of substantial knowhow support to increase absorption, this might not only be sufficient but feasible in budgetary and practical terms, allowing some funds for new objectives in combatting problems of urban areas and of migrants.

In NIESR (1991) we showed that, if the total budget of the Community continues to grow at 3 per cent a year in real terms, as it has done over recent years, the structural funds can increase by 60–70 per cent if spending on agricultural price support remains constant in real terms and all other programmes retain their share of the budget (that is, grow by 3 per cent a year). Redoubling of the structural funds requires some cut in agricultural spending or budget growth, but the magnitudes involved – 3 per cent a year – are not ridiculous. However, we doubt the political will of the member states to agree it.

Even so, it is unlikely that this will be enough to satisfy the Southern member states. Some rebalancing of the total budget will be required to relate net contributions more closely to ability to pay. A plausible mechanism has already been put forward in Padoa-Schioppa's (1987) book, *Equity, Efficiency and Stability*, and no doubt others can be devised. There must, nevertheless, be some doubts over whether Greece can reach the preconditions for convergence to monetary union and an explicit transitional package may be required at a later date with firm IMF style conditions. Implicit in this schema is that the richer countries, with objective 1 and other regional problems (Italy, France, United Kingdom and, if we treat the former DDR on the same basis, Germany) can handle both the preconditions for monetary union and the requirements for the cohesion of their less-favoured regions without any net contribution from the rest of the Community.

Achieving adequate cohesion to enable all the member states to enter EMU towards the end of the 1990s is thus a difficult but a feasible task. Currently, the signs are that the EC will struggle to attain it. Delaying will not assist the problem, as the pressures for widening the Community beyond the current EFTA members will grow and will entail further costs, whatever form such membership takes. Certainly, the problems of social and economic cohesion of central and eastern Europe make those of the current EC trivial by comparison.

The Maastricht agreement takes some of the initial steps, suggested in NIESR (1991), in the direction which is required if there is to be sufficient cohesion to achieve the preconditions for monetary union and to sustain the union thereafter. It has set up a limited Cohesion Fund for the environment and infrastructure. It has set up a consultative Regional Committee and strengthened the commitment to achieving cohesion in Article 130. However, the major step is still to come with the bargaining over the next five-year budgetary perspective. Only then could sufficient steps be taken to enhance the attempt to improve the competitiveness of the less-favoured regions and increase the fiscal capacity of some of the member states with the greatest problems in achieving the preconditions for monetary union through a more equitable budget. However, this is only part of the way to the system envisaged in the MacDougall Report as part of an ever closer union. Inter-territorial transfers, perhaps along the lines used in Germany, which might bring the treatment of regional disparities in the Community more in line with that practised in nation states, is an issue to be addressed after the establishment of monetary union (in 1999).

Notes

1 The European Community classifies its regions according to the 'Nomenclature of Territorial Units for Statistics'. This distinguishes 66 Regional units at level I and 174 at Level II. The United Kingdom standard regions are a Level I disaggregation.
2 The EC's structural policy allocates funds according to a series of objectives, three of which denote regions. Objective 1 regions are those judged to be lagging behind in their economic development with GDP per head substantially below the EC average and unemployment substantially above it. Objective 2 refers to industrial regions in decline, mostly areas of high unemployment in the northern member states. Objective 5b comprises rural regions in northern member states which have too high a level of income to be part of objective 1 but which face difficulties in development. Two further objectives (3 and 4) concern action on long-term unemployment and youth unemployment. Objective 5a is concerned with agricultural restructuring.
3 The principle of subsidiarity asserts that responsibility should as far as possible be allocated to the member state rather than to the Community providing this is efficient and does not involve substantial spillover effects in other member states. To quote the Delors report 'the functions of higher levels of government should be as limited as possible and should be subsidiary to those of lower levels. Thus the attribution of competences to the Community would have to be confined specifically to those areas in which collective decision-making was necessary.'

13

The Prospects for Monetary Union in Europe

Ray Barrell

This chapter attempts to summarise our conference discussion and put in context the preceding chapters. It also attempts to address the preconditions for union, both as set out in the Maastricht Treaty, and in a wider context. The chapter first of all attempts to address one of the questions asked in the preface by Michael Posner. Why has there been a slow shift of opinion in favour of fixed exchange rates? The answer must in part be because we did not fully enjoy the experience we had in the flexible rate system. There were also many, especially in France, who were never enamoured with flexible exchange rates in the first place.

Disenchantment with flexible exchange rates

The pressure for the creation of a monetary union in Europe has been rising over the last few years. Prior to the publication of the Delors report in 1989 the topic did not appear to be high on the political agenda anywhere in Europe. The Commission report, 'One market, one money' (1990), and the associated publications containing background research represent a major intellectual drive in the direction of a single currency for Europe. The significance of the debate on a common currency for Europe was recognised rather slowly in the United Kingdom, and there has been considerable political opposition to such a development. However the political debate has moved on and, even though the United Kingdom authorities have clear reservations about the process, the Conservative government signed up for the bulk of the Maastricht Treaty of December 1991.

The desire for a monetary union in Europe is not new. The Commission made a number of proposals for a monetary union in the early 1970s, but the intellectual and political climate was set against such a development. The Bretton Woods system, which had operated adequately in the 1950s and early 1960s, broke up because some of its members were unwilling to accept the consequences of a fixed exchange rate system. A small open economy in a fixed exchange rate system ultimately cannot control its price level or its real exchange rate. Without stringent capital controls it is not possible to have different interest rates from elsewhere in the world, and it is not possible to control the money supply. If there are capital controls then the price level will still depend upon developments elsewhere in the world, but as the channels of effect are purely based on trade it would be possible for the real exchange rate to diverge from its equilibrium for some period of time. Large open economies in a fixed exchange rate system may have some policy independence, but the abuse of this independence, especially by the reserve currency country (the United States in the 1960s), was the main factor behind the break up of the fixed exchange rate system.

The advocates of flexible exchange rates, and especially Milton Friedman and Harry Johnson, argued that a country with a flexible exchange rate would be able to control its own money supply, and hence it could control its own price level and rate of inflation. In the early 1970s policymakers saw this as a major advantage, as the combination of the Vietnam War and President Johnson's expenditure on social programmes had raised demand in the United States, and much of the expenditure was financed by money creation and balance of payments deficits. In the Bretton Woods fixed rate system the smaller economies had to accept the resulting balance of payments surpluses and increasing inflation. The nominal anchor of the system was seen as the source of inflationary pressure, and hence it was discarded.

The experience of flexible exchange rates in the 1970s and 1980s was not always as beneficial as their academic advocates suggested. Freedom to undertake policy initiatives is also freedom to make policy mistakes. Freedom to vary the exchange rate is also freedom to delay the costs of political compromises. These two problems were central to the European experience of flexible exchange rates. In a fixed rate system a country that expands its money supply excessively will, if the surplus countries are willing to hold the currency in question, experience a balance of payments deficit. Inflation is exported to the rest of the world, or at least shared with it. If the currency is not voluntarily held then the solvency of the expanding authorities is called into question and they may be forced to tighten their fiscal policy. On the other hand in a floating rate system monetary expansion is likely to be associated with a rise in inflation and a fall in the exchange rate. All of the resulting inflationary effects of a fiscal expansion are felt at home. Flexible exchange rates also gave policymakers the ability to validate excessive wage claims by devaluing the currency.

Many European countries faced severe inflationary difficulties in the 1970s and 1980s. The loss of the nominal anchor made France, Italy, the United Kingdom, Ireland and Spain much more prone to sudden bursts of inflation. Sometimes these resulted from monetary expansions, as in the United Kingdom in the early 1970s, sometimes they came from excessive wage push. Dissatisfaction with the experience of floating rates had led the European economies to search for a more rigidly fixed system. This search started with the 'snake' of the early 1970s. The ERM is the most recent and successful alternative.

We should not misinterpret the desire for fixed exchange rates as anything other than a desire for price stability. The European experience over the last two decades is discussed in Chapter 1. Only Germany, the Netherlands and Austria have consistently managed to keep inflation low. The desire for monetary union is a desire for German inflationary performance. A fixed exchange rate is one way of ensuring that the other European countries share German success. The ERM has seen a process of gradual convergence on German inflation rates, with France, Belgium, Denmark and Ireland having converged in recent years (albeit onto a rising German inflation rate). The United Kingdom, Spain and Italy still display substantial inflationary problems. However, all see German policy and German example as a new nominal anchor. Price stability (or inflation always averaging 2–3 per cent) is hardly questioned as a goal. The desire for fixed rates in Europe may, as Collignon argues in Chapter 10, also reflect a wish to pursue a more helpful and coordinated policy towards Eastern Europe. However, it is unlikely to lead to the Ecu taking on a dominant role in international finance. Indeed, Williamson, in Chapter 11, argues that its introduction will have little effect on the pattern of international monetary arrangements.

Preconditions for union in Europe

We are now facing the possibility of moving towards full monetary union in Europe by 1997 or 1999. The Exchange Rate Mechanism (ERM) of the European Monetary System (EMS) has been becoming increasingly fixed. The system was set up in 1979, and at that time most countries were allowed 2¼ per cent fluctuation bands around their central rates. Most of the initial members were operating effective ½ per cent fluctuation bands by the middle of 1991. The Italians were still in need of the full narrow band, and the late joiners, the United Kingdom and Spain, found it necessary to operate with 6 per cent bands.

The Maastricht Treaty set out numerous preconditions for the formation of a monetary union. These are all technical in nature, in that targets are set for inflation rates, for government debt and for government deficits. There is very little discussion in the Treaty about the conditions under which a feasible monetary union can be sustained amongst a group of essentially independent states. There is also no discussion about the timetable for the introduction of a common currency. This issue is addressed further in an appendix to this chapter.

There are three issues to consider in the run up to the formation of a monetary union. First, under what conditions is it possible to set up a monetary union, and how does one reduce the cost of doing so? Second, what criteria should one set for membership of the union, and how literally should we interpret such conditions? Third, what changes and policies are required in order that the union of independent states survives the difficult years as well as the balmy ones?

The conditions for the formation of an optimal currency area have been extensively discussed. The literature of the 1960s, as exemplified by Mundell and Mackinnon, suggested that strong trade links and similar output–inflation trade-offs were useful prerequisites for union. These characteristics were obvious in the monetary union between Ireland and the United Kingdom, and that union survived until 1979. However, developments in macroeconomic theory in the 1960s and early 1970s led to a revision of those views. Friedman and others suggested that in equilibrium a market economy would display no significant trade-off between inflation and unemployment. Hence it was argued that any group of countries could be brought together into a monetary union, as long as initial conditions were satisfactory, and the political will was present.

The costs of setting up a union depend upon the speed and size of any adjustment that is required. They will also depend upon the distribution of the effects of the transitional adjustment. Mayes and Begg argue in Chapter 12 that the poorer, peripheral countries will in general be losers in the process of economic and monetary integration. This, they argue, will reduce the cohesiveness of the potential union and this can only be ameliorated by substantial transfers of resources from rich to poor regions. These may be necessary for the political survival of the union, and they may take some time to put in place. Mayes and Begg see this as an argument in favour of a slow transition to monetary union.

The costs of setting up a union will be minimised if the participating countries are at or near their equilibrium real exchange rates. If a country is a long way from such an equilibrium then there are a number of ways to improve the situation. The most obvious is to realign the currency. In a monetary union this palliative is not available. If the price level is too high for the equilibrium real exchange rate then exports will be lower than they otherwise would have been, there will be a balance of payments deficit, wealth will be falling increasingly below its equilibrium trajectory, and as a consequence demand will be below full capacity output. There will therefore be downward pressure on prices. We argue in Barrell, Gurney and in't Veld (1991) that the process of adjustment to equilibrium will take place, but that if real exchange rates are overvalued even by 10 per cent at the inception of a union it could take five to ten years of below capacity growth for the disequilibrium to be removed. Once again, a slow process of adjustment indicates that a long preparation period for union may be necessary.

Is a realignment necessary?

We have argued (Barrell and in't Veld, 1991) that it is possible that the United Kingdom, France and Italy are all overvalued by 5–15 per cent, and that Germany is undervalued by a similar amount. Froot and Rogoff (1991) make a strong case for a final realignment of exchange rates before the formation of a union. They argue that a final realignment just before the introduction of a common currency will involve no loss of credibility, and it is possible that it would enhance the possibility of the survival of the union.[1]

There may however be good reasons for avoiding a general realignment. First, and possibly most important, the German authorities seem reluctant to contemplate one. Second the gains in credibility achieved over the last few years have been expensive, and it is not clear either how they have been won or how they affect the operation of the participating economies. Given this, it is not obvious that one last realignment would not damage the overall credibility of the system and change the behaviour of the economies involved. It is clear that the objective most participants have in mind in creating a monetary union is to make price stability the paramount goal of policy. A last realignment would be inconsistent with this goal. The gains from realignments are transitory, the costs may be longer lasting. However, there is still a policy choice to make.

The policy problem facing the authorities is quite clear. If an economy is not at its equilibrium real exchange rate then the forces of the market will eventually take it there. The price level will have to adjust, and if the real exchange rate is overvalued the price level has to fall relative to that in other countries. The target for the real exchange rate is in the long run essentially independent of the actions of the authorities.[2] The authorities are able to choose the instruments they use to approach the target and the speed at which they approach it. A nominal devaluation may be the least cost way of reaching the long-run equilibrium. However, although this move appears to be relatively costless, the gains have to be set off against the costs involved in higher inflation and in lost credibility. Given the opacity of the costs and benefits involved, an optimal policy may be hard to calculate (see Wren-Lewis *et al.*, 1991).

The preconditions for union membership set out in the Maastricht Treaty include a requirement that participating members do not precipitate devaluations in the two years before the union is set up. This precludes the Froot–Rogoff realignment, and this further weakens the case for a realignment now, as the credibility costs could be significant. The Maastricht Treaty requires that inflation rates converge towards the average of the best performing countries in the union.

We argued in Barrell and in't Veld (1991) that the equilibrium trajectory for current accounts in a monetary union could well be associated with sustainable inflation differentials of 1 per cent a year or more, even amongst the major advanced economies. If, for instance, German non-price competitiveness continues to have the same effects as in the last twenty-five years, then the German real exchange rate will have to continue to appreciate by around 1 per cent a year. This implies that in equilibrium in a fixed rate system the rate of inflation in Germany must be around 1 per cent a year higher than in France, Italy or the United Kingdom. Equilibrium inflation differentials can exist for other reasons as well. It is argued by Larre and Torres in Chapter 9 that the less-advanced economies, Spain, Portugal and Greece, have to undergo a process of catching up with the advanced economies, and that this will involve rapid increases in labour productivity in the tradeable sector. These increases in productivity will spill over into other sectors, either as higher productivity that is required to justify higher wages, or as higher wages and prices in the service sector where productivity is difficult to increase. The successful process of catching up could lead to a process of relative price change within the country in question that leads to a sustained equilibrium inflation differential.[3]

Public debt and the monetary constitution

Perhaps the most controversial, and most stringent, requirements in the Maastricht Treaty concern fiscal policy and debt. The decision to use a measure of gross public sector debt, and the ceiling chosen will, as Chapter 1 shows, put significant pressure on at least the Netherlands and Belgium. This is perhaps unfortunate as in all other respects these low-inflation, high-income countries are obvious candidates for the core of the monetary union. Large debt stocks were accumulated in the 1970s and 1980s to finance public sector deficits that were necessary during extended periods of below capacity growth. Although these debt stocks are in some sense sustainable, another period of significant debt accumulation might make the debt of some countries unsustainable without significant monetisation. This could easily put pressure on the political cohesion of the union.

The need for a monetary constitution has been recognised and it is often argued that an independent monetary authority is not sufficient to guarantee low inflation. As is stressed in Chapter 4, inflation has been low in Germany because the Bundesbank has been independent and competent, and also because there has been the will in the polity to have low inflation. A European monetary institution must be independent, but it is possible that extra sanctions and controls will be needed to ensure its efficiency. Debt stocks have risen because budget deficits have been used as stabilisers for the economies in the face of external shocks. The removal of fiscal policy as the shock absorber may be very undesirable, and Langfeldt argues that a strong monetary constitution is a much more desirable way of controlling lax fiscal policy than are rules for sensible behaviour on the part of the fiscal authorities.

There are many potential shocks to a union. Some may have long-run asymmetrical effects and they will require permanent adjustments of relative prices and wages. A good example of this type of shock would be the effects of German economic union. The accession of large quantities of skilled labour and of land may result in a change in relative factor prices, and this could require a permanent appreciation of the real exchange rate between Germany and the rest of the Community. We have stressed above that the necessary adjustment period in a fixed rate system may be rather extended. The union has to be able to deal with shocks efficiently. It also has to be able to deal with shocks that may be either transitory or symmetrical in the long run. These will cause problems for the cohesiveness of the union as they are asymmetric in the short run. Such asymmetries may arise from structural differences in the constituent members of the union.

Structural convergence in Europe

A set of countries with differing labour market structures will respond differently to shocks in the short run. If the authorities have lacked anti-inflation credibility then wage and price setters will pass shocks through to prices very quickly. They will not expect the authorities to adopt a restrictive stance in response to the shock. In Chapter 2 Anderton *et al.* discuss the speed of responses in European wage and price systems, and it is illuminating to note that the dynamic response of wages to prices has been considerably faster in Italy and the United Kingdom than it has been in Germany. This in part reflects the lack of credibility of the authorities' anti-inflationary resolve.

The mere existence of a monetary union may change the credibility of the authorities' stance, and anti-inflationary reputations may descend like manna from heaven. However, there is no evidence that such a process has taken place whilst the ERM has been becoming more hard. To the extent that there is evidence that labour markets have changed it is clear that the changes have been hard won. Where structural change has taken place it is clearly associated with a slow and painful process of institutional change. In particular in't Veld and Onofri and Tomasini argue that the removal of indexation mechanisms in Belgium, Denmark and Italy seems to have been associated with an improvement in the 'sacrifice ratio'. In these countries a given rise in unemployment seems to have been more effective in reducing inflation in the second half of the 1980s than it was in the 1970s. The labour market structures appear to be converging on that of the core European economies.

Anderton, Barrell and McHugh argue that the size of these changes in labour market structure should not be exaggerated, and the necessity for structural convergence cannot be ignored. There is some evidence that the 'sacrifice ratio' gains have been ebbing away, especially in Italy. Anti-inflationary credibility requires that a strong anti-inflationary stance is maintained, and it is argued by Onofri and Tomasini that the commitment of the Italian authorities has been declining in recent years. This appears to have reversed some of the early improvements in the functioning of the economy because informal indexation mechanisms have been replacing formal ones. Bordes and Girardin suggest that the example of the French authorities is particularly interesting. Inflation convergence has been achieved largely as a result of a tight policy stance. It appears that the gains from 'tying ones' hands' are expensive to achieve and slow in arriving. They are part of the process of the private sector learning about the resolve of the authorities, and it is as easy to lose reputation as to gain it.

It is often argued (Giavazzi and Pagano, 1990) that a contractionary fiscal policy in combination with a commitment to the ERM can actually produce an economic expansion. The channel of causation is supposed to be an accession of credibility on the part of the authorities in combination with a belief that interest rates, taxes and deficits will be continually lower. Bradley and Whelan and in't Veld argue that such expansionary contractions have not so far been observed in Europe. In Ireland and in Denmark in the late 1980s the expansions were driven more by the strength of demand in the rest of Europe. Bradley and Whelan in the case of Ireland, and Larre and Torres in the case of Spain, argue that inflation convergence is not a gift, it is a hard won prize from a long period of high unemployment and low growth.

The need for structural change

If the members of the union maintain diverse labour market structures then their short-term responses to shocks will differ. Diverse responses could put considerable strain on the cohesion and political sustainability of a monetary union. As Chapter 1 emphasises, there are three types of convergence in Europe to consider. Nominal convergence may be the easiest to achieve as it requires coordinated and similar macroeconomic policies. Real convergence is difficult, and perhaps should be left to the market mechanism. Convergence of economic structures is important if the union is to be sustained. A long transition process may be required, because there is nothing so good as the conquest of inflation to persuade wage and price setters that the authorities' resolve has stiffened. However, there may be a number of policies that can be adopted that make structural convergence easier. This may include the reform of wage bargaining and indexation mechanisms, and it may also involve the universal adoption of common labour market regulation. The social chapter of the Maastricht Treaty may indeed be the single most important plank in the building of a successful monetary union in Europe.

The first chapter of this volume suggests that a monetary union can be created, and sustained, if there is sufficient political will. This will require a continuation of the tightening of the monetary stance in some countries such as Italy. Our general conclusion is that, if a monetary union is to be a successful anti-inflation mechanism, we must see restrictive fiscal policies more generally adopted over the next decade. Debt burdens must be reduced. Labour market behaviour must be made more similar across the members of the union, and Anderton, Barrell and McHugh suggest that competition in the goods market must be enhanced by the single minded pursuit of a single market programme. Both of these will produce structural convergence in wage and price setting, and this will enable the system to copy more easily with transitory and asymmetric shocks. The transition to a single currency must also be achieved, and the problems that may be involved are discussed in the appendix below.

Notes

1 There can be no such thing as an irrevocable union of currencies between independent countries, or even between regions of the country. The British–Irish monetary union of 1826–1979 is an obvious counter-example.
2 Government financing decisions may have a second-order effect on the equilibrium real exchange rate.
3 The Maastricht Treaty does appear to make some allowance for such structural differentials.

Appendix to Chapter 13

Malcolm Levitt

The study, 'A Strategy for the Ecu' (Ernst & Young and NIESR, 1990) put forward a proposal for a rapid transition to a common currency. The Association for the Monetary Union of Europe subsequently set up a working group to examine some of the practical issues facing firms if the Ecu were to be substituted for national currencies. This appendix gives a personal report on the discussions that took place in this group between Autumn 1990 and Autumn 1991.

We asked a number of firms for their views, but many of them found it difficult to take the issue seriously because the substitution of the Ecu for national currencies seemed either unlikely or very far into the future. This view confirmed what had been emphasised in 'A Strategy for the Ecu', that is, that without a clear timetable for the introduction of monetary union the private sector would be unwilling to invest resources in planning and implementing the necessary changes. The Maastricht Treaty has removed much of this uncertainty. However, firms in the private sector still face considerable uncertainty in a number of countries, especially those in countries which will face considerable difficulty in meeting the convergence criteria, and also firms in the United Kingdom, where it is not yet clear whether the common currency will be adopted.

Nonetheless our discussions have made some progress and this appendix reports on the implications for firms and for the banking system, and also discusses other changes that will be necessary.

Industrial and commercial firms

Much discussion within the working party concerned the case for using the Ecu under current circumstances in normal commercial transactions. There are currently very few commercial users of the Ecu. However, it has found a use where a given organisation, such as the chemical company Tioxide, buys and sells across Europe in weak and strong currency markets. The Ecu not only provides the advantages of using a single currency for internal invoicing and accounting, it also provides a useful compromise between the interests of purchasing and selling bodies within the group. Groups of independent enterprises based in each of the Community countries, such as the Federation of European Railways, have also used the Ecu. The pattern of transactions amongst this group closely reflects the weights in the Ecu basket, and there are advantages in using the Ecu as the common unit of account and settlement currency. However most participants in the working party saw little current advantage to their own companies in the use of the Ecu for transactions. However, we envisage that even prior to EMU the use of the Ecu in commercial transactions will grow once national parliaments have ratified the Treaty.

Looking to the final introduction of the Ecu as Europe's single currency we can distinguish between the effects on the primary functions of companies and on their support systems. The principal effect on primary activities will be the removal of exchange risk within the currency union and this will have a number of implications. We would expect the willingness to source in other countries to increase. We would expect there to be an effect on the location of manufacturing facilities. A number of multinationals have located plants within their major markets so as to reduce currency risk. Over the longer term we may expect some rationalisation of plant distribution and size as currency risk declines.

We also expect that the removal of currency risk will increase the scale of sales and marketing activities. The scale of these effects is unlikely to be large and it will be very difficult to distinguish the effect of the removal of currency risk from effects of other changes, particularly those associated with the development of the single market.

The participants in our working group agreed to attempt to complete a questionnaire seeking to identify the changes which need to be made to support functions such as accountancy, treasury operations and training. We also decided to look at the potential costs of transition, and the length of time needed to plan and introduce the necessary changes.

Banks

The implications we considered for banks were largely related to markets and services, where the introduction of the single currency will have the greatest effect, and systems, where increased investment will be needed.

Foreign exchange markets and related revenue-generating services will clearly be affected by the substitution of a single currency for several existing ERM currencies. Cross-trades among the currencies for which the Ecu is substituted will obviously vanish. Ecu transactions will grow although we may expect a reduction in spreads and profits. The short-term effects of these developments will mean a reduction in Forex volumes, a squeeze on margins, and some reductions in capacity as banks scale down their operations and some may leave the market entirely.

However, the effects should not be exaggerated. The bulk (perhaps 95 per cent) of forex transactions – estimate by M. Deakin (Ernst & Young) – are between professional dealers in a market unrelated to trade, so the effect of the substitution of the Ecu for existing currencies in trade finance will be modest. Following reductions in capacity those remaining in the market may see an increase in volume with respect to Ecu-based transactions. Once the Ecu has replaced the principal currencies of Europe the market will grow in depth and liquidity to such an extent that the Ecu may well replace the dollar as the intermediary currency for transactions involving pairs of other currencies. It may also become the principal currency for trade and transactions between Europe and the rest of the world. In capital markets the replacement of domestic currencies by the Ecu will mean that banks which have dominant positions in lead management and underwriting in their domestic markets will see that position eroded. The emergence of a single European capital market through the removal of barriers created by the existence of national currencies will increase competition, put pressure on margins, and induce reductions in capacity including departure from the market of some small or domestically focused banks.

There are other potentially important developments induced by the substitution of the Ecu for national currencies. The emergence of Ecu-denominated bonds as attractive alternatives to dollar bonds may lead to difficulties in financing any potential United States deficit. There is likely to be increased use of the Ecu for pricing in commodity markets where Europe is the principal customer. There are also likely to be substantial reductions in revenues and capacity associated with personal foreign exchange transactions within Europe.

Banks will need to plan for major changes in support and operating systems such as customer payments services, client data, treasury support systems, accounting systems, and they will need to mount major training exercises for their branch networks. Participants in the study have been given a questionnaire asking them to detail the kinds of changes required, and the timescales and costs involved. To date a number of banks have indicated that they would need perhaps three to four years to plan and test the necessary systems changes for the substitution of the Ecu for the national currency.

An extended planning period is necessary if the national currency is used for domestic transactions prior to a 'big bang' and the Ecu is used afterwards. However, if the Ecu were to be used for domestic transactions on any scale prior to big bang the problems to be faced would be more complicated. At present banks offer the facilities of Ecu accounts in the same way that they provide a wide range of foreign currency accounts and it is quite likely that the use of the Ecu in cross-border commercial transactions within Europe will grow considerably prior to big bang and that will be handled in the normal way using Ecu foreign currency accounts. If customers were to require dual-currency domestic accounts permitting easy conversion between the domestic currency and the Ecu, then banks and the inter-bank payments systems would face a more strenuous task.

Inter-bank payments systems

The growth in the volume and value of cross-border transactions induced by the development of the single market together with the introduction of the single currency create a need for an improvement in cross-border payments systems within the Community. This system needs to be able to deal with both retail (high volume, low value) and wholesale (high value) payments.

The EC is currently reviewing arrangements for cross-border retail payments, where existing services have been strongly criticised on the grounds that low value irregular payments are too costly, subject to excessive delays, the fees to be borne by customers are unclear and there is excessive uncertainty about the date when and the amount which will be credited to recipients. To improve matters the Commission proposed that fee and cost structures should be more transparent and to facilitate the development of the single market and the transition to monetary union they propose to replace the 'patchwork quilt' of different national payments systems around the EC by developing a pan-EC network of automated clearing houses (ACHs), through developing electronic linkages between ACHs, possibly via a central body.

The question of the efficiency and the quality of service provided by retail payments systems merits attention in its own right, irrespective of monetary union. However a wide range of options for improving existing arrangements is under discussion, some of which involve market forces alone (such as improvements to correspondent banking, developments in branch banking by major international banks, technological developments for bulked payments and direct debits, and proposals for card networks and Swift to link national ACHs).

When we turn to large, wholesale payments the situation is rather different. We already have a wholesale Ecu clearing system, to which 45 Ecu clearing banks across Europe belong. Payment messages are passed via the Swift network and the system is operated by the BIS which does not, however, have any supervisory responsibilities. Volumes are large (over 38bn Ecu a day) and growing rapidly but the central banks are very concerned about the fragility of the system. There is no guaranteed finality of payment, the legal base for contracts is uncertain, there is a lack of transparency of risks involved, and most importantly, a lack of proper supervision.

Once we have a single European Ecu money market it is essential that we have a system capable of handling extremely large values efficiently, permitting guaranteed rapid settlement, and at minimum risk. However the construction of such a system will be a major undertaking and it would need to cope with large risks; for example, it could involve the establishment of a system capable of handling real-time bilateral net limits among participating institutions or perhaps fully collateralised real time gross limits, backed up by an adequate system of law.

This will be a major task for new European monetary institutions. The magnitude of the task is immense and possibly barely feasible within the time scale we now face before the introduction of the Ecu as the single currency. Given the time it is taking to get Taurus established in the United Kingdom, one can only speculate about the timescale involved in the construction of an efficient and effective wholesale Ecu clearing system.

Other issues

Many other issues remain to be resolved in order to minimise the commercial costs of a transition to EMU. The conversion rate between national currencies and the Ecu needs to be fixed well in advance of the big bang so that the necessary systems changes can be properly planned. A new legal framework needs to be established in order to support the use of the Ecu. It has to cover commercial contracts, tax assessment payments, financial reporting in advance of big bang, and the treatment of the Ecu as legal tender.

Decisions on regulatory and supervisory matters also have to be made. There needs to be a harmonisation of minimum reserve ratios across the monetary union. They currently range from the 0.45 per cent required by the Bank of England to 12.1 per cent for sight deposits over DM100 million in Germany to 25 per cent in Italy. Any moves towards a common ratio would have a significant impact on the financing costs and relative competitive position of commercial banks throughout the monetary union. The determination of responsibility for supervision and regulation also need to be decided.

Conclusion

Clearly time is rather short for planning and implementing the necessary changes which firms need to undertake in order to be able to handle the substitution of the Ecu for national currencies. Something of the order of three years seems to be required by banks which have major systems changes to introduce and one may assume that manufacturers would require much less time although retailers might well need as long as banks. The development of an efficient and effective wholesale Ecu clearance and settlement system is likely to take significantly longer than the three years needed within individual commercial banks.

In principal the monetary union could start in 1997 if a majority of EC countries meet the necessary convergence conditions; otherwise EMU will start in 1999. The preliminary results of the discussions in the working party so far suggest that if the Ecu were to be introduced as the single currency in 1997 decisions to that effect would need to be taken in 1993. If, on the other hand, decisions were not taken until July, 1998 on the countries which meet the convergence criteria it seems to follow that even if EMU were to start in 1999 in the sense of locked exchange rates the single currency could not be introduced before around 2002.

The longer political uncertainty remains, the less willing firms will be to make the necessary investments to enable the introduction of the single currency to become a reality within the sort of political timetable just agreed at Maastricht. What has been lacking from the debate among the visionaries so far is sufficient recognition of the need for an immense amount of detailed planning which firms throughout the Community need to undertake and which they will not commence until the political outlook is much clearer.

References

AMEX *Bank Review* (1991), 18 September 1991, vol. 18, no.7.

Abramovitz, M. (1986), 'Catching up, forging ahead, and falling behind', *Journal of Economic History*, vol. XLVI, no. 2, June.

Aglietta, M. (1990), 'La convertibilité du rouble' in *Monnaie et Finances Internationales*, Economie Prospective Internationale, no. 44, 4 trimestre.

Aglietta, M. and de Boissieu, C. (1991), 'Pour une organization des paiements entre les pays de l'Est', manuscript (mimeo).

Aglietta, M. and Coudert, V. (1990), 'Politiques budgétaires et ajustements macroéconomiques dans la perspective de l'intégration monêtaire européenne', *De Pecunia*, vol. II, no. 2–3, 275–306.

Albrechts, L., Moulaert, F., Roberts, P. and Swyngedouw, E. (eds) (1989), *Regional Policy at the Crossroads*, London, Jessica Kingsley Publishers.

Alogoskoufis, G., Papedemos, L. and Portes, R. (1990), *External Constraints on Macroeconomic Policy: The European Experience*.

Andersen, T. and Risayer, O. (1988), 'Stabilisation policies, credibility and interest rate determination in a small open economy', *European Economic Review*, Paper and Proceedings, 32, 669–73.

Anderton, R. (1992), 'Trade in Europe', NIESR mimeo.

Anderton, R. Barrell, R. and in't Veld, J.W. (1991), 'Macroeconomic convergence in Europe', *National Institute Economic Review*, no. 138, November.

Anderton, R., Barrell, R. and McHugh, J. (1991), 'Credibility, discipline or structural continuity: the effect of the ERM upon wage inflation', NIESR mimeo.

Artis, M.J. and Nachane, D. (1990), 'Wages and prices in Europe, a test of the German leadership hypothesis', *Weltwirtschaftliches Archiv*, 126, 59–77.

Artis, M. and Ormerod, P. (1991), 'Is there an 'EMS effect' in European Labour Markets?!' mimeo, Manchester University, paper presented at ESRC Macromodelling Bureau workshop, LSE, May.

Artus, P., Avouyi-Dovi, S., Bleuze, E. and Lecointe, F. (1991), 'Transmission of US monetary policy to Europe and asymmetry in the European Monetary System', *European Economic Review*, vol. 35, no. 7, October, 1369–1384.

Artus, P. and Bismut, C. (1986), 'Exchange-rate and wage–price dynamics: a theoretical analysis and econometric investigation', *European Economic Review*, 57–90.

Atkinson, A.B., Blanchard, O.J., Fitoussi, J.P., Fleming, J.S., Malinvaud, E., Phelps, E. and Solow, R. (1992), 'La désinflation compétitive, le mark et les politiques budgétaires en Europe', OFCE and Editions du Seuil.

Attali, J. (1991), 'Stabilisation of exchange relations between the Ecu and the currencies of central and Eastern Europe', speech delivered at the Annual Conference of the AUME, London, 30 May 1991, printed in AUME.

Bade, R. and Parkin, M. (1987), 'Central bank laws and monetary policy', Department of Economics, University of Western Ontario, June.

Balassa, B. (1964), 'The purchasing power parity doctrine: a reappraisal', *Journal of Political Economy*, vol. 72, no. 6, December.

Barrell, R.J. (1990a), 'European currency union and the EMS', *National Institute Economic Review*, no. 132, May.

Barrell, R.J. (1990b), 'Has the EMS changed wage and price behaviour in Europe?', *National Institute Economic Review*, no. 134, November.

Barrell, R., Britton, A. and Mayes D. (1990), 'Macroeconomic obstacles to the wider use of the ECU', NIESR Discussion paper no. 180.

Barrell, R., Darby, J. and Donaldson, C. (1990), 'Structural stability in European wage and price systems', NIESR Discussion paper no. 188.

Barrell, R., Gurney A. and Dulake (1990), 'Macroeconomic convergence and the prospects for monetary union in Europe', *Conjunctura Italiana,* November.

Barrell, R., Gurney, A. and in't Veld, J.W. (1992), 'The real exchange rate, fiscal policy and the role of wealth: an analysis of equilibrium in a monetary union', *Journal of Forecasting*, March, 1992.

Barrell, R. and in't Veld, J.W. (1991), 'FEERs and the path to EMU', *National Institute Economic Review*, no. 137.

Barro, R.J. and Xavier Sala-i-Martin (1990), 'World real interest rates', National Bureau of Economic Research Macroeconomics Annual, pp. 15–74.

Barry, F. and Bradley, J. (1991), 'On the causes of Ireland's unemployment', *The Economic and Social Review*, vol. 22, 253–286.

Basevi, G., Ferrari, M., Onofri, P. and Poli, G. (1991), 'Bilancia dei Pagamenti, posizione sull'estero e integrazione finanziaria', Paper presented to the Conference 'La posizione esterna dell'Italia', Rome, December.

Begg, I.G. and Guy, N. (1992 forthcoming), 'Structural change and the UK economy: the changing regional structure' in Driver, C. and Dunne, J.P. (eds) *Structural Change and the UK Economy*, Cambridge University Press.

Begg, I. and Mayes, D.G. (1991), 'Social and economic cohesion among the regions of Europe in the 1990s', *National Institute Economic Review*, November, no. 138.

Beregovoy, P. (1990), 'Pas d'indépendance monétaire de la Banque centrale dans l'ignorance des exigences politiques', Deutsche Bundesbank Auszeuge aus Pressartikeln, 22 November.

Bergsten, C.F. (1986), 'America's unilateralism', in Bergsten, C.F., Davignon, E. and Miyazaki, I., *Conditions for Partnership in International Economic Management*, New York, The Trilateral Commission.

Blanchard, O., Chouraqui, J.C., Hagemann, R.P. and Sartor, N. (1990), 'The sustainability of fiscal policy: new answers to an old question', OECD *Economic Studies*, no.15.

Blanchard, P. and Sevestre, P. (1989), L'indexation des salaires: quelle rupture en 1982?', *Economie et Prévision*, no. 87.

Blommestein, H. (forthcoming), *Reality of International Economic Policy Coordination*, Amsterdam, North-Holland.

Bofinger, P. (1991), 'Options for the payment and exchange rate system in

Eastern Europe' in *European Economy*, special edition no. 2, *The Path of Reforms in Central and Eastern Europe*, Brussels.

Bordes, C., Driscoll, M. and Strauss-Kahn, M.O. (1989), 'Price inertia and nominal aggregate demand in major European countries', *Recherches Economiques de Louvain*, no. 2, 103–128.

Brabant, J.M. van, (1991), 'Assistance to Eastern Europe and European economic and monetary integration 1991', *De Pecunia* (forthcoming).

Bradley, J. and Fitz Gerald, J. (1988), 'Industrial output and factor input determination in an econometric model of a small open economy', *European Economic Review*, vol. 32, 1227–1241.

Bradley, J. and Fitz Gerald, J. (1991), 'The ESRI medium-term economic model', *Medium-Term Review: 1991–1996*, Dublin, The Economic and Social Research Institute.

Bradley, J., Fitz Gerald, J. and Kearney, I. (1991), 'The Irish market services sector: an econometric investigation', *'The Economic and Social Review*, vol. 22, 287–309.

Bruno, M. and Sachs, J. (1985), *Economics of Worldwide Stagflation*, Cambridge, Mass, Harvard University Press.

Callan, T. and Fitz Gerald, J. (1989), 'Price determination in Ireland: effects of changes in exchange rates and exchange rate regimes', *Economic and Social Review*, vol. 20, 165–188.

Calvo, G.A. and Vegh, C.A. (1990), Credibility and the Dynamics of Stabilisation Policy: A Basic Framework, Preliminary draft.

Camagni, R. (ed) (1991), *Innovation Networks*, London, Bellhaven Press.

Centre for Economic Policy Research (1991), *Monitoring European Integration: The Making of Monetary Union*, London, Centre for Economic Policy Research.

Chan-Lee, J.H., Coe, D.T. and Prywes, M. (1987), 'Macroeconomic changes and macroeconomic wage disinflation in the 1980s', *OECD Economic Studies*, no. 8, Spring, 121–57.

Collignon, S. (1990), 'The consequences of European Monetary Union for Eastern Europe' in *De Pecunia*, vol. II, no. 2–3, October.

Collignon, S. (1990a), *Regionale Integration und Entwicklung in Ostafrika*, Institut für Afrikasforschung, Hamburg.

Collins, S.M. (1988), 'Inflation and the European Monetary System', in Giavazzi, Micossi and Miller (eds), *The European Monetary System*, Cambridge University Press.

Commission of the European Communities (1989), 'International trade of the European Community', *European Economy*, no. 35.

Commission of the European Communities (1989), 'Economic convergence in the Community: a greater effort is needed', *European Economy*, no. 41.

Commission of the European Communities (1990), 'One market, one money: an evaluation of the potential benefits and costs of forming an economic and monetary union', *European Economy*, no. 44, October.

Commission of the European Communities (1990), 'Annual economic report 1990–91', *European Economy*, no. 46.

Commission of the European Communities (1991a), *Europe 2000: Outlook for the Development of the Community's Territory*, Luxembourg, Office for Official Publications of the European Community.

Commission of the European Communities (1991b), *Fourth Periodic Report on the Social and Economic Situation and Development of the Regions of the Community*, Luxembourg, Office for Official Publications of the European Community.

Commission of the European Communities (1991c), 'Per capita GDP in the Community regions in 1989', Eurostat Rapid Report 1991. no. 2.

Commission of the European Communities (1991d), 'Unemployment in the Community regions in 1991', Eurostat Rapid Report 1991 no. 3.

Committee for the Study of Economic and Monetary Union (Delors Committee) (1989), 'Report on Economic and Monetary Union in the European Community', Luxembourg, April.

Cotis, J.P. (1991), 'Persistance du chômage et contenu en emploi de la croissance: quels progrès l'économie française a-t-elle réalisés sur la voie d'une plus grande flexibilité salariale?' *Direction de la Prévision*, Ministry of Finance.

Cotta, A. (1991), *La France en Panne*, Editions Fayard.

De Grauwe, P. (1989), The cost of disinflation and the European Monetary System, Discussion Paper no. 326, Centre for Economic Policy Research, July.

Demery, D. (1984), 'Aggregate demand, rational expectations and real output: some new evidence for the UK 1963.2–1982.2', *Economic Journal*, vol. 94, 847–862.

Dobson, W. (1991), *Economic Policy Coordination: Requiem or Prologue?* Washington, Institute for International Economics.

Dornbusch, R. (1987), *Dollars, Debts and Deficits*, MIT Press, Cambridge, Mass.

Dornbusch, R. (1988), 'Inflation stabilization and capital mobility' in Dornbusch, R., *Exchange Rates and Inflation*, Cambridge, Mass., MIT Press.

Dornbusch, R. (1989), 'Credibility, debt and unemployment: Ireland's failed stabilisation', *Economic Policy*, no. 8, April.

Dornbusch, R. (1991), 'Problem of European monetary integration' in Giovannini, A. and Mayer, C. (eds), *European Financial Integration,* Cambridge University Press.

Drazen, A. (1989), 'Monetary policy, capital controls and seignorage in an open economy' in de Cecco, M. and Giovannini, A. (eds), *A European Central Bank? Perspectives on Monetary Unification after Ten Years of EMS*, Cambridge, Cambridge University Press, 13–32.

Dreze, J. and Bean, C. (1990), 'Europe's unemployment problem: introduction and synthesis', in *Europe's Unemployment Problem*, Cambridge, Mass., MIT Press.

Edwards, S. and Edwards, A.C. (1987), *Monetarism and Liberalization: The Chilean Experiment*, Cambridge, Mass.

Ermisch, J. (1991), 'European integration and external constraints on social policy: is a social charter necessary?', *National Institute Economic Review*, August, no. 137.

Ernst & Young and NIESR (1990), *A Strategy for the ECU*, London, Kogan Page.

Fanning, R. (1978), *The Irish Department of Finance 1922–58*, Dublin, The Institute of Public Administration.

Fischer, S. (1986a), *Indexing, Inflation and Economic Policy*, Cambridge, Mass, MIT Press.

Fischer, S. (1986), 'Contracts, Credibility and Disinflation', in Fischer, S., *Indexing, Inflation and Economic Policy*, Cambridge, Mass, MIT Press.

Fischer, S. (1988), 'Real balances, the exchange rate and indexation: real variables in disinflation', *Quarterly Journal of Economics*, CIII, 1, 27–50.

Franzmeyer, F., Hrubesch, P., Seidel, B., Weise, C. and Schweiger, I. (1991), 'The regional impact of Community policies', report to the European Parliament.

Froot, K.A. and Rogoff, K. (1991), 'The EMS, the EMU, and the transition to a common currency', NBER Working Paper no. 3684.

Geary, P.T. (1976), 'World prices and the inflationary process in a small open economy: the case of Ireland', *The Economic and Social Review,* vol. 7, 391–400.

Genberg, H. and Swoboda, A.K. (1991), 'The provision of liquidity in the Bretton Woods system', paper presented at a NBER Conference at Bretton Woods, October.

Giavazzi, F. (1989), 'Italy: the real effects of inflation and disinflation', *Economic Policy*, April.

Giavazzi, F. and Giovannini, A. (1988), 'The role of the exchange-rate regime in a disinflation: empirical evidence on the European Monetary System', in Giavazzi, Micossi and Miller (eds), *The European Monetary System,* Cambridge University Press.

Giavazzi, F. and Giovannini, A. (1989), *Limiting Exchange Rate Flexibility: The European Monetary System*, Cambridge, Mass, MIT Press.

Giavazzi, F. and Pagano, M. (1988), 'The advantage of tying one's hands: EMS discipline and central bank credibility, *European Economic Review,* vol. 32, no. 5, June.

Giavazzi, F. and Pagano, M. (1990), 'Can severe fiscal contractions be expansionary? Tales of two small European countries', in 1990 *NBER Macroeconomic Annual*, MIT Press.

Giavazzi, F. and Spaventa, L. (1990), 'Il nuovo SME (con un poscritto)', *Politica Economica*, no. 3.

Giovannini, A. (1990), 'European monetary reform: progress and prospects', *Brookings Papers on Economic Activity*, no.2.

Godfrey, L.G., (1984), 'On the uses of misspecification checks and tests of non-nested hypothesis in empirical econometrics', *Economic Journal,* vol. 94, 69–81.

Godfrey L.G. (1988), *Misspecification tests in Econometrics*, Cambridge University Press.

Goodhart, C.A.E. (1989), *Money, Information and Uncertainty*, (2nd edn), Basingstoke, MacMillan.

Graafland, J.J. and Huizinga, F. (1988), 'Modelling a wage equation for the Netherlands: a cointegration approach', CPB Onderzoeksmemorandum, 51.

Greene, J. and Isard, P. (1991), 'Currency convertibility and the transformation of centrally planned economies', IMF, Occasional paper, no. 81, June, Washington DC.

Gros, D. and Thygesen, N. (1991), 'Towards monetary union in the European Community: Why and how' in Welfens, P. (ed.), *European Monetary Integration*, Berlin, Springer, 95–123.

Gudin, P. de Vallerin, Magnier, A. and Ponty, N. (1991), 'Taux d'intérêt: une asymétrie moins forte', *Economie et Statistiques*, no. 246–7, September–October.

Guillaumont, P. and Sylviane (1984), *Zone Franc et Developpement Africain*,

Paris.

von Hagen, J. and Fratianni, M. (1991), 'Monetary and fiscal policy in a European monetary union: Some public choice considerations' in Welfens, P. (ed.), *European Monetary Integration*, Berlin, Springer.

Hall, R. and Taylor, J. (1991), *Macro-Solve*, Norton.

Havel, V. (1991), 'Rede anlässlich der Verleihung des Internationalen Karlspreises zu Aachen 9 Mai 1991' in *Europa Archiv*, 11, 46, Johr 10.06.91.

Hellwig, M. and Neumann, M.J.M. (1987), 'Economic policy in Germany: was there a turnaround?' *Economic Policy*, 5, 105–40.

Henning, C. R. (1991), 'Economic and monetary union and the United States' in Weber, M. (ed.), *On the Road to Economic and Monetary Union*, Darmstadt, Germany, Wissenschaftliche Buchgesellschaft.

Herr, H., Tober, S. and Westphal, A. (1991), 'A strategy for economic transformation and development', *de Pecunia*, December.

Hingel, A. (1991), 'Archipelago Europe – prospective dossier, no.1, April.

Horn, G.A. (1991), Wage formation in Europe – comparison of modelling strategies, Paper presented at the SPES conference, Paris, June.

Horne, J. (1991), 'Criteria of external sustainability', *European Economic Review*, no. 35.

House of Lords (1991), 'Report on European regional policy', European Communities Committee, London, HMSO.

Jozzo, A. (1991), 'Eastern Europe and the Ecu' in *Ecu – A Currency for Europe*, Euromoney Books, London (forthcoming).

Kaldor, N. (1971), 'The truth about the dynamic effects', *New Statesman*, 12 March.

Keuzenkamp, H.A. and van der Ploeg, F. (1991), 'Savings. investment, government finance, and the current account: the Dutch experience', in Alogoskoufis, G., Papademos, L. and Portes, R. (eds), *External Constraints on Macroeconomic Policy: the European experience*, Cambridge University Press.

Keynes, J.M. (1923), *A Tract on Monetary Reform*, Macmillan, London.

Keynes, J.M. (1933), *National Self-Sufficiency*, Studies, vol. 22, 177–193.

Koen, V.R. (1991), 'Testing the credibility of the Belgian hard currency policy', IMF Working paper, 91/79, August.

Kremers, J.J.M. (1989), Gaining policy credibility in the EMS: the case of Ireland, IMF Working Paper 89/36.

Kremers, J. (1990), 'Gaining policy credibility for a disinflation: Ireland's experience in the EMS', *IMF Staff Papers*, vol. 37, no. 1.

Kremers, J. and Lane, T. (1990), 'Economic and monetary integration and the aggregate demand for money in the EMS' in *Staff Papers*, International Monetary Fund, vol. 37, December, 777–805.

Krueger, A. (1968), 'Factor endowments and per capita income differences among countries', *The Economic Journal*, vol. 78, September.

Krugman, P. (1991), 'Increasing returns and economic geography', *Journal of Political Economy*, vol. 99, 483–499.

Langfeldt, E., Scheide, J. and Trapp, P. (1989), 'The case for money supply rules', *Geld und Währung*, vol. 5, May, 30–47.

Layard, R. and Nickell, S. (1985), 'The causes of British unemployment, *National Institute Economic Review*, no. 111, February.

Layard, R., Nickell, S. and Jackman, R. (1991), *Unemployment: Macroeconomic Performance and the Labour Market*, Oxford University Press.

Leddin, A.J. and Walsh, B.M. (1990), *The Macroeconomy of Ireland*, Dublin, Gill and Macmillan.

Lee, J. (1989), *Ireland 1912–1985: Politics and Society*, Cambridge, Cambridge University Press.

Lindbeck, A. (1979), 'Imported and structural inflation and aggregate demand: the Scandinavian model reconstructed', in Lindbeck, A. (ed), *Inflation and Employment in Open Economies*, Amsterdam, North-Holland.

Lucas, R. (1990), 'Why doesn't capital flow from rich to poor countries?' *American Economic Review*, Papers and Proceedings, vol. 80, no. 2.

McAleese, D. (1971), 'Effective tariffs and the structure of industrial protection in Ireland', Dublin, The Economic and Social Research Institute, Paper nc. 62.

McCarthy, C. (1979), 'The European Monetary System and Irish macroeconomic policy', Annual Report, Central Bank of Ireland Spring, 109–122.

McCormack, D. (1979), 'Policy-making in a small open economy: some aspects of Irish experience', Annual Report, Central Bank of Ireland, Winter, 92–113.

MacDougall, D. (1977), 'Report of the study group on the role of public finance in the European Community', Brussels, Commission of the European Communities.

Masson, P. and Melitz, J. (1990), 'Fiscal policy independence in a monetary union', CEPR Discussion Paper.

Mayes, D.G. and Burridge, M. (1991), 'The impact of 1992 on the structure of UK manufacturing industry', chapter 8 in Driver, C. and Dunne, P. (eds), *Structural Change in the UK*, Cambridge, Cambridge University Press.

Mehta, F. and Sneesens, R. (1990), 'Belgian unemployment: the story of a small open economy caught in a worldwide recession', in Bean, L.R. and Drèze, J.H. (eds), *Europe's Unemployment Problem*, Cambridge, Mass., MIT Press.

Minczeles, A. and Sicsic, P. (1986), 'La désinflation 1982–1983: une analyse variantielle', *Revue Economique*, no. 6, November.

Morin, P. (1988), 'Une analyse du processus de désinflation', *Economie et Prévision*, no. 82.

Murray, C.H. (1979), 'The European Monetary System: implications for Ireland', Annual Report, Central Bank of Ireland, 96–108.

NIESR (1991), 'A new strategy for social and economic cohesion after 1992', report to the European Parliament.

Nam, C. W. *et al.* (1991), 'The effect of 1992 and associated legislation on the less favoured regions of the Community', Report to the European Parliament.

Neumann, M.J.M. (1991), 'Central bank independence as a prerequisite of price stability', in *European Economy, The Economics of EMU*, special edition, no. 1, 79–92.

Nickell, S.J. (1984), 'The modelling of wages and employment' in Hendry, D.F. and Wallis, K.F. (eds), *Econometrics and Quantitative Economics*.

Nicoletti, G. (1988), 'A cross-country analysis of private consumption, inflation and the debt neutrality hypothesis', OECD Economic Studies.

Nielsen, S.B. and Sondergaard, J. (1991), 'Macroeconomic policy and the external constraint: the Danish experience', in Alogoskoufis *et al.* (op. cit.).

OFCE (1991), 'Vents contraires: chronique de conjoncture', *Observations et Diagnostics Economiques*, no. 38, October.

O'Donnell, R. (1991), 'Policy requirements for regional balance in economic and monetary union', chapter 1 in Hannequart, A., *Economic and Social Cohesion and the Structural Funds*, Routledge.

Olson, M. (1982), 'The rise and decline of nations', New Haven.

O'Malley, E. (1989), *Industry and Economic Development: The Challenge for the Latecomer*, Dublin, Gill and Macmillan.

Padoa-Schioppa, T. (1987), *Efficiency, stability and equity: a strategy for the evolution of the economic system of the European Community*, Oxford University Press.

Pagan, A. (1984), 'Econometric issues in the analysis of regressions with generated regressors', *International Economic Review*, vol. 25 no. 1.

Perée, E. and Steinherr, A. (1989), 'Exchange rate uncertainty and foreign trade', *European Economic Review*, vol. 33, 1241–64.

Poret, P. (1990), 'Les salaires dans les grands pays de l'OCDE au cours des années quatre-vingt. Les comportements ont-ils changé?' *Economie et Statistique*, no. 235, September.

Portes, R. (1991), 'The path of reform in central and Eastern Europe: an introduction', CEPR Discussion Paper, no. 559, London.

Ralle, P. and Toujas-Bernate, J.(1990), 'Indexation des salaires: la rupture de 1983', *Economie et Prévision*, no. 92–93.

Riese, H. (1991), *Geld im Sozialismus. Zur theoretischen Fundierung von Konzeptionen des Sozialismus*, Regensburg.

Robertson, D. and Symons, J. (1991), 'Output, inflation and the ERM', Centre for Economic Performance, discussion paper no. 43.

Russo, M. and Tullio, G. (1988), 'Monetary policy coordination within the EMS: is there a rule?', in Giavazzi, Micossi and Miller (eds), *The European Monetary System*, Cambridge University Press.

Sachs, J. and Sala-i-Martin, X. (1989), *Federal Fiscal Policy and Optimum Currency Areas*, (unpublished) Cambridge, Mass., Harvard University.

Sachs, J. and Wyplosz C. (1986), 'The economic consequences of President Mitterand', *Economic Policy*, no. 2.

Schama, S. (1989), *Citizens: A Chronicle of the French Revolution*, London, Penguin Books.

Schatz, K.W., Scheide, J. and Trapp, P. (1988), 'Short-term prospects for the European economies', *Conjunctura Italiana*, 31, no. 5.

Scheide, J. (1989), 'A K-percent rule for monetary policy in West Germany', *Weltwirtschaftliches Archiv*, vol. 125, 326–36.

Scheide, J., Trapp, P. (1991), 'Etatdisziplin vom markt', *Frankfurter Allgemeine Zeitung*, 23 February.

Schlesinger, H. (1991), 'The establishment of a durable economic and monetary union in Europe', *Deutsche Bundesbank, Auszüge aus Presseartikeln*, Frankfurt, 1 October.

Stationery Office (1958), *Economic Devlopment*, Dublin, The Stationery Office, Pr 4803.

Steinherr, A. *et al.* (1990), *Reforms in Eastern Europe and the Role of the Ecu. A Report of the Macro-financial Study Group of the Ecu Banking Association*, Paris.

Svensson, L. (1990), 'The simplest test of target-zone credibility', NBER working paper no. 3394.

Ungerer, H. Evans, O., Mayer, T. and Young, P. (1986), 'The European Monetary System: recent developments', Occasional paper 48, International Monetary Fund, Washington D.C.

Ungerer, H., Hauvonen, J.J., Lopez-Claros, A. and Mayer, T. (1990), 'The European Monetary System: developments and perspectives', Occasional paper 73, International Monetary Fund, Washington D.C.

Vaubel, R. (1991), 'Die politische Oekonomie der wirtschaftspolitischen zentralisierung in der Europäischen gemeinschaft', *Beiträge zur angewandten Wirtschaftsforschung des Instituts für Volkswirtschaftslehre und Statistik der Universität Mannheim*, no. 456–91.

Vaubel, R. (1989), 'Ueberholte Glaubenssätze' in *Wirtschaftsdienst*, 1989/6, Hamburg, pp. 276–79.

Vinals, J. (1990), 'The EMS, Spain and macroeconomic policy', CEPR discussion paper no. 389, March.

Vizy, M. (1989), *La Zone Franc*, Paris.

Walsh, B.M. (1974), 'Expectations, information, and human migration: specifying an econometric model of Irish migration to Britain', *Journal of Regional Science*, vol. 14, 107–120.

Weber, A. (1991), 'Reputation and credibility in the European Monetary System', *Economic Policy*, no. 12, April.

Weber, A. (1991a), 'Stochastic process switching and intervention in exchange-rate target zones: empirical evidence from the EMS', CEPR Discussion Paper no. 554, July.

Whitaker, T.K. (1973), 'Monetary integration: reflections on Irish experience', *Quarterly Bulletin*, Central Bank of Ireland, Winter, 64–80.

Williamson, J. (1985), *The Exchange Rate System*, Washington, Institute for International Economics.

Williamson, J. (1991), 'FEERs and the ERM', *National Institute Economic Review*, August.

Williamson, J. and Miller, M. (1987), *Targets and Indicators: A Blueprint for the International Coordination of Economic Policy*, Washington, Institute for International Economics.

World Bank (1991), *The Transformation of Economies in Central and Eastern Europe: Issues, Progress and Prospects*, Washington, April.

Wren-Lewis, S. *et al.* (1991), 'Choosing the rate: an analysis of the optimum level of entry for sterling in the ERM', *Manchester School*, special issue, June.

Wyplosz, C. (1988), 'La libération des capitaux et le SME: un point de vue français', *Economie Européenne*, no. 36, May, 91–108.